The Laughing
Guide to Well-Being

PRAISE FOR *THE LAUGHING GUIDE TO WELL-BEING*

"In *The Laughing Guide to Well-Being: Using Humor and Science to Become Happier and Healthier,* Dr. Prilleltensky, a respected authority in the area of well-being, reminds us that humor is a key factor in coping with life stressors and being resilient in work and life. Drawing upon psychological insights, the scientific literature, and common life experiences this book provides an important contribution to positive psychology in general and our understanding of happiness in particular.

In each chapter, Dr. Prilleltensky uses a strengths-based orientation to provide both chuckles and chunks of wisdom that we can all use to create a greater sense of well-being in our lives. And for those who are in leadership roles, I suggest they make this book required reading for those they supervise. When leaders model the behaviors and attitudes described in this book, then they, their co-workers, and their workplace becomes healthier—and more productive!

The capacity to laugh is essential to our well-being and needed more today than ever. This book provides the evidence, both scientific and anecdotal, that we each have the capacity to incorporate humor to strengthen our sense of well-being. Be good to yourself, read this book!"
—Spencer Niles, dean and professor, School of Education, The College of William & Mary, co-author of *Career Flow and Career Development Interventions*

"A Revelation!

This is exactly what we need. *The Laughing Guide to Well-Being* shows the one little changeable thing in our life—a better sense of humor—that can transform relationships, visions toward the future, and our health. But as we've gotten more prosperous over the years, we've also gotten more serious, skeptical, and snarky in our humor. Prilleltensky's brilliant book shows how we can turn this around. There is no easier way to have a ripple across the rest of our lives than to realize that our laughing side is also our learning side."—Brian Wansink, PhD, Professor, Cornell University, Author of *Slim by Design and Mindless Eating*

"Who knew a self-help book could be funny, while being grounded in legitimate science; a guide to greater health or happiness, without being moralizing or prescriptive; or wise and insightful, without the self-directed blandishments from an author who can't see himself having the same problems the rest of us have. Dr. Prilleltensky has managed to pull off this hat trick – and produce a book that is fun to read and deeply educational." —Harold G. Levine, dean and professor, School of Education, University of California, Davis

"Don't let the lighthearted tone fool you! Dr. Prilleltensky provides witty descriptions of cutting-edge techniques and draws on the latest research to give you memorable, effective strategies for making your life meaningful and fun. Don't be surprised if you suddenly understand scientific thinking better, too. The guy entertained me immensely and taught me more than I would have ever guessed." —Mitch Earlywine, professor, SUNY Albany, author of *Humor 101*

"Isaac Prilleltensky has been long admired for his wisdom and insight about psychology, social issues, and well-being. His new book shines a light on his talents as a humorist, which allows him to generate incisive observations about the nature of the human condition. Reading this book will make you laugh and also will give you pause as you consider the complicated journey to a life of well-being, connection, and meaning. By weaving together humor, psychological insights, and compassion, Professor Prilleltensky has created a brilliant book, one that has enormous heart and a deep soul." —David L. Blustein, professor, Boston College, author of *The Psychology of Working*

"*The Laughing Guide to Well-Being* changed my life! I gained two hours a day of productive time by simply washing my Senokot down with pomegranate juice . . . who knew. . . . Isaac did! You will learn and laugh; a great prescription for well-being." —Kenneth A. Rosen, chief executive officer, Infinity Sales Group

"This book takes the 'tense' out of Prilleltensky. It is not only funny, but also instructive, practical, and deeply thought-provoking. Prof. Prilleltensky's accessible text reminds us of the healing power of gentle satire and laughter, while also sharing important insights about the sources of personal and collective well-being across Interpersonal, Community, Occupational, Physical, Psychological, and Economic domains (I COPPE)." —Dr. Iain Butterworth, manager; Liveability and Sustainability, Eastern & Southern Metropolitan Health, Victorian Dept. Health and Human Services, Australia

"This book not only tickles your belly and makes your heart glad, but it contains important health information—laughter is seriously good for you! It's a fun read that present slaughter as a tonic with powerful healing properties.You'll be convinced that a sense of well-being is good for your health and laughter is way more fun than surgery." —Eduardo J. Padrón, president of Miami Dade College

"Reading Isaac Prilleltensky's book is like having him as your own funny, irreverent, warm, and wise friend. For years, he's been a scholarly mentor in matters of social equity and well-being; now he offers caring guidance in living a healthy, connected, good life—all in the context of his hilarious observations of human nature (most often his own). Open and personal, informative but never preachy, Prilleltensky shows that we can take our wellness seriously without taking ourselves too seriously." —Laura Smith, associate professor, Teachers College; author of *Psychology, Poverty, and the End of Social Exclusion*

"Prilleltensky adeptly tackles the challenges that confront most humor scholars. How can the science of laughter be taken seriously? This book provides entertaining stories to illustrate and validate the psychology of humor as integral to the search for well-being." —Mary Kay Morrison, president, Association for Applied and Therapeutic Humor; author of *Using Humor to Maximize Living*

"In *The Laughing Guide to Well-Being*, Isaac Prilleltensky combines humor and science to provide readers with an in-depth understanding of the six areas of well-being. His approach is unique and innovative. Each chapter begins with the Laughing Side, then the Learning Side, which makes for a most engaging, informative, and, at times, hilarious read. His use of amusingly constructed acronyms makes it easy to remember key concepts. This book is an important contribution to the field of happiness, laughter, and well-being. I learnt and laughed a lot!" —Ros Ben-Moshe, director of LaughLife Wellbeing Programs and lecturer, School of Public Health, LaTrobe University

"One need only spend a leisurely lunch with Isaac Prilleltensky to know you're in the presence of someone who sees the world from a unique perspective. Even the most serious of subjects are broached with a sense of charm and humor that's very rare these days. I've had the pleasure of engaging Dr. Prilleltensky in a variety of settings, and, knowing him as I do, it makes so much sense that he has written this wondrous new book, *The Laughing Guide to Well-Being: Using Humor and Science to Become Happier and Healthier*. In his own words: 'All of us can use a little help to become happier and healthier,' and that's just what he provides in this lively, funny, and abundantly useful guide to leading the most fulfilling life possible. This is a book I know will resonate with my customers and all readers everywhere!" —Mitchell Kaplan, owner, Books & Books

"This is a humorous and entertaining book about matters of great seriousness and importance. Prof. Prilleltensky touches on central points related to human functioning and our experience of well-being. He draws on his rich experience, as well as providing support from contemporary research, ultimately providing profound insights about our lives. The humorous perspective complements the theoretical and empirical material, rendering it accessible to all." —Amiram Raviv, professor and dean, School of Psychology, The Center for Academic Studies, Or-Yehuda; former chief psychologist, Department of Education, Israel

"The two most difficult tasks for a writer are, one, to make us laugh and, two, to get us to live healthy lifestyles. Isaac Prilleltensky has succeeded admirably with the humorous half of the equation and I trust is on his way to the second half as readers chuckle their ways through his book. Now, either laughter will help us live better or we can go back to the old method of scaring ourselves to death. I prefer his way, and so will you." —Michael Lewis, editor and publisher, *Miami Today*

"This is vintage Prilleltensky: a sharp, witty, compassionate, and insightful approach that deftly handles the serious ways in which humour and laughter can enrich our capacity for individual and communal wellbeing. A knowledgeable, deeply human, and very funny piece of work that encourages us not only to see but also to see through ourselves, and come out healthier and happier on the other side." —Professor Michele Grossman, director, Centre for Cultural Diversity and Wellbeing Victoria University, Melbourne

The Laughing Guide to Well-Being

Using Humor and Science
to Become Happier and Healthier

Isaac Prilleltensky

ROWMAN & LITTLEFIELD
Lanham • Boulder • New York • London

Published by Rowman & Littlefield
A wholly owned subsidary of The Rowman & Littlefield Publishing Group, Inc.
4501 Forbes Boulevard, Suite 200, Lanham, Maryland 20706
www.rowman.com

Unit A, Whitacre Mews, 26-34 Stannary Street, London SE11 4AB

British Library Cataloguing in Publication Information Available

Library of Congress Cataloging-in-Publication Data

Names: Prilleltensky, Isaac, 1959- author.
Title: The laughing guide to well-being : using humor and science to become
    happier and healthier / Isaac Prilleltensky.
Description: Lanham, Maryland : Rowman & Littlefield, 2016. | Includes
    bibliographical references.
Identifiers: LCCN 2016004231 | ISBN 9781475825732 (cloth : alk. Paper) | ISBN 9781475825749
(pbk : alk. paper) | ISBN 9781475825756 (electronic)
Subjects: LCSH: Well-being—Psychological aspects. | Health—Psychological
    aspects. | Laughter—Psychological aspects. | Wit and humor—Psychological
    aspects.
Classification: LCC HN29 .P595 2016 | DDC 301—dc23 LC record available at http://lccn.loc.
gov/2016004231

∞™ The paper used in this publication meets the minimum requirements of
American National Standard for Information Sciences—Permanence of Paper
for Printed Library Materials, ANSI/NISO Z39.48-1992.

Printed in the United States of America

Contents

Preface

All of us can use a little help to become happier or healthier. Unfortunately, the help we get is often too serious or too scary: "if you don't do this or that, some catastrophic event of epic proportions will happen." My approach, in contrast, is to help you become healthier and happier through laughter. In the book I laugh mostly about myself, but also about Miami, from which I learned so much. Here I learned that a city can run without a prefrontal cortex.

As a professor of psychology, I spent the last twenty-five years studying, teaching, and writing about different aspects of well-being. This was after I worked as a clinician for several years. Along the way, I consulted with individuals, families, organizations, and communities striving to improve their well-being. As a humor blogger and columnist, I spent the last few years writing about the funny side of life. In the summer of 2015 I received an award from the National Newspaper Association for my humor writing, which nudged me to publish *The Laughing Guide to Well-Being*. The book combines my knowledge of well-being with my interest in humor, hoping to prevent illness and promote wellness in amusing ways. I believe that we can do better than scaring people, which is what health messages often do.[1]

Research shows that humor can contribute to learning, positive emotions, happiness, and health.[2] That's why I start each chapter with *The Laughing Side*, a series of funny stories. This is followed by *The Learning Side*, in which I analyze the topic in light of research and science. The first chapter provides an overview of well-being, while subsequent chapters cover each of its six domains: Interpersonal, Community, Occupational, Physical, Psychological, and Economic, which form the mnemonic I COPPE (pronounced *I cope*). As we'll see, the level of well-being we experience in each domain of life is a matter of fit, fitness, and fairness. My hope is that when you finish the book, you'll have a greater understanding of your life, and ways to make it better.

The chapters combine humor with science. Each one has a serious side and a comic side. But just to be sure, if you're having a medical emergency, don't rely on this book to get better; call 911 or go to the nearest emergency room. Do take the book with you, though. Chances are you'll wait there for several days until somebody sees you.

1

Your Six Areas of Well-Being

THE LAUGHING SIDE

I'm fifty-six years old, and I want to spend the remaining three-quarters of my life doing something useful, which is why I wrote this book. If by reading it you laugh, or improve your well-being, I'd be ecstatic. If you do both, I'd be euphoric.

The book uses a simple method called *smarter through laughter*. The whole point of this approach is to get you thinking about parts of your life where you can do better, not through threats or sermons, but rather through laughter and fun. Most people are defensive about their health and wellness habits. You don't need to feel defensive here. Just get ready to laugh at me, and try to laugh a little at yourself too. Laughter and humor open up all kinds of possibilities for thinking about well-being.

The book is organized around six domains of well-being which form the acronym *I COPPE*:

- Interpersonal well-being
- Community well-being
- Occupational well-being
- Physical well-being
- Psychological well-being
- Economic well-being

Each chapter, including this one, starts with the *Laughing Side*, which is a series of humor stories illustrating certain aspects of well-being. In the *Learning Side*, we review what we know about the various domains of well-being, building on the funny stories.

Now that you know the plan, we can get started. Each of the following humor pieces relates to an I COPPE domain of life. We go in order, with interpersonal well-being first.

Gossip

Working at a university, I have great access to unique resources. Using the latest software from our Center for Computational Time Wasting, I came to the conclusion that the average human being spends on average seven million hours gossiping. This amounts to eight hours a day. The average goes up considerably when Lindsay Lohan goes into rehab, but using a smoothing function that controls for celebrity addictions over the last ninety years of available data, we are pretty sure that eight hours per day is about right.

Given that most people sleep for about eight hours, watch TV for about six hours, and struggle with constipation in the toilet for about two hours, it is abundantly clear that ALL of their gossip is done at work, which explains why our economy is in such abysmal state and why GM had to recall 2.6 million cars.

Gossiping is such an epidemic that I decided to do some research on it. I, of course, never gossip, so I lacked any personal experience with this phenomenon threatening interpersonal well-being. As a result, I had to rely on validated tools to collect data: random eavesdropping. I chose a representative sample of visitors to the broadwalk at Hollywood Beach, Florida (don't even dare calling it the boardwalk, the locals will lynch you). The two-and-a-half-mile stretch by the ocean invites multilingual populations from all over the world to congregate for daily gossip conventions. I can detect what passersby are saying only in a few languages, but using the latest Google glasses I surreptitiously record and translate what I did not get, which is usually in Russian and involves the words *vodka* and *morgaly vikalyu, padla* (which more or less means "I will poke your eyes out," followed by an expletive unbecoming of a dean of education).

This is a list of the ten most frequent gossip statements emitted by broadwalk visitors:

1. Pepe (not his real name, his real name is José) never pays child support.
2. Sofia's plastic surgery came out awful (her real name, used with permission).
3. Castro, Castro, Castro, Castro (real name, used without permission).
4. Dovid is a putz.
5. Faigel (real name) is such an *Alte Makhsheyfe* (old witch, in Yiddish) (reproduced with permission from Faigel's daughter-in-law).
6. They don't know how to make poutine here (Quebecois visitor).
7. They don't know how to run a dictatorship here (Russian couple).
8. Yolanda cheats on him.
9. Dovid is going out with Victoria/Gabriela/Yolanda/Amanda, and none of them are Jewish.
10. Faigel has no idea that Dovid (the putz) paid for Sofia's plastic surgery, before going out with Victoria/Gabriela/Yolanda/Amanda, who now want him to pay for their plastic surgery too.

Gossip serves many evolutionary functions such as self-protection. Talking ill of others fills the air and prevents people from contemplating their own foibles. This is a well-known psychological defense mechanism characteristic of three year olds, Kim Kardashian, Silvio Berlusconi, Donald Trump, Vladimir Putin, Dovid the putz, and mayoral candidates in South Florida. Gossip is essential for procreation too. If people ever stopped gossiping and realized who they were procreating with, it would be the end of the human species, causing the demise of the diaper industry.

Gossip comes in several forms and levels of sophistication, from the pedestrian (Dovid is a putz) to the refined (Something has been on my mind lately. I wonder if you happen to know the whereabouts of the famous banker, Faigel's former husband, Dovid the putz.).

My observations also revealed that gossipers come in different personality types:

- *The diarrheic gossiper:* Cannot contain herself. Gossip is a force of nature that needs to come out no matter what. Gossips without regard for personal credibility. Procreates a lot.
- *The constipated gossiper:* Really wants to gossip but cannot get it out. Early trauma involved. Victorian upbringing. Sexually repressed. Has problems procreating.
- *The closeted gossiper:* "I'm going to tell you something that you cannot repeat to anybody." Gossip usually involves self-aggrandizement and false humility.
- *The obsessed gossiper:* Focuses on a single subject: Kardashians (half of the US population), Obamacare (John Boehner), missing flights (CNN), and catastrophes (Anderson Cooper).
- *The benign gossiper:* Harmless. Gossips mostly about people you don't know.
- *The toxic gossiper:* You know who you are.

For many people gossip is a form of sublimation. Sublimation is a big word that psychoanalysts invented when pharmaceutical companies threatened to put them out of business. The word refers to the expression of aggression by acceptable means. Instead of killing each other in duels, we invent and leak embarrassing information about our opponents through Facebook, Twitter, and Fox News. All things considered, sublimation through gossip is not a bad thing for interpersonal well-being.

Prefrontal Phontex

A new region of the brain, called the Prefrontal Phontex, is poised to replace the Prefrontal Cortex in people who constantly use their phones to text, posing a great threat to community well-being. The startling discovery, published in the most recent issue of *Nature*, reveals that the obsession with texting now has a physical representation. The brain of compulsive texters contains an android-like cellular mass, surrounded by flickering lights that resemble iPhone apps. The Prefrontal Phontex sits between the Prefrontal Cortex and the skull. Researchers at MIT found that the more you text, the larger the Phontex gets, and the smaller your Cortex becomes. Scientists predict that avid users of text will lose their entire Prefrontal Cortex in six to seven years, unleashing catastrophic consequences for themselves and society at large.

For those unfamiliar with the functions of the Prefrontal Cortex, it is a part of the brain involved in decision making, complex cognitive processes, planning, predicting outcomes, suppressing unacceptable behavior, distinguishing between good and bad, and overall ethical demeanor. While health professionals warn against the disastrous consequences of a Prefrontal Cortex–free society, Dr. Tranquillo from the Miami Institute of Psychiatry thinks otherwise. He told me that "80 percent of the people in the city already behave as if they had no Cortex whatsoever and we are all still here. It's the way of the future. Miami is a harbinger for the entire country." The Chamber of Commerce of Miami-Dade County sees this as a great opportunity to attract new businesses and research centers. "This development builds on our strengths," said a spokesperson for the chamber. "We have gotten so used to people without a Prefrontal Cortex that other cities can learn from us." "Come to a World Like No Other. Visit Miami, City with no Prefrontal Cortex."

Meanwhile, the South Florida Union of Convicted Politicians issued a statement announcing its intent to call for a mistrial in the 278 cases that resulted in jail terms for their members.

"Everybody thought that we were crooks, but we are not to blame. Texting was part of our job. It's not our fault. This discovery proves that we are innocent. It's not our fault that we lost our Prefrontal Cortex to texting. When we get out of jail, we will sue mobile companies for inventing texting."

Speaking anonymously, an executive with the telecommunication industry told the Associated Press that they are already saving money for the lawsuits. "This will be big! It will be much bigger than the tobacco settlements." Besides, he told me, "Texting will be nothing compared to selfies." Selfie, the act of taking your own picture with a smartphone and uploading it to social media, has become so popular that *selfie* was named word of the year for 2013. "More and more people are selfing and driving."

For their part, texters claim that the state is not doing enough to protect them from their devices. "They recently passed a law in Florida to prevent texting while driving that is totally unenforceable," a twenty-six-year-old told me while he was texting and driving on US 1 next to a police officer, who was also texting and driving. Indeed, an investigation into the conviction rates under the new law shows that fewer people have gotten convicted than were able to access the HealthCare.gov website the first time around.

When I approached the governor's office about the dismal rate of convictions in Florida, a spokeswoman told me that "texting is here to stay, it's the way of the future, and besides, there is no room in our jails for texters. We have too many Medicare fraud and political corruption cases in Florida. There is only so much our jails can handle." "Does it bother you that people are getting into accidents because they are distracted by their phones?" I asked. "It's a free market," she said. "The government should stay away from our lives. Texting and driving is a personal choice," she said. "What about the NSA spying on all of us?" I said, to which she replied, "When Mr. Scott becomes president of the United States, he will do away with the NSA and the entire Department of Justice. He will privatize law enforcement and the Supreme Court." But he is working on a fix, she said. "One solution that Governor Scott is exploring is to give every Floridian a Google car—those that don't require a driver—and a pair of Google glasses to spy on Democrats." "And how is he going to pay for that?" I said. "Google will give every Floridian a car and a pair of glasses and the governor will give Google all of Miami, present and future residents included."

Lawyers show no interest in enforcing the law either, as they are now charging clients by words texted. "If our clients are in jail, they cannot text us because they take their phones away from them, depriving us of a new source of revenue," Mr. Suetime told me. "It's much better for us to keep our clients on the streets, where they can text and drive." Mr. Suetime also told me that the legal profession is looking forward to many more Cortex-free clients. Law schools also welcome a Cortex-free society, especially at a time when enrollments are down.

When I interviewed several compulsive texters about their habits, they told me that they are afraid of FOMO: Fear of Missing Out. They are constantly texting and looking at their Facebook page because they want to be the first one to know that their best friend had diarrhea.

Getting Organized

Getting organized is fundamental to occupational well-being, but unfortunately, only 0.000000000000001 percent of the population can legitimately claim to be organized: my aunt Eusebia and I. Since she passed away over twenty-five years ago, it is now my sole responsibility to make sure there is order in the world. To be organized you need either paper and pencil, or one of the three million apps that claim to help with organization, time management, priorities, schedule, goals, objectives, and bad breath—all essential for success at work.

If you are like most people, you are going to spend 278 hours choosing the right time-saving app from the app store. After you download it, you are going to use it for about three minutes until you get an email from your brother telling you that you must watch the latest TED talk on productivity. As you are about to click on the link, you are distracted by various pop-ups with offers to purchase cruise tickets, Viagra, and houses in foreclosure. By the time you are ready to watch the video on productivity you realize it's time to go home.

After dinner you get your iPad and finally have time to watch the talk on productivity. The speaker recommends that you download a goal-setting app. Because you are a discerning customer, you are not going to download just the first app that appears on your screen, so you are going to spend fifty-nine hours comparing features, at which point you forget what you were looking for and settle for the latest version of Angry Birds.

My identification with the prophet Job has grown considerably since marrying my wife. When our son was old enough to be expected to carry out tasks, my identification with the prophet was complete. I felt that God had presented me with the toughest cases of disorganization to prove my conviction with the mission to bring order to the world.

Soon after Ora and I started living together in Israel, I remember a weekend when we decided to clean our apartment. We literally turned everything upside down to do a thorough job. In the middle of the chaos, Ora found an old letter I had sent her, and she decided to stop everything, lie on the unmade bed, and start reading the letter for nostalgia's sake. I found this episode totally endearing but profoundly disorienting and stressful. In the house I grew up in, you finished what you started before you moved on to other activities, let alone frivolous ones, like reading an old love letter. I did my best to act normal in the face of her spontaneity, but later that night I threw up.

My befuddlement was alleviated when I met Ora's parents, who had just come from Canada for our wedding. I understood then that the gene responsible for tidiness had fallen off her family tree. I slowly moved from perplexity to acceptance.

Our son Matan showed no inclination to be organized until he turned twenty-two. These were the most disorganized and distressing years of my life. Nothing had prepared me for it. When we lived in Australia, Matan used to go to summer camp. Upon return from one such adventure, we picked him up from the drop-off point and drove home. On our way home we spotted one of his shoes in the middle of an intersection. I am sure that the shoe had an irrepressible urge to jump out of the bus. Anything to get away from my kid's smelly feet after a month-long camp.

Over the years, however, we saw signs of hope. Matan could be disorganized at school, but when it came to chess, there was a level of neuroticism that gave us real hope. When his working life started revolving around chess, everything came together. There is a big lesson here for all of us: go with your strengths. Let your passion drive your life, and the rest will come together.

I used to have a recurring nightmare that I would die and that Ora and Matan wouldn't find the life insurance policy and instructions for burial. I feared they wouldn't find my will and that my entire pension plan would go to fund the forty-eighth year of the war in Afghanistan; but no more. I'm pleased to report that in the last seven years Matan has become dangerously like me. When he started graduate school, he bought a BlackBerry and started getting his act together, big-time. He had about a dozen chess students spread out all over New York City, and his system worked like a Swiss clock. For several years, Matan was a chess teacher in NEST+m, a school for the gifted and talented in the Lower East Side. He had about six hundred students in the school, was supremely organized, and was slowly but surely becoming quite obsessive-compulsive like his old man. His students won several major national tournaments, which says something about being organized.

Ora has also become much more organized, threatening my supremacy as the most neurotically habitual member of the house. Don't give Ora amaranth instead of organic gluten-free steel-cut oatmeal from Whole Foods in the morning, and please, please, don't overcook the broccoli. Twelve extra seconds can make a big difference in the nutritional chemistry of a crucifer—not to mention the divorce rate in North America.

Gluteus Maximus

In an effort to improve my physical wellness, every day my sexy 55 kilograms (122 pounds) of muscle go through the humiliation of being the skinniest athlete in the Northern Hemisphere. Yes, I'm healthy, but I have yet to encounter a woman in the gym who would ask me about my biceps, serratus magnus, or pectoralis major, let alone my gluteus maximus. I keep telling myself that I'm beautiful and strong on the inside, but women at the gym prefer a big gluteus maximus.

At the gym, I keep looking for something that I will be the best at, but I'm at a loss. For a while I kept thinking that I was probably the most obsessive-compulsive person in the entire Wellness Center at the University of Miami. That was a source of real pride, until I saw a couple of guys compulsively recording their every move. They extend an arm, they write it down. They lift a ten-pounder, they write it down. They smell their armpit, they write it down. Much to my chagrin, I lost that competition too.

Then I went for the best-dressed athlete. That was an easy one. I spent $4,592 on Nike shorts, shirts, shoes, and socks. The only problem was that I had to get rid of all my Adidas shorts, shirts, shoes, and socks. I've seen enough people mix Adidas with Nike to give me an aesthetic thrombosis. What I still can't reconcile is the fact that now I'm wearing a Nike shirt that says Pro Combat. For the life of me I can't imagine anyone taking me for any kind of combat, other than a self-deprecation duel.

In all honesty, that was not a difficult contest to win. Other than women, who spend on athletic wear almost as much as I spend on brown Tumi bags, I knew I could beat the guys. There are two types of guys in the gym: those who don't know how to match colors and those who use their T-shirts to clean their garage. This one was easy.

But if you thought that going to the gym was tough for me, going to restaurants is a nightmare. There was a brief period of time when my eating disorders were a little out of control (1963–2012). Concerned with the unpleasant side effects of white flour (obesity, constipation, and sudden death syndrome), I used to spend hours searching for bagel places that served 100 percent whole wheat. Much to our son's mortification, I used to go to bakeries and ask what percentage of the bagel was whole wheat, and if the poor folk at the counter didn't have an answer, I used to send them to the back to read the list of ingredients. While my wife and son pretended they didn't know me, I kept pressing for an exact answer.

I'm happy to report that I stopped eating bagels altogether, but not before bakeries in all major North American cities put a picture of me next to the cash register with a warning: DO NOT SERVE THIS CUSTOMER.

Being a vegan is tough, especially when you're on the road. About two years ago we took a vacation in the Blue Ridge Mountains of Virginia. We flew to DC and rented a car. On our way to the hotel we got hungry. After a futile search for gourmet vegan restaurants in rural Virginia, we settled for a Cracker Barrel. We discovered at the end of the menu a section called *vegetables* with three items: macaroni and cheese, sugar-added applesauce, and green beans with pork. Following a conversation with the manager, you can now find my picture next to cash registers in Cracker Barrels all around the country ALSO with the warning DO NOT SERVE THIS CUSTOMER.

Crowdsourcing Psychiatric Conditions

Mental health is an important part of psychological well-being. To make sure that mental health professionals are up to date with the latest discoveries, every few years the American Psychiatric Association (APA) updates its *Diagnostic and Statistical Manual of Mental and Emotional Disorders*. The manual, usually called the DSM, is now in its fifth edition and sells like hotcakes. It is worth noting that the number of psychiatric conditions has grown approximately 7,982 percent from the first edition to the latest, leaving only three people on the planet who can legitimately claim they are not kookoo. I'm not going to mention who these people are, because the remaining 6,334,999,485,230 will likely sue me for defamation, and Obamacare doesn't protect you from kookoos. You will have to guess if you are one of these people. If you don't want to guess, you will have to buy a copy of the DSM and review its 27,812,903,225 conditions to see if any apply to you. The problem is that if you did not have a psychiatric condition when you started reading the manual, you surely will have one by the time you finish the book, leaving only two sane people on the entire planet.

The APA is unfairly accused of inventing new psychiatric problems to provide (a) job security for psychiatrists and (b) Nespresso machines for all its employees. To assist the APA with its current woes, I have devised a system that would turn the DSM into an engine of economic opportunity for the entire nation and make APA the most loved professional organization in the world: crowdsourcing updates for the DSM.

This is how this would work. People would submit new psychiatric conditions to the APA. If accepted, submitters would receive a $5 rebate every time they saw a psychiatrist and a 15 percent discount on future medications developed to treat the condition they proposed. Given that only three people on the planet are not diagnosed with a psychiatric condition, most of us will benefit from this win-win-win solution: patients get a discount and participate in the democratic and scientific process of inventing diseases, the APA improves its tarnished reputation, and pharmaceuticals have a never-ending stream of conditions on which to try medications that never worked for their intended purpose.

In anticipation, I came up with fifty-four psychiatric conditions I wish to submit for inclusion in the next DSM. My top three:

1. Voice-induced gender identity confusion
2. First-class envy
3. Big-ears trauma

For years I have suffered from people confusing me with members of the opposite sex on the phone. I have yet to come up with a proper response when people on the other end of the line call me Mrs. To prevent such embarrassment I have occasionally tried to project a very manly voice on the phone, especially with service people I don't know. Alternatively I say, "This is *ISAAC* Prilleltensky calling," to which people often reply, "How can I help you, ma'am?"

I'm sure I'm not the only person suffering from such a common but yet-undiagnosed condition. Therefore, I came up with a solution that would solve the problem forever and provide jobs not just to psychiatrists but also to surgeons and music engineers: vocal cord transplant. Enterprising music engineering students would devise a menu of manly voices to choose from:

1. Luciano Pavarotti
2. Placido Domingo
3. Frank Sinatra
4. Marlon Brando

"I'll take Placido, please, with a little more baritone." I'm sure by the time I finish publishing this, there will be a dozen start-up companies working on my cure.

First-class envy is a condition afflicting millions of people who fly economy, especially those who fly long hours with their knees up to their chins. We recently flew to Israel with our knees and feet kissing our foreheads. To make sure we didn't think much about our leg problems, two adorable brothers aged eight and five kept kicking the back of my seat every time I started falling asleep. All I could think of was how nice it must be to fly first-class.

To cope with this malady I have a number of recommendations:

1. Overthrow the government, nationalize the airlines, and eliminate first-class.
2. Develop an envy elimination pill.
3. Stay home.

Big-ears trauma is a particularly challenging condition, especially because I can hear so loud and clear when people on the phone say to me, "How can I help you, ma'am?" This is probably a case of co-morbidity: big ears, girly voice. The only thing that stops me from doing plastic surgery on my ears is saving for vocal cord transplant and first-class seats.

Experiences Are Better Than Purchases, If You Survive Them

My adorable and inquisitive wife Ora, who keeps up with the latest research on well-being, read that experiences are a much better investment than purchases.[1] Serious studies, with more than two participants unrelated to the researcher, show that if you have a little extra cash, it is better to invest it in experiences rather than in objects. This is provided you don't get killed or traumatized during these experiences.

Investigators have demonstrated that buying things does not improve your well-being much. Experiences, on the other hand, have the potential to improve happiness by providing a source of distorted memories that make family vacations sound idyllic. Study after study proves that buying a pair of red shoes, or a red Corvette, does not improve your happiness as much as having a meaningful experience with loved ones.

Persuaded by the research, Ora decided to improve our well-being by having a new experience: five consecutive days of shopping at Miami's finest malls.

Day 1: Aventura Mall
Day 2: Dolphin Mall
Day 3: Merrick Park
Day 4: Dadeland
Day 5: The Falls

I tried telling Ora that by the end of day five she would be the only one with memories because I would be dead, but she told me to quit whining and get some extra cash from the ATM in case we maxed out on our credit card. Of course she had a perfectly good excuse to drag me into this. Our son Matan was about to get married in the summer, and she insisted that I buy some new clothes to impress our future in-laws. To say nothing of what Ora had to buy for the occasion. It's not every day we marry our son, and I did need new underwear.

What I thought was going to be a horrible experience turned out to be a sequence of atrociously traumatizing near-death experiences, which will be very memorable indeed. I give Ora that much. On the first day alone we spent close to eleven hours in Aventura Mall buying and returning items in a never-ending cycle of hunting for bargains, comparing prices, losing my wife, calling each other on the phone, not hearing the phone because of the obnoxious music in stores designed to replace Guantanamo, matching colors, fighting for a dressing room, dressing and undressing, trying on fifty-three items, leaving a complete mess in the dressing room, buying items, refusing to get a new credit card from Banana Republic, schlepping bags to the car, going back to the mall, finding a better bargain, fighting for a dressing room, standing in line behind twenty-seven Brazilian women and twenty-seven nannies maneuvering strollers the size of an SUV, paying, and going to the car to leave the new purchases and retrieve the old ones, which Ora decided we needed to return because she found a comparable item for 34 cents less in Chico's, which usually charges 0.34 percent more than Express, which offers discounts on Thursdays and Fridays from 9 to 11 a.m. that are 0.00021 percent better than the bargains at Ann Taylor Loft.

Meanwhile, I could never find Intimissi underwear, which I usually buy in Europe. If they have it in Europe, I figured they would have it at Aventura Mall, which is the size of Montenegro and Luxembourg combined. To my dismay, no store in Aventura carry Intimissi cotton briefs with elasticized waistband, 93 percent cotton and 7 percent elastane.

Determined to get the only underwear especially suited for my European anatomy, I used my iPhone to check the Intimissi website while Ora left me in the husband deposit area of the Loft with other comatose males. The Intimissi website listed twenty-nine countries where you can find a store, including Qatar, Croatia, and Saudi Arabia, but the United States of Consumerism was not one of them. Resigned to have to buy online, I discovered that you CANNOT BUY INTIMISSI UNDERWEAR ONLINE FROM THE UNITED STATES, which is grounds for retaliation and military invasion of whichever country manufactures Intimissi. Undeterred by setbacks, I thought that I would be the first one to open an Intimissi store in the United States, which would make us rich enough to clone myself and send my alternate ego with Ora to the mall.

THE LEARNING SIDE

The ultimate in gossip is discovering who is cheating on their spouse. In August 2015, hackers published personal information about users of Ashley Madison, an online service promoting extramarital affairs. The tagline for the company says *Life Is Short, Have an Affair.* Gossipers had a field day. Discovering the identity of cheaters filled them with schadenfreude. This is a German term meaning "pleasure derived from another person's misfortune." That's the main theme of the hilarious Broadway show *Avenue Q*, and it's the engine behind gossiping.

But why would human beings derive pleasure from someone else's woes? Basically, it is a form of self-defense. We are forever comparing ourselves to other people. Our worth as a person is determined by how well we do in life compared to others. Instead of focusing on what we can do to improve our lot in life, which is hard, we take the easy route of maligning others. We put down others to elevate ourselves. The internal unconscious talk goes something like this: "If David is promiscuous, and Vanessa is an idiot, I must be so much better than them."

Spreading rumors and putting others down creates a noxious culture. Susan Fiske, a psychologist at Princeton University, wrote a book called *Envy Up, Scorn Down.*[2] The book details our proclivity to compare ourselves to others, and our temptation to either put them down or envy them. While some benign gossip can be fun, we have to make sure we don't cross the line. To be sure, gossip is only one side of the relationship coin. People act also empathically, with many positive results for the giver and receiver of compassion. In this book we will explore both sides of relationships, negative and positive, and see how they relate to overall well-being.

The *Gossip* story begins to show how various aspects of well-being relate to each other. Our interpersonal well-being is closely tied to our psychological well-being. Emotional insecurities lead to cheap talk about others, which, in turn, can erode community well-being, which leads me to the *Prefrontal Phontex* story.

At first blush, this does not seem a story about community well-being, but when you think about the impact of texting and driving on the entire community of commuters, you pretty quickly realize the collective impact of irresponsible drivers. Compare in your mind a city where commuters engage in texting and driving, causing accidents right and left, with a place where drivers are courteous and polite. By the time you get to work in the former scenario, you are a bundle of nerves. In the latter, you feel pretty good about living in a civilized place. The impact, by the way, is felt not only by drivers, but by pedestrians as well. When we lived in Canada, as soon as we approached the crosswalk, drivers would decelerate. In Miami, when drivers spot you near the crosswalk, they accelerate.

Assuming you made it to work safely, and hopefully on time, you want to do your best. Being organized is the subject of our third story. This is a challenge for many people driven to distraction by the cacophony of stimuli bombarding computer screens. If you don't perform well at work, your psychological well-being is likely to suffer, your stress might go up, and your financial well-being might go down. To cope with it all you go to the gym, but if you're highly neurotic like me, instead of having a good time you fret about your looks, compare yourself to others, and feel hopeless about the size of your muscles, which brings us to acceptance.

Feelings of shame are not uncommon. Our unconscious deals with shame in different ways. Many dreams revolve around it. Shame is the enemy of psychological well-being. Coming to terms with our own looks (and sounds) is a big psychological task. The leader of the opposition in Israel, Mr. Herzog, takes voice lessons to sound manlier. The ways we look and sound make a difference in how we are perceived.

Acceptance of all kinds of looks and voices is within our control. We have to love ourselves, but to do so it helps to feel loved and accepted by others. I've come to live well with my big ears and with my girly voice, but it would help if people at the other end of the line would listen when I say my name is ISAAC. Come to think of it, I should probably say this is MR. ISAAC speaking.

As the *Gluteus Maximus* and *Crowdsourcing* stories illustrate, I've had my share of self-perceived imperfections. Perhaps you had some too. Some may still cause you to ruminate or to act compulsively. It really helps if you can build on your strengths in other areas of life. Hugh Jackman's muscles I will never have, but perhaps I can excel in other domains of life, such as work, family, or relationships. After all, these are big parts of life. This is why, despite my hatred of shopping, I sometimes accompany my wife to the mall. I never miss an opportunity to have unique experiences together. Shopping is obviously not my ticket to happiness, but I learned to compromise, and Ora learned to limit my exposure to sale signs.

Well-Being Defined

As shown in the stories, well-being is a positive state of affairs in six domains of life: Interpersonal, Communal, Occupational, Physical, Psychological, and Economic. In short, I call these the I COPPE spheres. The various I COPPE domains correlate to overall well-being.[3] The higher the level of well-being in a particular domain, the higher our overall satisfaction with life. The key is to learn how to make progress in each domain, one step at a time. While we should strive to do well in all domains of life, the good news is that we can start improving our life by focusing on areas of strength and opportunity. We don't need to make a dramatic change in all areas at once. We can start to make some small changes in one aspect of life. This will build our confidence to improve other parts. Research shows that small wins can build confidence in our ability to make bigger changes.[4] As we will see throughout the book, there are plenty of opportunities to promote our well-being.

When people think of well-being, they often think of physical health, but this is just one aspect. The other domains are equally important. What's more, they all work in concert. Healthy relationships lower stress and improve psychological and physical well-being. They also strengthen immunity and boost resilience.[5] A sense of community increases psychological and physical vitality.[6] The same goes for occupational well-being.[7]

The I COPPE domains interact in interesting ways. The more satisfied we are in one, such as interpersonal, the higher the chances that we will be overall pleased with our lives.[8] In addition, strengths in a particular I COPPE area can compensate for weaknesses in others. You may experience physical challenges, or even a disability, but high levels of satisfaction in the interpersonal, occupational, or psychological domains can lead to general satisfaction with life. Knowing that some strong domains can compensate for weak ones is very useful. Instead of focusing only on ways to overcome deficits, we can also think of creating wealth in more malleable aspects of life.[9]

Wealth is not just about money, though; far from it. Wealth refers to capital also in the interpersonal, communal, occupational, physical, and psychological facets of life.[10] We all know about financial capital, and since the nineties, we've heard a lot about social capital. My approach goes further in claiming that we can build capital and wealth in all I COPPE domains. A reservoir of positive emotions, built on supportive relationships, can serve us well in times of distress.[11] A caring community, rich in compassion, can help us buffer sickness and isolation.[12] Financial resources enable us to go on memorable vacations and form bonds with family and friends.[13] Psychological and intellectual capital can translate into great jobs. Wealthy pillars can sustain fragile ones.[14]

Well-being flows from health, wealth, and mattering in all facets of life. We should strive to excel in all I COPPE domains. The good news is that there are so many areas of life and so many ways to get happier, wealthier, and wiser that some are bound to appeal to you. You can start in any of the I COPPE areas that interest you the most, or that seem easiest, and then progress to more challenging ones. If you want to be wealthier, there are several I COPPE domains. Each chapter contains two sections with practical applications: *Know Yourself, Help Yourself* and *Know Others, Help Others*. There I discuss how to use in real life what we've learned from I COPPE.

Happiness and Well-Being

I aim to promote happiness as well as well-being, but do you think that these two things are synonymous? They are related, to be sure, but they are not the same. Happiness refers to momentary enjoyment and pleasure. When you laugh and have a good time, or when you eat your favorite ice cream, you experience happiness. Well-being, in turn, refers to feelings of satisfaction with life overall, and with specific aspects of it. To make a well-being judgment, you have to think and evaluate your life and its unique elements. Whereas happiness is based on momentary emotions, well-being relies on assessments over time.

But there is one more way in which happiness and well-being differ. To experience well-being over time, the pursuit of meaning must be present. Sometimes we suffer as we struggle to achieve our goals. We work and study hard. We delay gratification. We forgo fun activities to finish a project. These sacrifices do not necessarily make us happy, but they make us proud to have achieved something meaningful.[15]

Meaning is about devotion to a worthy cause: love, compassion, faith, peace, or the environment. Personal achievements in sports, science, or business can provide a sense of meaning and purpose. They go beyond momentary pleasure and happiness. These activities represent engagement and alignment with goals and values. People find meaning in wildly different ways. Some may bring happiness and some may not, but they all seem purposeful and value-driven.

For all their differences, however, happiness and well-being are related. It is hard to imagine high levels of well-being when all the moments you recall are awful. After all, when we are asked how satisfied with life we are, we think about experiences. If most memories that come to mind at the moment are depressing, it is hard to report high levels of well-being. By the same token, we may struggle as we work to achieve meaningful goals, but accomplishing them can make us happy and proud.

Meaning and Mattering

Joy and laughter make for good and happy moments. Meaning and mattering make for well-being. As you learn about the components of well-being, and strategies to improve it, we will see how they relate to feelings of mattering and meaning. Meaning is about making a difference in the world through passion, devotion, dedication, achievement, and commitment to a set of values and beliefs. Mattering, in turn, is about feeling that we count, that we are important, and that we can make a difference. In short, it is about *recognition* and *impact*.[16]

We need to feel valued, and we need to feel useful. When we fail to fulfill these needs, we engage in unhealthy behaviors that result in either deficits or excesses. Recognition derives from the nurturance that we receive from others. The more we benefit from positive messages and attention in childhood, the more secure we are going to be in adulthood. But for kids to grow into fair and caring adults, they also need to be taught how to care for others.

Our need for affirmation requires that other people notice our presence and our worth. When this need is thwarted, or overly indulged, we risk either demanding too much attention or fearing social interactions. The former will lead to entitlement and narcissism; the latter to invisibility and self-denial. If you've had interactions with entitled people, you can tell that they speak mostly about themselves, rarely show interest in others, and care very little about you. It is mostly about them. On the other hand, if you've had interactions with socially anxious individuals, you can tell that it is hard for them to be heard. We need talent to engage the anxious and restrain the pompous.

To experience mattering we need external validation as well as self-affirmation. The love, attention, empathy, and acceptance we receive from others are exceptional nutrients of well-being. The more nurtured we are, the higher the chances that we would want to assert ourselves and make a mark in the world.[17] As unique individuals, we want to exercise autonomy and self-determination. We seek autonomy and independence from external control. We value voice and choice. We seek opportunities to pursue our goals without interference.[18]

When you feel you don't have a voice—at home, school, work, or community—you feel disempowered. Lack of self-determination damages our integrity. Oppressive situations rob people of their ability to exercise independence of mind and spirit. But too much self-determination, to be sure, may come at the expense of other people. *My way or the highway* is not a great motto for conviviality. This is why mattering is not all about me. Caring for others leads to meaning and is an antidote to egocentric behavior.[19]

The best gift we can give one another is a nurturing environment. Many studies document the benefits of growing up in caring families. Unfortunately, many studies also show the deleterious effects of growing up in stressful environments, where adults are absent and children neglected. Nurturance will have enormous impacts on kids. The repercussions can last a lifetime. Unless we experience a caring and nurturing environment in early childhood, we are not going to feel as valued and appreciated in adulthood.[20]

It is part of our nature to pursue self-efficacy. Children and adults alike want to feel mastery and control over their environments. We want to feel that we can do things. This is obvious in children, who enjoy learning new skills, such as walking and feeding themselves. As adults, we engage in art and work to make a difference. We crave a sense of agency. We want to be active participants in the world.[21] When this wish is blocked, or too indulged, we end up with one of two unattractive options: desire to dominate others, or fear of impotence. If we don't experience enough opportunities for mastery and self-efficacy, we will either try to compensate by becoming bossy and domineering, or we will stop trying to make a difference altogether, leading to feelings of helplessness and depression. This is why nurturing a healthy sense of mattering is vital.

Recognition and impact, the essential components of mattering, are present in all I COPPE domains. The interpersonal domain affords many opportunities to feel loved, valued, and appreciated. The same goes for community and occupational settings, where we interact with peers and bosses who can support or ignore us.

Impact, the feeling that we can make a difference, is also at play in interactions with family, friends, coworkers, and community members. We can also feel effective in physical, psychological, and economic domains, conquering challenges and making progress toward well-being.

To summarize, in response to neglectful environments people respond in one of two main ways. They either shy away from contact due to fear of rejection, or compensate by demanding too much attention. Neither pathway is healthy. When the need for recognition is blocked, or overly indulged, negative processes ensue. Similarly, when the need for making a difference is thwarted, or overly indulged, we risk domination or helplessness. Recognition and impact are at play in all domains of life, and, as we shall see, they represent a set of fundamental human needs.

Needs and Values

Needs must be represented in values and actions. To promote personal, relational, and communal well-being, we have to be clear about what values to espouse and what actions to pursue.[22] Implicit in the previous section were some basic needs. In this section we make them explicit and translate them into values.

Self-Care

This value reflects the need for safety and personal well-being. Our very survival depends on self-care. It may seem superfluous to talk about it, but there are people who neglect their bodies and punish their minds. Think of people with eating disorders, or self-mutilating behaviors. To some extent, people with depression are very harsh on themselves too. They ruminate and engage in punitive self-talk. Judging by the number of people suffering from depressive symptoms, lack of self-care is a real challenge.

Of course, we can take self-care too far, obsessing about our looks, image, and power. This is counterproductive. Self-care is about acceptance too. While I still try to project a manlier voice on the phone, I've come to accept my vocal cords. I suppose I get affirmation in other ways, especially from my adorable wife, who swears that she loves my voice.

Indeed, self-acceptance is foundational to psychological well-being. Being overly judgmental, toward self and others, is very harmful. Mindfulness is a powerful technique for self-acceptance. When we cannot prevent negative thoughts, we can learn to see them just as thoughts. Like menacing waves, they too shall pass. They may be there, but they don't have to dictate how we feel about ourselves.[23]

Self-Determination

Voice and choice are essential to mattering. Our very integrity depends on our ability to make decisions. This is what self-determination is about. The inability to control our destiny has risky consequences, for body and mind. Living under the threat of coercion, however subtle, predisposes us to respond in fear. This constant state of stress produces toxic hormones that harm our physiological system.[24]

Throughout the world, people rebel against oppression and subjugation. Individuals, groups, and nations have fought tooth and nail throughout history to protect their self-determination. This is why the French promoted liberty as the first value of their revolution.

In children, you see the need for self-determination when they say, as early as they can, "I can do it by myself." This assertion of personal control motivates a lot of our behavior. If you are feeling unhappy, chances are that something, or someone, is interfering with your self-determination.

Like self-care, however, this can be taken too far. If all I care about is my own self-determination, few people will play with me. The unrelenting pursuit of self-determination can easily turn into the pursuit of domination and narcissism.[25] To coexist, our wishes must be tempered by the needs of others. This is to say that self-care and self-determination must be balanced by mutual care and mutual respect.

Relating with Care

The need for recognition, crucial to mattering, depends on caring. As infants, we depend on the care of others, but as we mature we become agents of caring ourselves. From infancy, we empathize with others who seem to be suffering. We are born with prosocial tendencies. At the same time, without caring from others we could not survive, let alone thrive.[26] And the beauty of it is that helping others is one of the best forms of helping ourselves.

Nurturing environments don't just happen, though. They require careful planning and design. Attentive parents think well in advance when to have kids, how to provide a caring and enriching environment, and how to keep their sanity at the same time, which can be a challenge. The enemies of mutual care are violence, coercion, neglect, rejection, and abuse. While abuse is an error of commission, neglect is an error of omission.

Lack of caring is often internalized as lack of worth. Children often interpret lack of caring as a reflection of their own personal faults. As a consequence, they stop loving themselves. Lack of caring often turns into lack of self-care. Lack of self-care, in turn, leads to lack of self-determination. But the opposite is also true. Caring by others turns into self-care, which bolsters self-determination and control over one's life.

Relating with Respect

Not all our relationships are of an intimate nature. We come into contact with many people with whom we don't really have a deep and caring relationship, but to whom we owe respect. Recognition, the first element of mattering, is premised on mutual respect. The need for respect is as basic as the need for self-care. We cannot establish deeply caring relationships with many people, and that is understandable, but we can establish mutual respect.

Mutual respect says "I value you, your voice matters, and what you are thinking is important to me, even if it's not what I'm thinking." If I respect you, I will ask for your opinion, involve you in decisions affecting your life, and I will never diminish your worth as a person. Furthermore, I will never belittle you, threaten you, or coerce you in any way. These are the main tenets of respect. In relationships, we are agents as well as recipients of care. We demonstrate caring and respect for others, regardless of their background, and we expect to get it from others as well.

Mutual care and mutual respect bolster mattering. The more we engage in these behaviors, the more we contribute to the recognition of others. Similarly, the more we care for our kids, the more we strengthen their self-determination. This will make for a challenging life as a parent, but you can take solace in knowing that it's the right thing to do. As the father of a highly self-determined son, I know it only too well. I know the challenges but I also know the rewards.

Sense of Community

We seek belonging and a sense of community. We have a need to feel part of a family and a community. The need to belong complements the need for self-determination. We want to be our own person, but we also want to be part of a tribe. Negotiating this tension is not always easy, which is why we need the values of caring and respect. If I care for you, despite our differences, I will have a respectful conversation about how to get along and how to reconcile differences. Mutual care and mutual respect are a bridge between self-determination and sense of community.

Sense of community is an antidote for isolation and a tonic for self-preservation. We cannot experience mattering in isolation. In a state of loneliness, we can neither feel recognized nor make a difference. Without a sense of community we fail at mattering. With a sense of belonging we flourish and thrive.[27]

Sense of Fairness

As soon as kids can string words together, you can hear them say "that's not fair." We hear it on the playground, at home, and at school. A sense of fairness, that you get what you deserve, is crucial to well-being. We respond vehemently to violations of fairness. We are acutely sensitive to it. Violations of this type are perceived as infringements on our dignity, making us feel that we are less worthy than others. This is a major assault on mattering and recognition. Lack of fairness has proven deleterious to our health and well-being. To restore our health and wellness we sometimes have to restore our sense of fairness.[28] As we shall see next, well-being can be enhanced through fit, fitness, and fairness.

Together, these six values are a pretty good guide for mattering. The first two deal with personal needs, the next two with relational, and the last two with communal needs. All of them are important, and all of them respond to different needs.

Fit, Fitness, and Fairness

We meet needs and cultivate mattering through fit, fitness, and fairness. Fit is about the right match between person and environment.[29] The context of life—family, work, community—has to be responsive to human needs, and human beings need to adjust to the context. Life is a dance between what we want and possess and what the context can offer. Sometimes we have to change the environment to make it more in line with human needs. For example, we can make it more nurturing and accepting. Sometimes we have to change human tendencies—selfishness, aggressiveness—to maximize fit with the situation. Families and workplaces that provide caring and respect foster mattering. Settings that ignore you create alienation.

Shopping malls are a terrible fit for me. If I spend too much time there, I become insufferable. My wife knows it, so she tries to take me there as little as possible. My family, in turn, is a good fit for me. We support and love one another. We do our best to provide a fun and caring environment. My workplace is also a good fit for me. I have lots of freedom to pursue my interests and work with great colleagues. But this hasn't always been the case. I used to work at a place that was very supportive, but not very stimulating. Overall the fit was not great, so I left. In general, though, I feel pretty lucky, as many people work in toxic environments.

Outside family and work, the community can also provide a good fit, to a lesser or greater extent. Crazy drivers make for stressful environments, as shown in *Prefrontal Phontex*. Restaurants in rural Virginia are a poor fit for vegans, as seen in *Gluteus Maximus*. If you are the subject of gossip, at work or in the neighborhood, I guarantee that your fit will deteriorate. A chaotic household or workplace can be deadly for some people. If you are neat, you want to live and work with folks who pick up after themselves. If you want to survive in Miami, you want to live near work, and avoid the lunatics behind the wheel, as we do. Knowing my sensibilities, Ora insisted that we buy a house near campus. We reap the benefits of this decision every single day.

There is a very practical side to this discussion. Is there a good fit between your needs and aspirations and your social environment? Are you surrounded by supportive or judgmental people? Are there lots of barriers for you to achieve your goals? Have you thought of changing the environment to improve your life?

I made some major changes in my life to obtain a better fit between my needs and living conditions. To begin with, I moved countries four times, which sounds crazy, but it's true. I grew up in Argentina under a dictatorship that was both brutal and anti-Semitic. Terrible fit, especially if you opposed the military dictatorship and were Jewish, like me: two for two.

I moved to Israel when I was a teenager. After nine years there, Ora and I wanted to pursue advanced degrees in Canada, which we thought would present better opportunities for us. After fifteen wonderful years in Canada, the winter started getting to us. Ora, who uses a wheelchair, was restricted by the constant presence of snow and slush. There were many wonderful things about Canada, but weather was not one of them. In pursuit of better weather, we moved to Australia. We had three amazing years in Melbourne, but my occupational fit was not great, so we moved to the United States, where I had some interesting job opportunities.

These are obviously major life changes, but let me be clear: a better fit does not require emigrating four times. People make smaller changes to improve their fit all the time. All of us pursue a better situation. This is the reason why people change jobs, change partners, and learn new skills. This may require moving, making changes to the relationship you have, or going back to school, which leads us to fitness. Fitness is about acquiring skills to improve the fit with the environment. We need skills to promote meaning and mattering. The more we refine them, the higher the chances that we will matter to ourselves and to others.

To be clear, fitness is not just about physical well-being; far from it. Fitness refers to the entire set of skills we should have to promote well-being in all domains of life. We can pursue fitness not just in physical, but also in interpersonal, psychological, and occupational well-being. To succeed in the world of work we need to refine our attitude and aptitude. These are things we can work on.

Good listening is an acquired skill, as is teamwork. Both are part of caring and respect. These have to do with attitude. Writing computer code, cutting hair, or doing hip replacements is a matter of aptitude. They all can be learned. Saving money is also a skill. The same can be said for avoiding junk food. These are all things we can learn. Some, like doing hip replacements, will take quite some time to learn, but others, like eating better, lowering your stress, or improving your listening don't have to take years of training. In the next section, *GREASE the Plan*, we review an approach for goal attainment that makes fitness doable.

Fitness is a necessary but insufficient condition for well-being. The right fit between person and environment requires fitness but also fairness. Fairness relates to the role of justice in mattering and well-being. If injustice prevails, improving our fitness may not be enough. If you find yourself in a domestic abuse situation, improving your communication skills may not stop the abuse. You may be the greatest communicator on earth, but this may not prevent a physically abusive partner from acting violently. This is a profound lack of fairness. Without fairness, you can't achieve wellness.

Fairness, or lack thereof, can take place in relationships, families, workplaces, or the community. Women are still getting paid less than men for similar work. People with disabilities still encounter barriers. Children are abused by ill-prepared parents. Minorities are discriminated against due to racism, bias, and stigma. Poor children, due to no fault of their own, go hungry. Workers are exploited by callous employers. These are injustices afflicting large parts of the population, worldwide.

While these may be egregious violations of human rights, injustice also takes place in subtle ways. In fact, it may be so subtle that you are not even aware that it's taking place. If you always give in to your husband's wishes—if he is the one deciding what movie to watch, what car to buy, and who to invite for dinner—your voice may be slowly but surely drowning. Human beings are so good at coping and adjusting to the environment that sometimes we learn to live with unlivable situations.

What's more, people make excuses for inexcusable behavior of others. Just like children of abusive parents make excuses for them, so do folks in the workplace and the community. This is when fitness needs to help fairness. We should learn how to detect signs of unfair treatment. Bullying does not have to be overt to be harmful. Insidious ways can be just as damaging to our soul. Harassment can take many forms: sexual, psychological, social. Once we learn how to recognize these transgressions, we can improve our fitness to enhance fairness. Being assertive is part of interpersonal and psychological fitness.

To achieve an optimal fit between person and environment we need fitness and fairness. We need to improve fitness in all I COPPE domains of life. But we also need to strive for fairness. If you are a woman in an abusive relationship, you have to call it for what it is: an injustice. If you are prevented from taking a job due to your ethnicity, you have to call it for what it is: discrimination. While injustice harms health, fairness improves wellness. When we are treated with respect, our overall well-being improves. In the next six chapters we explore how fit, fitness, and fairness play out in I COPPE.

GREASE the Plan

Understanding must be followed by action. To improve fit, fitness, and fairness, we need a method. We call it *GREASE the Plan*, and it consists of six strategies:

- *Gradual*:   Taking small steps, one at a time, to achieve a goal.
- *Rewarded*:   Praise and reward yourself for accomplishing small steps.
- *Easy*:   Make it simple for yourself so that you can experience success quickly.
- *Alternatives*: Always have an alternative available for the behavior you want to replace.
- *Supported*:   Get your friends and relatives to help you and cheer you on.
- *Educated*:   Learn and inform yourself about the issue you want to tackle.

Let's talk about gradual steps. Your system gets addicted to many things: cigarettes, donuts, betting, beer, sodas, email, Instagram, Facebook, and Donald Trump insults. If you give up these things cold turkey, you are at risk of falling off the wagon. Let's say you eat too many donuts: five per week. You want to bring it down to zero. How about reducing your donut intake to three the first week? If you are successful at that, you will feel better physically and psychologically and will be ready to conquer the next challenge: two donuts the week after.

Once you conquer a small wellness objective, chances are you will also want to get healthier in other ways. You start small. Then you feel great about your accomplishments, and then you get ready to tackle the next goal: fewer sugary drinks. Many people give up on their goals because they think they don't have enough willpower. Well, let me tell you: willpower is overrated. Don't blame your lack of willpower.[30] Instead of blaming your lack of motivation, create a positive habit gradually. Habits are routines that can be formed and reformed. Instead of five donuts per week you eat four, and on Fridays you snack on an apple instead. Instead of yelling at your kids for leaving the house late, you create a new habit of getting up thirty minutes early and rewarding them for doing so.[31]

The key to achieving your goal gradually is having a SMART goal: specific (eating fewer donuts), measurable (four instead of five the first week), achievable (reducing one donut per week does not seem too hard), relevant (you worry about your cholesterol), and time-limited (your plan is to bring down the consumptions of donuts from five to two in three weeks). In addition to selecting a SMART goal, you need to reward and reinforce yourself. You need to celebrate small accomplishments. I get rewarded by telling myself that I'm getting close to the finish line.[32]

In the case of publications, it is a very long process from the moment you write a paper or a book and the time it gets published and you hear—hopefully—some positive feedback. If you just reward yourself at the end of the process, it is very frustrating because you have to wait so long to hear anything about the value of your work. But if you break down the task into small pieces, and reinforce yourself for accomplishing tiny steps along the way, the job becomes less arduous. I usually reward myself by thinking that I'm on track to finish a certain part of the book by a certain date. Of course you may not be as self-disciplined as me, and in all likelihood you need a more tangible reward for good behavior, so go ahead and watch another episode of *Seinfeld*. Choose a reward that works for you—in moderation, and most importantly, one that does not work against your goal, like having chocolate cake because you avoided a donut.

Having someone to cheer you on is very rewarding. Tell your friends to reinforce you for taking the first step toward a healthier you. Rewards come in many shapes: a good word from your spouse, your doctor, or your boss. You can invite yourself to the movies, or a walk. Celebrate your accomplishment. Make a big deal out of it.

The E in GREASE stands for *easy*. The goal is to get you to experience success quickly, so pick something really doable. You can increase the level of difficulty later, but to begin with, stick with easy targets. If you prove to yourself that you can take control of your donut or soda intake, you will grow your self-efficacy and the belief that you can change other aspects of your life. Think of the E in GREASE as the motivator in chief. Set easy goals and share with friends your success. If you can eliminate one donut a week, you can surely eliminate two.

Without alternatives it is difficult to renounce bad habits. If you are accustomed to something sweet in the middle of the afternoon to pick you up, don't give up on something sweet. You can replace the chocolate bar with a fruit. If you want to lose weight, PLEASE do not starve yourself. Your body wants and needs nutrition. You just need to consume better nutrition, not to eliminate nutrition. Please do not go hungry. Your organism does not like hunger. If you starve it, it will come back with a vengeance. The trick is not to starve your system, but to give it the right amount and the right type of fuel.[33]

I eat five times a day, but small portions. Hearty breakfast with gluten-free steel-cut oatmeal (cooked with water, not with milk), berries, an orange, almonds, and pecans. For a change, sometimes I eat shredded wheat, with extra bran of course. Before that I drink a big cup of hot water with lemon. During the day I drink lots of water. I always keep a tall refillable bottle of water next to me. Midmorning I have a healthy snack like almonds or veggies. For lunch, we usually have a soup with a big and colorful salad. In the afternoon I snack on a granola bar, a fruit, or some veggies, and in the evening we usually have a grain like quinoa with beans and blanched vegetables.

Before you say you could never do this, let me remind you that I grew up in Argentina, where we used to eat meat three times a day, and not just steaks, but brains, bull testicles, and coagulated blood in the form of sausages. Change is possible. I eat now mostly a vegan diet. The exception is when we go out to eat and there aren't healthy vegan options. Then we eat fish.

In the unlikely event that you become vegan, check your B12 levels, because that is a risk factor, and make sure you get enough iron. I eat so much spinach and other green leafy vegetables that I'm okay with iron, but I do take a vegan source of B12. No fun being low on B12. But I have to warn you, if you eat like me you may end up with a girly voice, a funny accent, and big ears.

Just as there are alternatives to eating junk, there are alternatives to yelling at your kids. Rewarding them for good behavior is a substitute to screaming. If you feel you interact with your children mostly through arguing, create alternative habits. Remember when they were little and you used to read them bedtime stories? That was quality time, to use a cliché. You can find ways to interact with your grown kids by asking them open-ended questions. Make a point of interacting with them on a positive note. Praise them for their effort to help out at home. Ask them about sports. Refrain from being judgmental. Show interest in their friends. Listen and avoid lecturing them.

The S in GREASE is for *supported*. You might think that you are not influenced by other people. You think that only people with weak character are affected by what others do and say. WRONG! All of us are highly susceptible to other people's opinions and perceptions of us. To achieve goals, we need to recruit supporters and avoid naysayers. At first, your health habits might be threatening to others who are still very much engaged in a junk lifestyle. You can practice what to tell them when they invite you to go out and get drunk, or when they make fun of you for your new lifestyle. Great opportunity to practice your assertiveness skills!

Some people, like most of my extended family, are slow learners. It took most of them about ten years to stop telling me that I look thinner than the previous time they saw me (I've had the same weight for the last twenty-five years). Every single time they used to see me they would tell me that I'm getting thinner while I hadn't changed at all. They, in turn, kept getting bigger and bigger.

Naysayers will find many opportunities to critique your new lifestyle: "You're not fun anymore, you don't drink anymore, and it's hard to go out to eat with you." The more you get your friends and family to support the new YOU, the easier it will become. Better yet, you can ask your immediate family to join you in your pursuit of a happier and healthier you.[34] Cook together, go to the gym together, and talk about how to reduce stress in the family. Practice nonjudgmental listening. You might think that happy and healthy equals boring, but nothing could be further from the truth. If you are organized and your routine is healthy, you will have more time and energy to do fun things instead of worrying about being late with work or feeling sluggish.

Finally, the second E in GREASE stands for *educated*. There is so much misinformation about dieting, nutrition, happiness, and health that we are all at risk of being taken for a ride. Do yourself a favor and explore the issues afflicting you. There is really no substitute for educating yourself by reading and learning and talking with a variety of experts. Remember that at the end of the day, you are the best EXPERT on YOU. Do not relinquish control of your health and well-being to other people. Professionals have a lot to offer, but don't just go with the opinion of the first professional you encounter.

There are psychological interventions like meditation that can do some good. For some people, nurturing their spirituality is the royal path to happiness and meaning in life. Most physical ailments are related to lifestyle, and the best solution is improving your wellness, not necessarily taking more medications with noxious side effects. The point is to resist the lifestyle dictated by commercials pushing a consumerist agenda—except for brown Tumi bags that fill my life, and my closet.

Know Yourself, Help Yourself

Let's apply what we learned in this chapter to your own life. To evaluate how well you're doing in the various domains of life, you can start by taking the I COPPE self-assessment. This validated tool, which I developed with my colleagues, can be taken online. Go to www. funforwellness.com/icoppe. In a few minutes you will get an I COPPE profile that can help you reflect on your life. There you will see your areas of strengths, and areas in need of improvement (if you don't have access to the online version, you can do the paper and pencil version found in the appendix).

Next you can go back to the humor stories and ask yourself if there are things that make you self-conscious. I told you about my physical imperfections: nose, ears, voice, tiny muscles. I also shared with you some of my obsessive-compulsive behaviors with neatness and eating, and I revealed my hatred of shopping, to say nothing of texting and driving. I'm trying to grow more Zen in all these aspects of life, which can be challenging when you live in Miami—world capital of plastic surgery, reckless driving, and shopping. Luckily, other aspects of my life are going pretty well. I feel like I matter at home, work, and the community. I feel well psychologically, physically, and occupationally, which reminds us that we can always leverage strengths to compensate for difficulties.

What are some issues affecting your well-being? What are your areas of strengths? Can you use some of your personal assets to cope with more challenging areas of life? Success in some I COPPE domains can compensate for weaknesses in others. When you look at the result of the I COPPE self-assessment, which domains require more attention?

Do you feel a sense of mattering? Are you engaged in meaningful activities? What are some barriers for you to feel recognized at home, work, and community? When it comes to values and needs, how well are you doing in self-care, self-determination, mutual care, mutual respect, sense of community, and sense of fairness? Do you feel that these needs and values are present in your life?

Finally, is there a good fit in your life? Do you feel that your relational, occupational, and communal contexts are good for you? Similarly, do you feel that you possess the right skills to promote your well-being? What about fairness? In the next chapters we explore in more depth all these elements of well-being. For now, I recommend just reflecting on these questions. Sometimes we are not even aware of what is preventing us from achieving higher levels of well-being. The point of this chapter is to provide a vocabulary that can help in growing your awareness of what can be improved, and what personal strengths you can leverage.

To change any aspect of your life, you have to set a SMART goal: specific, measurable, achievable, relevant, and time-limited. It can be as simple as eating fewer donuts or reading more with your kids. But it can also be more complex, such as getting a better job or finishing a degree. In all cases, you need to set a goal and find ways to GREASE the plan. Remember that every major accomplishment in life starts with small and gradual steps. Take time to reinforce yourself for taking initiative, and try to make the first step easy. If you want to change a negative behavior, such as eating too many sweets, try to find an alternative first, such as fruits. And it always helps to get support from family and friends. Make a commitment to your spouse and ask for her support. Change is a team sport.

Finally, get educated about the change you want to make, and the solutions you implement. There is so much propaganda for miracle cures that people can get confused. Don't jump to the first diet you see on TV, and don't rush to purchase pills before you explore their effectiveness. There is a lot of evidence that many physical and psychological ailments have to do with lifestyle, quality of relationships, self-care, caring, and mattering. Feeling recognized by others, and making a difference in the world, are indeed wonderful and invigorating pathways to wellness. To matter is to feel engaged. To feel engaged we need to create spaces that afford recognition and opportunities to make a difference. To build that space we need to know ourselves, but we also need to know others. Healthy and nurturing places require that we know others and help others.

Know Others, Help Others

A significant piece of well-being is the feeling of mattering. Mattering consists of feeling recognized and useful. To create a family, workplace, or community where everybody experiences mattering, we have to promote certain values: self-care, self-determination, caring, respect, sense of community, and sense of fairness. These values are important because they represent basic human needs. Our own self-care and self-determination depend on caring, respect, sense of community, and sense of fairness. For us to experience mattering, we have to get some care and compassion from others. We have to be treated with respect and fairness, and we have to feel part of a community. For others to experience mattering, we have to treat them with respect, care, and fairness. It is all about mutuality and reciprocity.

To create a nurturing environment for others we can start by asking if they feel like they matter. Do they feel affirmed, appreciated, valued, and cared for? Do they have opportunities to make a difference in the world? Do they experience self-determination? Are they treated fairly and with respect? And the most important question we can ask, what can we do to facilitate these feelings and experiences? Are we enabling these feelings or are we blocking them? Do we open doors or put up walls?

Making a difference starts with the people close to you. Some people may achieve great fame and recognition for liberating nations or discovering vaccines, but for most of us, the biggest opportunity to make a difference and experience mattering is with folks close to us, at home, at work, and in the community. If we want to experience impact, and derive meaning from being helpful, helping others close to us is the proverbial low-hanging fruit.

Just like we help ourselves with the GREASE method, we can start helping others gradually. Remember to start small and get some small wins under your belt. Before you know it, you will be feeling better by making an impact in somebody's life. As you help others, you will be helping yourself. Creating a nurturing environment for our family, colleagues, students, clients, patients, and friends is a great way to start. If you want to help me, for instance, don't call me Mrs. Prilleltensky on the phone, and don't gossip about my voice, nose, and ears. Don't laugh at my gluteus maximus, don't text and drive next to me, and no matter what, please don't take me shopping.

2

Interpersonal Well-Being

THE LAUGHING SIDE

The previous chapter provided an overview of the various areas of well-being. In this chapter we explore more in-depth interpersonal well-being. I start with three stories that highlight the comical side of relationships with family, friends, and foes.

Looks, Smarts, Money

There are two main threats to interpersonal well-being: insecurities, and INSECURITIES. People have a hard time getting along with others because they fear that at some point they will be wrong, and God forbid, they may have to apologize. People hate to be wrong, but hate to apologize even more. As a social scientist intrigued by these phenomena, I developed a mathematical formula according to which the "need to be right about everything all the time and never apologize" is inversely related to looks, smarts, or money.

The more insecure you feel about your looks, intelligence, or pocketbook, the more you feel you have to be right about everything else in life. This is called a compensatory model. You compensate for your incompetence by feeling that you are right about everything. So depending on your gender, our model has four or five variables:

Women
1. Need to be right about everything all the time
2. Looks
3. Smarts
4. Money

Or,

$$\mathbf{y}_{p\,x\,1}^{g} = \mathbf{v}_{p\,x\,1}^{g} + \mathbf{\Lambda}_{p\,x\,m}^{g} \mathbf{\eta}_{m\,x\,1}^{g} + \mathbf{\varepsilon}_{p\,x\,1}^{g}$$

Men:

$$\mathbf{y}^g_{p \times 1} = \mathbf{v}^g_{p \times 1} + \mathbf{\Lambda}^g_{p \times m} \mathbf{\eta}^g_{m \times 1} + \mathbf{\varepsilon}^g_{p \times 1}$$

DIVIDED BY HOURS SPENT WATCHING FOOTBALL

Sometimes the need to be right about everything all the time is conflated with smarts. Take universities for example, where most professors are dreadful, and don't make a lot of money, but think they are very smart. In that case, our subjects compensate for being obnoxious and underpaid by coming across as smarter than they really are, which only reinforces the need to be right about everything all the time, which makes universities as much fun as the Inquisition.

Sometimes, looks and money are not enough to conquer insecurities. People work hard to come across as smart. A wealthy and good-looking acquaintance, with the intellectual curiosity of an ant, was spotted lounging next to a swimming pool pretending to read *From Nietzsche to Foucault*. Either pretentiousness got the best of her or she thought *Nietzsche* and *Foucault* were the latest European shoes. But I shouldn't be saying these things. It probably means that I have no money, or don't look great, both of which are right, and for neither of which I'm going to apologize because I'm a university professor.

Another acquaintance, big on money, has a very bad case of *need to be right about everything all the time and never apologize*, including things he has absolutely no idea about. But if might makes right, money makes wise. Tevye from *Fiddler on the Roof* got it right: "When you're rich, they think you really know!" Worse than that, when you're rich, you think *you* know.

"If I Were a Rich Man" is the most evocative and artistic expression of my mathematical formula (minus the virility part). "If I were a Rich Man . . . I'd see my wife . . . looking like a rich man's wife . . . supervising meals to her heart's delight . . . screaming at the servants, day and night."

Primal insecurities get in the way of enjoying vulnerability and the liberating ability to say "I'm sorry" or "I don't know." We fear that if we admit ignorance or mistakes, something terrible will happen. Sometimes I fear that if I make a mistake I will be fired, anti-Semitism will rise, Jews will be deported to Iran, UPS will change the color of its fleet, and the pharmacy will run out of Senokot.

Beset by the need to be right all the time, and the obsession with money, looks, and smarts, humanity has two options: Elect Donald Trump to replace Barack Obama or move to Miami, which leads me to a local corollary of my main thesis: smarts and cognitive capacity in Miami are inversely related to the number of plastic surgeries, which says nothing about money, because in Miami Medicare pays for everything, including colonoscopies for dead people in Havana.

It is really too bad that we spend so much time compensating for our insecurities that we miss the entire point of relationships, which is to have someone who can love you despite your big ears, someone who can put up with your terrible real estate decisions, and someone who lets you think you are funny. What really matters in life is not how we look on the outside, but what happens on the inside, like your digestive system. If more people could talk about their bowel movements without feeling defensive, or self-conscious, we could reverse the divorce trend and bring peace to the Middle East.

To conclude, what I really want to say about relationships is that if

$$f(x) = a_0 + \sum_{n=1}^{\infty} \left(a_n \cos \frac{n\pi x}{L} + b_n \sin \frac{n\pi x}{L} \right)$$

then stay away from university professors.

Truth, Trust, Trauma

I trust people. I tend to believe what they tell me. I'm big on trust. If they tell me they will do something, I believe them. If they share with me information, I take it at face value. In short, I'm an idiot. It takes me a while to see that not everyone is as well intentioned as I want them to be. I suffer from high expectations, which is why I was crushed when I realized that some people LIE.

Before coming to Miami Ora and I were very trusting people. So trusting in fact that we let several folks come and work in our house without any precautions whatsoever. We were still idiots. However, we were quickly reminded that Miami was not Melbourne (the one in Australia, not Florida).

It all started with Ana (not her real name, her real name was Anna), who came to the house to help us with various domestic chores. Within a few days, Ora and I discovered that a few things were missing, and I went crazy. I DO NOT misplace things. I may be totally naïve and somewhat of a moron sometimes, but I'm NOT disorganized. I'm an obsessive-compulsive neat freak.

First, my iPhone charger disappeared. This was a small thing, so against my best judgment, I resigned myself to the fact that I had probably misplaced it. Then one of my expensive brown Tumi bags disappeared. I DO NOT misplace Tumi bags. I had not devised a system for storing them for nothing. Then it was one of Ora's skirts. This went on for a few weeks until Ora and I dared question Ana's integrity. When we gently asked Ana if she had seen the missing items, she denied ever encountering them. We had a thief in our midst, and we kept employing her for fear of offending her. We had reached a new level of stupidity. It took us months of missing items and lies to realize we had been had.

When we finally said enough is enough, I warned my friend, who had also employed Ana. Our friend, in turn, warned her daughter, who warned her husband, who was home when Ana worked there. The husband was under strict orders not to leave Ana by herself. When he left her for a minute, Ana stole none other than the doghouse before leaving the premises.

Enter Victoria, who stole jewelry from us after Ora had gone out of her way to be helpful to her. Among other things, Ora had bought her books to help her with college. Oh, the value of education. This is typical of us. But this time we were smarter. We waited only a few weeks, not months, to fire her. Soon after we parted company she went on a trip overseas with the proceeds of Ora's necklaces.

For years we had gardeners who neglected our yard. We did not want to fire them because they just had a baby, and we felt for them, and they did show remorse once in a while. These guys had a special talent for driving their lawn mower over our sprinkler system. Not a single visit went by without warning them not to destroy it, to no avail. Occasionally, they would charge us double. We ignored that. We thought it was an honest mistake. After eight years of secure employment, and after dozens of warnings, pleas, reminders, and requests to be more careful, we fired them. The next thing you know we got a bill that was triple the usual. All of a sudden, after we fired them, they sent us a bill that included dandruff treatment for our grass, pedicure for our trees, and manicure for our plants. The sprinkler system had been driven over again.

Compared to the pool guy, the gardeners were beyond reproach. One day Ora and I returned from the university to find our pool empty. Where did the water go? It was hot, but seventeen thousand gallons of water do not just evaporate. Being the handy man that I am, I immediately reached for the phone. I called the pool guy and asked if he had visited today. After the affirmative reply I asked if he did something to empty the pool. "Nothing, just the usual," he said.

Our pool guy, let's call him Innocencio, was vehement that somebody else must have tampered with the pool. I thought I could trust these guys, but something was fishy. After talking with the owner of the company and pressing the issue, they told me that I must have done something wrong, that it was my fault. Innocencio thought nothing of lying. At that moment I remembered that we had installed security cameras on top of the pool whatchamacallit. I ran to the control panel, rewound the tape, and could clearly see Innocencio moving a lever to "empty pool"—an oversight. There he was, caught on tape, in the act. Oh, the sweet taste of revenge. After producing the evidence, the company stopped sending Innocencio to the house and paid for the zillion gallons required to fill the pool again.

Strangers, okay, we were fools with strangers sometimes; but friends, that's another story. A childhood friend needed some money, and shelter, and a lot of TLC, a lot. He had just separated from his wife, who used to beat him up; rare, but true. Ora and I immediately responded to the call, opening our house and our ears and our wallet. The promise of immediate return of the money was sufficient for us to lend a few thousand dollars so that he could pay the lawyers. When we shared this with a colleague, she told us to kiss the money good-bye. Cannot be true! A childhood friend would not do this to us.

The money was eventually returned, but not before my friend completely disappeared from the face of the earth for several years, and not before I expressed my indignation, which I've come to cultivate since coming to Miami. Thank you, Miami; nowhere else could I have grown out of my innocence so fast.

Fun Summer Travel

Travel can be very detrimental to your well-being, especially if it involves other people. For me, the trauma began as soon as we approached the Delta counter at Miami International Airport. I was quizzing the customer representative about my usual list of concerns: Does the airplane have a toilet? How many years of experience does the captain have? What if Delta is bought by Aeroflot in midair? Do we have seats together? Do we have vegan meals? She gave me sort of acceptable answers to the first few questions but stumbled on the meals. She said that Ora, my wife, did have a vegan meal booked but I did not. We were about to embark on a long trip to Israel with a seven-hour layover in Newark, which is not known for its vegan gourmet cuisine.

While I was going through divorce proceedings in my head on account of Ora neglecting to order a vegan meal for me, the customer service representative called on a senior person for help. After staring at the screen for what looked like eternity, she finally said that I did have a vegan meal on the flight from Newark to Tel Aviv. Ora smiled: "I told you that I ordered vegan for BOTH of us."

The first flight was uneventful, but we arrived in Newark quite hungry. The flight to Tel Aviv was departing in another seven hours, so we decided to eat something. The closest to vegan food we found was a veggie burger. After we explained to the waitress that we were vegan, and what that meant, we waited for forty-five minutes. Eventually she brought us two veggie burgers smothered with cheese on top. We told her that vegans do not eat dairy, but she probably thought that cheese and dairy were two different things. We were so famished that we decided to forgo the ordeal of returning the burgers. We tried to peel off the cheese from top of the burger, which ended up eliminating 95 percent of our meal. At least we had vegan meals waiting for us on the flight to Tel Aviv.

Although we sent two suitcases directly to Tel Aviv, I still had to schlep four carry-on bags with rocks that Ora took for self-defense in case a third intifada suddenly erupted in Israel. Looking forward to resting my back, no sooner did I take my seat than two kids entertained themselves by kicking the back of it. While I was fantasizing what I would do to these kids, my vegan meal finally arrived, which guaranteed a bit of distraction removing the foil, discovering what's inside the little plastic container, rearranging the little tray to make sure that nothing spilled on my lap, and making sure that Ora did the same so no part of her food ended on my lap either.

I usually calculate the digestive quotient of each meal by examining its fiber content. It turns out that the only part with roughage in our meal was the carton in which it came, which reminded me that I had not brought with me Senokot or Metamucil, which meant that I was not going to go to the toilet for the duration of our visit to the Holy Land.

We visit family in Israel often, so this time I came equipped. On our trip last year I bought an Israeli cell phone for $50, which was way cheaper than paying the usual $2,773 roaming charges from AT&T. Now when I go to Israel I just add minutes to the $50 cell phone and I'm in touch with all our relatives and friends, which of course turned out to be a curse because I hate phone calls, especially to cell phones because, as everybody knows, the radiation causes cancer, flat feet, Alzheimer, blindness, and testicular evaporation. Every five minutes the phone would ring with one of the following typical conversations:

Conversation #1:

Relative: *What are you guys doing today?*

Us: *We are not sure yet.*

Relative: *Okay, we will call you in ten minutes to plan the next conversation in another ten minutes until we figure out what we are doing today.*

Conversation #2:

Relative: *We will call you in five minutes to let you know if in five minutes we are ready to leave to pick you up.*

Us: *Okay.*

Conversation #3:

Relative: *We thought we would be ready in five minutes but now we will have to call you in five minutes to give you an update.*

Us: *Okay.*

Conversation #4:

Same relative, now from second car on a family trip: *We made a wrong turn and are headed for Syria.*

Us on another car: *Good luck.*

Israel is so small that a wrong turn can take you in no time to Jordan, Syria, Lebanon, or Egypt. Indeed, in Israel you always have to be a little vigilant about security issues, which is why Ora brought from Miami four bags full of rocks. If Arabs didn't start a new intifada, there was always the chance that Orthodox Jews would throw rocks at you for driving during the Sabbath. It's good to be ready for any kind of multicultural aggression, especially if you carry within you millennia of persecutory paranoia fueled by multilingual crusaders and dictators, which is what led me to be a little apprehensive when my brother-in-law took me to the Muslim quarter in the old city of Jerusalem.

We were roaming around the Muslim quarter during Ramadan, trying to find the Nablus Gate to meet our family. As we approached the gate we discovered there were 23,556 people in ten square feet trying to exit the Old City through the Nablus Gate, out of whom 23,554 were Muslim Arabs. It was peak pedestrian traffic time, as it was the end of the business day and folks were eager to have a meal after the fast. Feeling a little claustrophobic and a little paranoid, I had an irrepressible urge to shout "LET'S BE FRIENDS, I AM IN FAVOR OF RETURNING ALL THE TERRITORIES, INCLUDING BROOKLYN . . . AND MIAMI." I am sure nobody cared that there were two Jews among 23,554 Arabs in ten square feet, but I felt a little self-conscious. Blame it on 5,774 years of persecution, 3,370 pogroms, 4,898 forced migrations, 7 wars, 2 intifadas, Hitler, and Bernie Madoff.

Israel has changed a lot since Ora and I lived there in the early eighties. Every time we visit we are impressed by the speed of development. Buildings pop up in every corner, languages you've never heard of are spoken everywhere, and the country is more technologically advanced by the day. Something that never changes, however, is the heat in July. I found myself missing Miami's humidity in July.

We had a very well-planned itinerary to avoid sitting around and talking on the phone. The only problem was that our itinerary included being outside, which was many degrees hotter than Miami, in July. We had to stop every five minutes for water or pomegranate juice, which turned out to be much better than Metamucil. I discovered that three gallons of pomegranate juice is the equivalent of a teaspoon of Metamucil, or one Senokot tablet, which meant that I had to find bathrooms among the many ruins we visited. It turns out that the Romans and Greeks did not build many bathrooms for the colonized Jews, which explains why my people have so many bowel problems.

Looking forward to restful nights after exhausting days outside in the heat, we would wake up early every morning to the sound of Arab laborers picking up construction materials right outside our door. Ora, who is no less paranoid than I am, would wake me up in a panic, every single morning, telling me that there is a terrorist attack. Turns out that the unit we rented belonged to a contractor who kept his tools in a shed next to our unit. This was the second time we stayed there. We had met the landlord many times, and we knew that his employees came every morning to pick up the tools, but for some reason, Ora thought that every morning we were going to be the victims of a terrorist attack. "Isaac, there is a terrorist attack, bring your Metamucil!"

It was so hot outside, I could not just go for a run, so I meant to return to the gym I had visited last year. The only problem was that the rules had changed and they now required a doctor's note. I tried to explain to the Russian fitness instructor that I could not get a certificate now, to which he replied, in Hebrew and in a heavy Russian accent, that if I'm wearing such nice clothes, I must not be homeless and I must have access to a physician. Although my Hebrew is excellent, I could not understand whether he was serious, joking, or using Russian sarcasm, which we all know where that led the Soviets.

I went for the jovial side and told him in Hebrew that it would be "a pain in the a_ _" for me to get a health certificate from my doctor in Miami, to which he said that "they must have a fax machine in Miami," to which I said, in Hebrew, that it would be "a pain in the a_ _," at which point I discovered that he was not joking because he lectured me about civics and the proper use of the Hebrew language. Not only could I not exercise, but I got chewed out by a humorless, KGB sympathizer, smoking fitness instructor who told me to wake up my physician at 2 a.m. in Miami and ask her to fax a health certificate, at which point I went out for a pomegranate juice.

THE LEARNING SIDE

Mattering depends on feeling recognized and making an impact. When either experience goes awry, problems emerge. To compensate for lack of recognition, some folks become too controlling, like the fitness instructor, while others become too entitled. Yet others feel so deprived that they resort to stealing. Needless to say, none of them related with much care or respect, and none of them held fairness in high regard. Surely there was a lot of self-care and self-determination, but not enough attention to mutual care and mutual respect. Too much self-determination can easily degenerate into selfishness. Relating with care and respect builds trust. If in order to get your way you resort to lying or stealing, trust will never emerge, let alone a sense of community or sense of fairness.

We are forever communicating with others, either verbally or nonverbally. Some of these communications, to be sure, can be aggressive. The accumulation of microaggressions—such as the abusive treatment I got from the fitness instructor—can take a toll on our well-being. These microaggressions create stress and frustration that flood the body with cortisol and other toxic substances. This is why we have to teach the essentials of relating with caring and respect. It is very easy to cut someone off on the road because you don't feel accountable to somebody you will never see again, but should this give you license to be impolite? Infrequent microaggressions are unlikely to create permanent damage, but frequent ones will.[1]

In the absence of truth and trust it is virtually impossible to build healthy relationships.[2] The indignation revealed in these stories demonstrates how deeply we feel about loyalty and lying. We feel offended when people lie to us and betray our trust. This is not just a matter of fitness, of knowing how to communicate and what to do, but also a matter of fairness. In work settings there is a particular transgression called *informational injustice*. Lack of transparency and misinformation generate strong negative feelings. The same happens in relationships.

Lying and cheating in romantic relationships is quite prevalent. By some estimates about 10 percent of married individuals will engage in infidelity, a phenomenon that is more prevalent in men.[3] We live in a society that fosters immediate gratification over and above meaning-making.[4] We have a skill and a value deficit at the same time. Consequently, we promote an environment poorly suited for interpersonal well-being. Healthy relationships require an investment of time and emotional commitment. Fitness and fairness can prevent many of the ills associated with lack of truth and lack of trust.

Interpersonal Well-Being Defined

Interpersonal well-being refers to the level of satisfaction in relationships that matter to us. How we get along with family, friends, and fellow workers determines our interpersonal well-being. We may have great relationships at home and lousy interactions at work, or vice versa, but we're always trying to improve relationships. The quality of our interactions makes a difference in our overall, physical, psychological, and occupational well-being.

What happens in relationships matters a great deal to our physical and emotional health. People who enjoy supportive relationships have lower stress and are more resilient. In addition, they recover faster from disease and live longer. Loneliness, on the other hand, can do great damage to our health.[5] When we were living in Nashville, music legend Johnny Cash passed away a few months after his wife. This is not an uncommon pattern for males who lose their wives. Isolation makes them sick.

Whether we like it or not, we are wired to seek connections.[6] What other people think of us matters a great deal. We are programmed to compare our looks, smarts, and achievements. We are obsessed by what other people say about us.[7] And yet, for all the stress that comparisons and gossip can cause, we need one another. We want to prevent loneliness at all costs. We are social creatures through and through. Because humans are comparing machines, and because we judge our worth mostly on conventional measures of looks, smarts, and money, we can spend a lot of time on the wrong priorities. Yes, it is nice to be good-looking, to be smart, and to have money, but there is more to wealth than money, and there is more to sexy than looks. Rigid definitions of beauty and wealth exclude most of us from what is regarded as worthy of value.

To overcome this exclusionary standard, we have to create more diverse definitions of wealthy and sexy. I happen to have big ears, a funny nose, a girly voice, and a very skinny physique. If my worth were to be determined by conventional norms, I'd be under a rock right now. We have an opportunity in relationships to propagate more inclusive standards of beauty. If you are stuck evaluating yourself and others through the eyes of popular media, and you don't measure up, you are likely to be frustrated and act in either domineering or helpless ways. If you are insecure about your looks or smarts, the traditional yardsticks of worth in our culture, and you buy into the Hollywood culture, you are in trouble. Which standards of beauty and worth do you hold? How much do you buy into cultural norms of looks, smarts, and money? To understand these social and cultural dynamics, and how they affect our interpersonal well-being, we can use the fit, fitness, and fairness framework.

Interpersonal Fit

A good fit refers to a positive outcome resulting from an interaction. A good person-environment fit means that the environment meets a person's needs and that the person can thrive under these conditions. A poor fit means that the environment is not the right one for the person, or that the person is not the right one for the environment. If you are psychologically shy, you'll be happier in a place that doesn't require constant interactions. If you're very gregarious and end up in a warehouse job, stocking merchandise by yourself all day, you'll be miserable. A good fit between your temperament, preferences, and environment is a wonderful thing. Your biology, psychology, and environment have to work in sync. Kurt Lewin, a famous social psychologist, introduced the notion of person-environment fit. For a good fit to take place, the interacting parts have to complement one another.[8]

When it comes to relationships, we want a good fit between what we need and expect and what others can give us. Reciprocity is the name of the game. When we engage in mutually beneficial interactions, we experience a sense of mattering. We all want to experience recognition and impact, which are the essentials of mattering. Table 2.1 shows the feelings and behaviors associated with differing degrees of mattering. As can be seen, too much or too little creates problems.

Mattering derives from being recognized, acknowledged, and affirmed by others. We want approval. We want people to tell us that they love us. That is all good, in good measure. The problem starts when we feel so entitled and self-centered that it is all about us. We so want to feel valued and appreciated that we take more space than we deserve. We take center stage in relationships, cocktail parties, classrooms, and boardrooms. These folk are likely to suffer from three deficits: lack of appreciation, lack of skill, and lack of fairness. They lack the skill to modulate their hunger for attention, and they lack a sense of fairness because they consume all the attention.

On the other end of the continuum, we have people who feel invisible. For different reasons, they don't get enough attention and end up feeling marginalized. Think of discrimination against sexual minorities. For decades, they were afraid to come out due to repressive social norms, resulting in literal and metaphorical invisibility. The same goes for other minorities who feel ostracized, minimized, and invisible.[9] Make no mistake, though; this happens in society, but it can also happen at home and at work. Neither *entitled* nor *invisible* is a desirable state.

The second part of mattering is feeling like we are making an impact; that we matter through our actions. Feeling valued and appreciated is good, but we also need to feel like we are engaged and making a difference in the world. Here we also need to make sure that we do this in good measure. Otherwise, we end up controlling too much or feeling helpless.

Some seek mattering through the control of other people. They control their spouses, children, peers, and employees. The need for mattering grows into need for domination. This is a recipe for disaster. On the other hand, feeling helpless—that you cannot make a difference, no matter what—is equally unwelcome. In all these cases, *entitled*, *invisible*, *domineering*, or *helpless*, there are problems in the fit, skill, and fairness departments.

Table 2.1. Mattering

Mattering Type	Mattering Level		
	Too Little	*Just Right*	*Too Much*
Recognition	Feel invisible	Feel valued	Entitled behavior
Impact	Feel helpless	Feel effective	Domineering behavior

In large part, our interpersonal behavior depends on the fit and type of attachment we had with caregivers early in life. Parents who are responsive to their babies tend to build a secure base, while those who are less responsive lay the foundation for anxious, ambivalent, or avoidant attachment styles later in life. As infants learn about the world, the ability to trust adults around them is crucial. We learn from childhood, through our interaction with caregivers, that the world is either a secure or threatening place. Naturally, some kids are more temperamentally anxious than others. And others are more resilient to inattentive parents, but the best outcome derives from parental attunement to the child's needs. An anxious baby requires a more reassuring environment, especially at a young age. Eventually, we want our kids to become independent, but at the beginning of life, when the surroundings are ominous, and the baby is totally dependent on us, we must provide a secure base. We do so by being responsive and caring. This is the beginning of mattering.

When babies realize that they are well cared for, they develop trust in the world. They tell themselves that help is on the way. If they feel hungry or afraid, mom or dad will come. This is the ultimate in recognition: my needs are met, other people care about me, and I can trust my caregivers.

Research shows that a secure attachment in early childhood will serve us well in adulthood, especially during stressful periods and when we seek romantic relationships.[10] The opposite is also true. Insecure attachment early in life will tend to be reproduced in intimate relationships, leading to distrust and ambivalence. Although these early experiences can be highly influential, they are not deterministic of our happiness and well-being. Lack of interpersonal fit early in life can be addressed later in life. Repeated positive interactions can teach a person with anxious attachment style that trust is possible after all. Consistent experiences of love and attention can be highly therapeutic.

For intimate relationships to succeed, we have to be aware of each other's needs. For some with a history of secure attachment, forming and maintaining romantic relationships will be relatively easy. For some with a background of insecure attachment, starting and keeping intimate connections will be more of a challenge. But understanding where anxiety comes from is always helpful. Are we jealous and overly possessive? Are we insecure in the relationship? Do we fear rejection and abandonment? If we do, can we see connections to early experiences of neglect? Understanding the precursor of our own behavior can open the door to improvement.

While some adults may be anxious in intimate relationships, others may be avoidant. The difference is that while the former is insecure, the latter is aloof and removed. Avoidant types have a hard time with intimacy and closeness. This behavior represents an attempt to protect oneself from possible emotional pain. There is a psychological logic behind it: *If I get too close, and things go wrong, I will get hurt very badly. Better keep my distance.*

This learned behavior is beneficial in the short term because it prevents pain, but detrimental in the long term because it prevents intimacy. Guided by such logic, people behave in ways that create a poor fit in relationships, especially if the partner wishes greater closeness. As with the anxious and the secure type, the avoidant kind has its origins in interactions with caregivers early in life. Avoidant and anxious individuals benefit from cumulative experiences of care, affirmation, validation, and recognition. Such an environment has the potential to produce therapeutic experiences that can lead to happiness and well-being.

Responsive parenting is influential in secure attachment styles and in providing much-needed recognition, but it is also important in nurturing self-efficacy. Caring parents know how to foster a sense of mastery in their infants. Affording kids an opportunity to exercise control over their environment is the precursor to feeling competent later in life. Creating opportunities for children to feel in control—from choosing a pajama to feeding themselves—builds a sense of self-efficacy. This, in turn, grows into feelings of mattering.

The ability to exert control over the environment, by learning how to read or ride a bike, is foundational for self-esteem. With time, kids acquire thousands of skills, from doing math to solving interpersonal conflicts. The more successful they feel in their cognitive, emotional, physical, and social development, the more robust their sense of mattering is going to be. Moreover, when kids encounter challenges in one area of life, such as scholastic ability, they can call on other areas of strength to regain a sense of control. This is why it's crucial to nurture strengths in a variety of fields, not just academic. Interpersonal intelligence, in particular, is a great investment for life. But before we get to interpersonal fitness, let's explore further what adults look for in close relationships.

In friends, adults look for acceptance, support, trust, and joy. First of all, we want to feel accepted and supported. We expect friends to be trustworthy, keep secrets, and be there for us when we need them. Finally, we want to have a good time. Humor is an expectation of friendship. Laughing together creates bonds of connection. Reciprocity in these four domains fulfills the two requirements for mattering: recognition and impact. We want to be accepted and appreciated because that is part of recognition, but we also want to be helpful and make others laugh because that is part of impact.[11]

We want our friends to be there for us when we are in trouble, but we also want them to be there for us when we have something to celebrate, like a promotion or an accomplishment. We relive happy moments when we retell them to our friends. Their reactions to our story can be very meaningful. Excitement about our good news can make us feel appreciated and valued. Lack of interest can make us feel lonely. There is nothing worse than coming home with exciting news and feeling ignored. Sensitivity to the fit requires a proper response. If my friend got an award, and I fail to acknowledge him, I'm sending a message that he is not that important to me. Friends know how to cherish each other.[12]

In intimate relations we expect more than in friendships. In addition to trust, we expect commitment, caring, interdependence, and self-disclosure. This last one is particularly important in developing intimacy. Sharing hopes, fears, dreams, and aspirations builds connections. The richer the self-disclosure among intimate partners, the thicker the connection. Self-disclosure is an accelerator for intimacy. If all we talk about with our partner is the weather or sports, it will be hard to grow close. We expect our partners to share with us their thoughts and feelings. In addition, we expect them to stick around and not vanish at the first sign of conflict.

Romantic relationships come in different forms, depending on the interactions among three factors: intimacy, passion, and commitment. The first factor relates to closeness built on mutual concern. The second refers to sexual attraction and physiological arousal, while the third relates to dedication to the long-term health of the relationship. Ideally, we would excel in all three, but realistically, couples vary in their degree of intimacy, passion, and commitment. It is hard to maintain a relationship based solely on passion and sexual attraction. Without intimacy and self-disclosure it is hard to build a life together. Over time, couples change in terms of the prominence given to each factor, and each couple is unique. Some feed the relationship with great intimacy and others with sex. But it is hard to derive great meaning from it without investment and commitment.[13]

Interpersonal Fitness

To feel like we matter through recognition and impact we need skills. Just like we need physical fitness, we need interpersonal fitness. We must practice the craft of healthy relationships. We require competencies related to listening, connecting, communicating, and empathizing. To feel recognized, we need to know how to assert ourselves without being aggressive.

Not all of us end up in a great person-environment fit, so we need competencies to maneuver relationships at home and at work, to say nothing of schools, neighborhoods, financial institutions, and the health care system. We need to learn how to start, grow, and repair relationships. We need to practice good listening and assertive communication all day. If we want to achieve high levels of interpersonal well-being, we need to work at it. We have to have a fitness program.

Never assume that you or your close ones have mastered all the skills of interpersonal well-being. But even if you have, these skills are like your muscles; they require training and use. To improve our interpersonal fitness, we have to master three sets of actions: responding to others, expressing ourselves, and creating together. As can be seen in table 2.2, these actions pertain to needs, feelings, and beliefs.

Responding to Others

This refers to how we react to what other people are saying to us. To respond appropriately, we have to be good listeners. To listen well, we have to pay attention to three things embedded in what other people are telling us: needs, feelings, and beliefs. These elements are present in most communications. Even when people are seemingly conveying trivial information, they are expressing a need, feeling, or belief. Take the following statements:

- I finished the report on sales you requested.
- It's your time to pick up the kids from the babysitter.
- There are great vacation packages to the Bahamas.

In the first one there is probably a feeling of pride. In the second one there is a need, and in the third there might be a belief that it is time for us to go on a vacation.

The art of listening requires that we identify what is the need, feeling, or belief embedded in what people are saying. If my employee is handing me a high-quality report on time, he is probably expecting a good word in return. I have to listen for that, even if it's not an explicit request. After all, he didn't say "I finished the report, give me a cookie." But if you get into the habit of recognizing the feeling associated with a certain action or communication, you're connecting to the other person at a deeper level. When you say, "Thank you for giving me such a useful report, on time," you're speaking to the other person's feelings and needs.

Table 2.2. Skills for Interpersonal Fitness

Actions	Needs	Feelings	Beliefs
Responding to others	He or she needs . . .	He or she is feeling . . .	He or she believes that . . .
Expressing yourself	I need . . .	I'm feeling . . .	I believe that . . .
Creating together	We need . . .	We're feeling . . .	We believe that . . .

The second factual statement about the babysitter is clearly expressing a need, even though the word *need* does not appear in the sentence. This trivial statement can encapsulate multiple meanings, such as "I'm the one who always picks up the kids" or "It's about time you did your share in this house."

The last bullet can also contain multiple meanings. Depending on the context of the relationship, this statement of fact—there is a sale on trips to the Bahamas—can be saying many things: "We never take a vacation together," "You don't pay attention to my needs," "You're a workaholic," or "I really need a break from the kids." These possible interpretations contain needs (I need a break), feelings (I'm resentful of your work habits), or beliefs (couples should take breaks once in a while).

If you're interested in refining your listening skills, table 2.2 offers a few tips. Upon hearing others talk, you can be looking for needs, feelings, or beliefs in what they are saying. In the case of the first bullet, the employee may be fishing for a compliment. In the second bullet, a wife may be expressing frustration. In the third one, a husband may be voicing a need for a break or a little excitement. Of course, not all statements emitted by others contain deep psychological meaning. Sometimes a cigar is just a cigar, as Freud, the master of interpretations, famously said. But you would be surprised how many statements do contain a need, feeling, or belief embedded in them.

To enhance your listening skills, it helps to get into the habit of identifying the psychological state of the person talking to you. What is the person needing, feeling, or believing right now? The more accurate your perception, the more meaningful the conversation will be. To become more empathic, ask yourself what are the needs, feelings, or beliefs contained in this communication. This requires training and knowledge.

For example, there are dozens of ways to feel bad. You can feel sad, frustrated, disappointed, neglected, rejected, fearful, anxious, depressed, angry, tormented, remorseful, or annoyed. Likewise, there are many ways to feel good: happy, content, energized, invigorated, stimulated, healthy, exuberant, excited, and rewarded. When you get the feeling right, and you express it, the other person will usually say something like "Yeah, that's exactly how I feel."

The mechanics of good listening are not very complicated. The first step is not to say the first thing that comes to your mind, such as:

- Yeah, I also feel that way.
- It will go away.
- Don't worry about it.
- Who cares?
- The Heat won last night.

If you want to be a good listener, you need to control what you say. It's okay to think whatever comes to mind, but if you are committed to interpersonal excellence, you will park these thoughts somewhere and focus instead on what the other person is saying to you. So first step: park your intrusive thoughts.

The second step is to search for needs, feelings, or beliefs hidden in what the person is telling you. To help you with this step, ask yourself the following question: What is the need, feeling, or belief underneath what I just heard? Is the person frustrated, annoyed, elated or just drunk? Once you ascertain the psychological message of the communication, you can summarize it in your head: he is feeling disappointed, or he is ecstatic that he won the tournament. So second step: identify the need, feeling, or belief in what you just heard or saw. It helps if you try to put yourself in that person's shoes. If I were in their shoes, how would I be feeling right now?

The third step is to put into words what you think you just heard. For example, you might say: "You're feeling frustrated that we haven't had a vacation in three years." In response to a conscientious employee who produces high-quality work you might say, "You deserve to be proud of your work. You've done a great job." You are responding to the psychological content of the exchange, as opposed to facts. Your job is to put these feelings into words that resonate with the experience of the other person. But when you do that, remember to be humble and don't pretend to know exactly what the other person is feeling or thinking.

It takes experience to get it right, so don't pretend to know what the other person is experiencing better than she does. To avoid coming across as a know-it-all, you can say something like: "I'm not sure, but it seems to me that you're frustrated about our meeting with the sales rep." By saying *I'm not sure*, you're showing humility. By saying *it seems to me that you're frustrated*, you're showing empathy. The combination of humility with empathy is very important. So third step: express what you think the other person is feeling or believing, humbly.

Sometimes it's not clear what the other person needs, feels, or believes. In these cases, you just want to encourage them to say more. You just need to say something like: "I'm not sure I understand what you're saying. Tell me more." It also helps if you ask open-ended questions, such as "How did you feel when that happened?" or "What were you thinking when you heard the news?"

Finally, do not be judgmental. If you want to learn more about the other person, adopt a curious attitude, as opposed to a judgmental one. The moment you tell the other person that he is wrong to think or feel in a certain way, it's the moment you're closing the door to communication. This doesn't mean that you have to accept whatever other people do. You may get to that, but in order to build a healthy relationship of trust, you should first try to understand the other person the best you can. Passing judgment is a sure way to interrupt the flow of mutual understanding. The minute you attack, the other person has to defend. When we attack or defend, we're not interested in reciprocity, but in victory. We may win the argument but lose the relationship.[14] There is obviously more to good listening and to empathy, but these five tips can get you started:

1. Park intrusive thoughts.
2. Identify hidden needs, feelings, and beliefs.
3. Share, with humility, what you think the other person needs, feels, or believes.
4. Ask open-ended questions.
5. Refrain from judgment.

Practicing these five techniques will make the other person feel recognized and heard. By doing so, you're responding in ways that enhance mattering. In fact, nonjudgmental listening is primordial in mattering. Other people need your empathy and care. Using these tools, you're breathing life into the values of relating with care and respect. This is a big part of interpersonal fitness. Another part is being able to express yourself. When we do so successfully, we are enacting the values of self-care and self-determination.

Expressing Yourself

Interpersonal well-being is about reciprocity. In the previous section we learned how to make other people feel heard. In this one we are going to explore how to assert our needs, feelings, and beliefs in respectful ways. In a sense, we have to mirror the process of responding to others. We have to identify the needs, feelings, and beliefs associated with a particular relationship? Do I need more attention? Am I feeling discounted? Do I believe that you're being unfair to me? These are important questions. To get started, then, we have to have an internal conversation with ourselves to distill what are our needs, feelings, and beliefs.

Then we need to formulate an appropriate way to express them. This can be risky because we often tend to blame people for relationship problems. Blaming here is the equivalent of judging in the previous section. It is bound to shut down conversation prematurely. Therefore, I recommend making "I" statements. Instead of saying, "You should think about me also once in a while," you can say, "I wish you considered a little bit my needs before you make decisions." The message in both sentences is similar, but the tone is very different. Whereas the first one shuts down conversation, the second one invites dialogue. This is not to say that judgment is never appropriate.

If you're living with a violent person who abuses you, you should judge that person and say that what he is doing is wrong. It all depends on the context. If you are living with a person you love, and with whom you can build a good future, you can establish norms for how to deal with conflict and difficult emotions. If you're living with an abusive partner, you need to take immediate action to stop the abuse. Context is everything. If both parties are invested in their mutual well-being, you'd want to foster communication. If one is violent, we're moving from the realm of fitness to fairness, and you need to assert your needs in unequivocal terms.

Sometimes people internalize blame. This happens in kids and adults who experience abuse. The abused person has heard so many times that she is useless or stupid that she ends up believing it. As a result, she ignores her own needs and feelings. In cases like that, reality testing is required. Talking to friends and relatives can help. If you're suffering in an abusive relationship, talk to others. This is what it takes sometimes to realize that you are living in an untenable situation and that you need to get out, or that something ought to change in the relationship. If you're just having a conversation with yourself, you may be in an unhealthy loop. You know that you're suffering in a relationship, but you see no way out because you blame yourself for it. In cases like these, someone else needs to tell you that abuse is never acceptable.

In other cases, people refuse to call abuse for what it is. As I shared in one of the previous stories, I had a friend who got used to getting beat up by his wife. This went on for a long time until I said to him that this was totally crazy. He had convinced himself that this was "normal."

If you're failing to assert your needs, ask yourself why. Is it because you learned that it doesn't make a difference? Is it because you had experiences that made you feel helpless in the past? Remember that it is your right to assert your need for recognition and impact. You have the right to feel safe and the right to express your needs. If these rights are violated, you may live in an oppressive situation. The cure for oppression is not understanding the oppressors, let alone making excuses for them, but rather liberating yourself from them.

In summary, expressing yourself consists of a few steps:

1. Identify your personal needs, feelings, and beliefs.
2. Express them in non-blaming terms.
3. Make "I" statements.
4. Assert your rights for safety and self-expression.
5. Distinguish between relationships that need dialogue and ones that need termination.

Together, these five steps can help you make a difference for yourself. The key is to assert your needs while respecting the needs of others. You don't want to dominate others, but you don't want to be dominated either. If you're not sure if a relationship is healthy for you, seek advice from friends, relatives, or professionals.

Creating Together

There is you, there is me, and there is us. To build nurturing relationships, we have to create a sense of community and a sense of fairness. To do that, we have to use the language of "we." In table 2.2 there are three conversation starters: *we need, we feel,* and *we believe.* People get along when they have norms of conviviality. This creates a sense of community and a sense of fairness. In most cases, families and couples do so implicitly. They don't sit down to write a family constitution, but if you look at healthy families, you'll see that they respect one another, take each other's needs into account, and treat each other with kindness.

Implicitly or explicitly, healthy relationships abide by a few norms and values. The first conversation starter is "we need." You can decide, as a couple, some of the following:

- We need time together.
- We need to respect each other.
- We need to learn how to disagree without becoming aggressive.
- We need to be fair.
- We need to stop driving each other crazy.

As a family, you can also share a set of beliefs:

- We believe that everyone should pick up after themselves.
- We believe that all of us should share in carrying out chores.
- We believe in helping each other.
- We believe we should limit screen time to be together.

Perhaps the biggest *we need* that relationships have is the need to have fun together. There are four major tasks in relationships: start, grow, maintain, and repair. If you are in start, grow, or maintain mode, you need to accumulate positive experiences together. Relationships need nurturing in the form of outings, conversations, vacations, decisions, work, and mutual disclosure. The more positive experiences you collect, the wealthier the relationship is going to be, and the easier it will be to repair it when things go south.

John Gottman figured that it takes three to five positive interactions to counteract the negative effect of a bad one. [15] You cannot remain stagnant, because you run the risk of negative interactions exceeding the reservoir of positive ones. This means that you are always re-creating or enriching the relationship. For some, this may mean working together on projects—my wife and I write and teach together, which sounds easier than it actually is, but it strengthens our bonds nonetheless. For others, it may mean traveling together or going to the movies.

There are as many ways to enrich a relationship as there are people in relationships, but the main lesson is that relationships that stagnate run the risk of ending. If intimacy, passion, and commitment slowly evaporate, so does the relationship. It takes a conscious effort to nurture interpersonal well-being with spouses, children, friends, relatives, and coworkers.

Needless to say, some people require more interaction than others, and this is perfectly fine. The key is to find the right fit between your needs and the wishes of your partner. Once you reach common ground, build from there according to the terms of your mutual understanding. Creating together means nurturing what you have built as families and friends. With some friends, this means periodic visits. With others, it means working together or emailing. With families, it means building positive norms and beliefs.

Just as there are many dos in families, there are also many don'ts. Gottman identified four negative patterns of conflict management that spell disaster for married couples. They are stonewalling, criticism, defensiveness, and contempt. Stonewalling refers to avoidance on the part of a spouse. He removes himself from the situation, goes silent, pretends you're not there, and does whatever he can to ignore you. This can be rather infuriating, and it's one of the best predictors of divorce.

The second one is criticism. Attacking the person, rather than expressing a wish, is very toxic. You express your discontent by making personal attacks. Instead of saying, "I wish we had more time to talk about my issues at work," you say, "You are so selfish; you never pay attention to my needs."

Defensiveness is the third negative way of dealing with conflict. Instead of taking responsibility for your behavior, you accuse the other person: "You should not have asked me to pick up the dry-cleaning because you knew how busy I was going to be today. You should have known." This shifts the blame to the other person and does not resolve anything.

The last and very pernicious way to handle conflict is through contempt. This involves put-downs, sarcasm, and hostility. You make the other person feel inferior by diminishing her dignity. Together, these four horsemen predict problems and ultimately divorce.

These four don'ts should be taken seriously. Although they were studied in the context of marital relationships, they apply to other contexts as well, such as parenting and work. Some parents ignore their kids and stonewall. Colleagues at work criticize and act defensively. Others are contemptuous. Instead of creating together, these four strategies destroy together.

In combination, responding to others, expressing yourself, and creating together form the basis of interpersonal fitness. None of us can be in listening mode all the time. After all, we're not therapists to our spouses or colleagues. But if we're interested in refining our communication skills, the tips presented here can be helpful. As you build trust in relationships, you can afford slips and falls. The wealthier your relational bank account, the easier it is to handle conflict, which is bound to happen. And when it does, try to prevent the four horsemen of the apocalypse: stonewalling, defensiveness, criticism, and contempt. It is actually in moments of conflict when you need to enlist good listening. These techniques help improve your interpersonal fitness, but as we'll see next, they also come in handy to protect interpersonal fairness.

Interpersonal Fairness

When you take up too much space in relationships, it's not just a skill problem; it's also a fairness problem. You may be supremely skilled and unfair at the same time. Fairness involves thinking about the right amount of attention and control we need and deserve. It is always a balancing act between what I need and want and what others wish and deserve. This is what fairness is all about: making sure that all of us involved in a relationship get our fair share of attention, appreciation, decision making, resources, time, and space.

In relationships, you can't have wellness without fairness. When you are trying to create, maintain, or repair a relationship, don't just think about what to do or say to make it pleasant. Think also about what to do or say to make it fair. You can think of fairness in terms of outcomes and processes. Outcomes refer to who gets *what* piece of the pie—distributive justice.

Processes refer to *how* the decision was made—procedural justice. Both animals and human beings are exquisitely sensitive to issues of fairness.[16]

If two monkeys are trained to give a pebble in exchange for a piece of cucumber, and all of a sudden the experimenter gives one monkey a grape instead of cucumber, the other monkey becomes stressed and protests vehemently. This is an instance of distributive injustice. Both monkeys played by the rules, but one of them got a grape instead of a cucumber. When the first monkey saw the second monkey getting a grape instead of the vegetable, it went berserk. Many studies document the deleterious effects of unfair relationships in animals and humans. Frans de Waal has done these studies with different species, and they all react the same way: lack of fairness creates anger, frustration, and even aggression.[17]

At home, you may not fight over a grape but may argue over mortgage payments, shopping, taking out the garbage, picking up the dry-cleaning, or doing the dishes. In all these exchanges there is fairness involved. If you always end up giving in, and your wishes are not taken into account, the relationship may be failing you. If, on the other hand, you are always the one getting to decide, it is time to think what this is doing to your partner. What is the outcome of the conversation? Do you always get your way? Do the two of you cooperate? These are all fairness questions. How you answer them can increase or decrease stress and strain in the relationship and can augment or reduce the secretion of cortisol, a very unhealthy stress hormone.

To foster interpersonal well-being we have to pay attention not only to the final decision (who takes out the garbage), but also to the process of reaching decisions (my way or the highway). We have highly refined antennae to detect lack of fairness, and we are badly hurt when we pick it up. Have you been consulted on decisions affecting your life? Did you have an opportunity to express an opinion? Did you have time to digest what you discussed with your partner, or were you forced to make a quick decision? These are all process questions. If you have a fair relationship, you would have answered yes to most of them. In healthy relationships you make decisions together, as developmentally appropriate. But don't let age interfere with playing fair. Children as well as the elderly deserve fair game.

To experience fairness in relationships it helps to have some social skills—turn taking, naming your feelings, listening nonjudgmentally, making "I" statements, compromising, empathizing—but skills are not enough. You have to bring into the relationship justice. Remember, healthy relationships thrive with fairness and languish with unfairness.[18] This, of course, makes perfect academic sense, but, as we saw in *The Laughing Side* of this chapter, human beings don't behave according to academic theories. Instead of refining their interpersonal skills, they spend time hiding their insecurity and proclaiming their superiority.

Know Yourself, Help Yourself

It is time to bring home the lessons of this chapter. To make it all relevant, you can ask yourself a few questions: How do you relate to people in your inner circle? Are you anxious, avoidant, ambivalent, aggressive, or comfortable? Where do these styles come from? Have you experienced rejections before? Have they taught you that people cannot be trusted? Are people close to you creating a good or a poor fit for you?

Our interpersonal behavior is the result of genetic predispositions, environmental influences, and our own efforts to change and improve. It helps tremendously if we can look at ourselves in the mirror and honestly answer the questions I just posed. Some of our tendencies might be inherited, and some might be the outcome of negative experiences. Self-awareness can elucidate the source of avoidant, anxious, or aggressive tendencies. That much we learned in the interpersonal fit section.

In the interpersonal fitness section we reviewed a few techniques to help us become better listeners and communicators. The ability to express your needs, feelings, and beliefs can improve your interpersonal well-being. This requires an internal dialogue. Once you formulate what you need to feel recognized and significant, it is time to express it in nonthreatening ways. This is part of self-care and self-determination.

If you are having trouble asserting yourself, you can use the GREASE technique introduced in chapter 1. First, set a goal. Let's say your goal is to express your needs. To make it more manageable, you narrow it down: when you go to the movies, you want to have a say in the pick. This is certainly specific. Instead of talking about all the things you need at once, which can be a little overwhelming to your partner, you start gradually—the G in GREASE. In this case, you start by having a say in the choice of movie and restaurants you go to. This is gradual and good.

You then reward yourself for having asserted your opinion. It is also an easy thing to do, which meets the third criterion of GREASE. You found an alternative to being silent. Now you express your views. Next, you need to be supported in your change efforts. This might come in the form of a request to your partner. Can you say something like: "Tim, when we go to the movies, you always pick. I want for us to think about what I want to watch as well, and I want you to help me with that"? The final component of your assertiveness plan with GREASE is to get a little education on the issue. You can certainly learn how to become more assertive. You can make "I" statements, learn about the consequences of not being assertive, and review the patterns of your interactions.

Instead of lacking in assertiveness, some people can be overly assertive, or even a little aggressive. Do you engage in such behavior from time to time? Do you find yourself losing your temper with your kids and spouse? Do you argue a lot with people at work? Unlike the previous example, you may need to work on toning down your overly assertive tendencies. The principles in GREASE would apply all the same.

First, set a goal (argue less with my wife). Then try to make it gradual (lowering the number of arguments from over ten in a week to fewer than eight). Reward yourself for achieving the first step. Make it easy and don't be overly ambitious. Find alternatives. Tell yourself that instead of getting into a shouting match you're going to call time-out and cool off for ten minutes. Alternatively, go for a walk and resume the conversation when you're feeling calmer. Ask for support. Tell your wife to raise her hand when you're about to get into an argument. You can decide that this is your signal to lower the temperature. Finally, get a little education on how to resolve conflict, and what negative patterns to avoid, such as Gottman's four horsemen.

Know Others, Help Others

You are only one part of the interpersonal well-being equation. You can take responsibility for your own behavior, which is great, but sometimes you need to help others as well. To know others, you can use the *need, feel,* and *believe* formula. In every interaction one or more of these psychological elements are present. The best way to know other people is to learn about their needs, feelings, beliefs, stories, fears, and aspirations. Nothing can replace a quiet conversation where you practice your listening skills. Take time to get to know them. Ask open-ended questions and adopt a curious, as opposed to a judgmental, attitude. When you do that, remember to park your intrusive thoughts. Give other folks ample time to express themselves. Self-disclosure leads to intimacy, and intimacy strengthens relationships.

If you want to help others, think about the most appropriate fit for them. If you are a manager, or a school principal, try to assign jobs based on assets and interests. Some teachers are great with little kids. Some employees are tremendous team leaders but not very good with details. Think about your own children. Would they enjoy playing football or chess? Are they introverts or extroverts? How do they respond to stimulation? Do they need a quiet environment to do their homework? Do they thrive on interactions? Does your second child need more reassurance than your first child?

Helping others is an exercise in diversity. We are all different, and the best fit for one person may not be the right one for another. If you are in charge of individuals, at work as a manager or at home as a parent, your job is to enable experiences of recognition and impact. The more you practice interpersonal fitness and fairness, the more successful you'll be.

3

Community Well-Being

THE LAUGHING SIDE

As a community psychologist, I'm a purveyor of fit, fitness, and fairness in neighborhoods, cities, and nations. What I observe is not always pretty, but it is often funny. Fit is rarely there, fitness is missing in action, and fairness is in back order. Feeling welcomed and accepted by our neighbors is wonderful, but communities consist of PEOPLE, and PEOPLE can be irrational, uncivil, insensitive, dirty, messy, and smelly, not to mention clueless. We all have a need to belong, to a family, group, or community, but as we'll see, there are many barriers to overcome. Luckily, some of them can make us laugh.

Culturally Clueless, Linguistically Lost

With all the talk about immigration reform, it is about time I weigh in. I know immigration only too well. I was way ahead of the curve on this one. Anticipating waves of globalization and mass migration, I decided at a young age to be more culturally clueless and linguistically lost than anybody else. I knew that eventually seven billion people would feel that way in the age of globalization, so I set out to beat the crowd by living in several countries and learning a few languages.

If I could figure out how to survive in places and cultures foreign to me, I could monetize that by creating the First International Online Academy for the Culturally Clueless and the Linguistically Lost, better known for its simple acronym FIOAFTCCATLL, which rhymes with Quetzalcoatl, who, as everybody knows, is a midfielder in the Mexican national soccer team. I know a good brand is very important, and that is exactly why I came up with FIOAFTCCATLL; short and memorable, just like Xerox, or Kinko's.

To build the curriculum for FIOAFTCCATLL I started traveling and moving places. To prepare myself for my first move from Argentina to Israel I went to Hebrew school for eleven years, at the end of which I could say, but not necessarily spell, three things: shalom, bar mitzvah, and Yom Kippur. To add to my cluelessness and linguistic incompetence, I quickly discovered that in Israel many of my new friends expressed animosity in other languages I've never heard of. First lesson for my curriculum: if you want to survive in Israel, study anatomy, in Arabic, Russian, Moroccan, and Yiddish.

As if I didn't feel incompetent enough in Hebrew, and Arabic, my wife's parents were both Hebrew teachers, who subjected me to etymological colonoscopies and grammatical torment for hours on end. They loved me so much that they wanted me to speak perfect Hebrew. Second lesson for my curriculum: practice selective deafness with in-laws.

Then we moved to Canada, and I finally had to study English properly. All I could say after fifteen years of English study in Argentina and Israel was "CNN," which is admittedly easier to pronounce than FIOAFTCCATLL. After fifteen years in Canada I was also able to say "NHL," "Wayne Gretzky," and "eh?"

In my eagerness to show that I was not a complete idiot, I tried to anglicize many Spanish words, hoping they would make me sound smart. Little did I know that these "false friends" would lead me into a whole lot of trouble!

Instead of the word *commit*, I used *compromise* liberally, leading to many puzzled looks (*compromiso* in Spanish means a commitment). Instead of success I often used the word *exit*, asking people to head for the exit when I thought I was congratulating them (*exito* in Spanish means success). But I got into real trouble when I confidently asked a young lady at a store "if I may molest you?" In Spanish *molestar* means to disturb. *La podria molestar* means "may I disturb you?" I thought I was being polite by approaching the store clerk with my respectful "may I molest you?" She thought otherwise.

These words are not called "false friends" for nothing. Before I knew of their existence I wanted to move to Brazil. Guess what the meaning of *constipaçao* in Portuguese is—cold, or constipation? The right answer is cold! Yeah, I was also surprised. To make sure I wasn't confused when I discovered this, I went online to my English-Portuguese dictionary. I typed *constipation*, hit "translate," and what did I find? No matches. Imagine! I discovered that over two hundred million people don't even know what constipation is. No wonder Brazilians are happy people. Lesson number three: avoid false friends.

As if my linguistic challenges were not enough, I faced my share of cultural cluelessness. Nothing prepared me for what folks in North America call football, which is a strange form of wrestling played with a giant suppository. For me, there was only one kind of football, and that was soccer.

Moving to Australia was most confusing, especially because I had to unlearn a lot of what I learned in Canada. When I finally got what football was in North America, I was introduced to an even stranger form of footie, which is part bull stampede and part Cirque du Soleil.

I also had to learn a bunch of new sayings, such as "chuck a sickie" (stay home from work pretending you are sick), "chuck a wobbly" (throw a temper tantrum), and "crack a fat" (get an erection, for which they recommend Crackiagra or Crackialis).

Aussies are so averse to arrogance that they created "figjam" (F**k I'm Good, Just Ask Me; a person with Mel Gibson's ego), and "tall poppy" (successful people who rise above the rest—do not even try it!). Lesson number four: before you move to Australia, put www .australianexplorer.com/slang in your favorites.

In Australia we naturally befriended Argentinean Jews. We had quite a nice group of friends. Of all our friends, Roberto was the nicest. He was the gentle giant, taller than Yao Ming and sweeter than Mr. Rogers. Roberto was a caring medical technician who had recently arrived in Melbourne from Buenos Aires. When we met him he was still struggling with English. With tears in his eyes, he told us that one of his new patients in Melbourne, an elderly gentleman, had not shown up for a test. Concerned, Roberto called his home to find out why he missed the appointment. The gentleman's daughter answered the phone and told Roberto that her father had passed away. Unaware of what "passing away" meant, Roberto said to the daughter, "No problem, can you bring him tomorrow?"

In contrast to Roberto's sad story, my Portuguese teacher shared with me a funny one. When she came from Brazil to the United States she was a tour guide, but her English wasn't great. She was taking a bunch of kids to a McDonald's while their parents went shopping. As the kids were getting bored waiting for their parents, she decided to teach them some Portuguese. She proceeded to teach them about eating. She wanted to teach them how to say "fork," "spoon," and "knife." In Portuguese, fork is *garfo*, spoon is *colher*, and knife is *faca* (yes, *faca*). First, she taught them how to say "fork." As she gestured what to do with a fork, she kept saying out loud "*garfo, garfo*." Then she moved on to "spoon." As she gestured with her hands how to eat from a soup bowl, she repeated out loud "*colher, colher*." When it got to "knife," *faca*, she gestured with her hand a rapid back-and-forth cutting motion while saying out loud "*faca, faca, faca*." While the kids and other customers were really amused, she had no idea what was going on.

After Australia we moved to Nashville, which was a cultural and linguistic surreal experience. It turns out that my wife, son, and I were the first immigrants Nashvilleans ever saw, and heard. I did my best to enunciate clearly every word I said, to which the locals consistently replied with a blank stare and a yawning "WHAAAAT?" Lesson five: skip Nashville.

The least we could do to fit into American culture was to get a DVR. After pressing buttons at random for seventeen hours, I thought I'd figured out how to record the *Daily Show*. It took me several months to learn how to play back what I recorded. When I finally figured it out, I realized I had recorded 239 episodes of *Best Monsoon in History* from the Weather Channel. The *Daily Show* was nowhere to be found. Lesson number six: marry a techie.

Then we moved to Miami, the land of *quitar* and *freakar* (to quit and to freak out, respectively, in Spanglish). I learned these from my hairdresser, who told me in Spanish about a friend who *quiteo* her job and started to *freakar* because she had no money. Lesson number seven: if you don't know Spanglish, just add *-ar* to any English verb and you will get by in Miami just fine.

With all the talk about immigration reform, it is about time President Obama called me to lend my expertise to the country. My first move would be to teach all 117 million Mexicans proper English. The second move would be to create a wall separating the United States and China. Next I would send all members of Congress to the Sahara Desert for six months, followed by a team-building exercise in the Arctic for three months, with the proviso that they are not allowed back in the country until they come together on immigration reform. If they don't, they will have to go through cultural sensitivity training at FIOAFTCCATLL, or debate Donald Trump.

Condo Living

Just outside the door of our condo in Hollywood Beach there is a fire extinguisher with an ominous warning: if you tamper with it you will go to RAIFORD PRISON. Apparently previous signs with mere warnings of incarceration did nothing to deter the elderly Jewish ladies from having wild foam parties. What the sign does not mention, however, is that the town of Raiford is home to both Union Correctional Institution AND Florida State Prison, leading to great confusion among residents. This is especially the case since Wikipedia states that both prisons "house inmates in death row facilities, but only Florida State Prison does executions." Keep the bastards guessing!

Indeed, condo associations all around the world spend precious time during board meetings deciding how to traumatize residents. This usually appears on the agenda as "other business." While living in a condo in the nineties, I attended a board meeting where the fate of a hard-of-hearing woman and her service dog was going to be discussed. The association did not allow dogs on the premises, but somehow this woman had managed to get herself a service dog. I went to the meeting to show support for the old lady.

Imagine my surprise when I was the only resident, other than the dog owner herself, who voted in favor of keeping the dog. Not only was I chewed out during the meeting for not respecting rules, but my family had to endure the disapproving looks of the self-appointed vigilante squad of the building, which made condo living as much fun as the Inquisition. To make sure my family did not forget our transgression, the squad always had a vigilante on call to make sure that our son, younger than twelve years old at the time, would never enter the swimming pool without adult supervision.

But don't get me wrong; not all condo boards provide shelter to vigilantes. Some very nice people get on boards to make sure they spend all the reserves on building a mini-Disneyland for their grandchildren. God forbid their grandkids from New Jersey would get bored.

Condo associations serve many other important roles in society, such as fighting unemployment. Were it not for the job-creation efforts of condo associations in South Florida, the level of unemployment among gardeners, security officers, garage door supervisors, pool attendants, and valet boys would be totally untenable. That, in turn, would lead to the ruin of the local mortgage industry and induce more folks to partner with operators of bogus health clinics to defraud Medicare, which is not necessarily a bad thing since prosecutions offer employment to many lawyers who would otherwise be suing condo associations for not displaying signs that tampering with the fire extinguisher would result in a trip to RAIFORD PRISON, which would result in higher condo fees for people like me.

For years I've complained to my wife that I'm tired of paying for pool services and gardeners for our house, not to mention high property taxes and all the extra fees charged by Coral Gables, which I'm sure go to buy Nespresso machines for all the city employees. When my wife suggested that I do the upkeep myself, I decided it was time to buy a condo, so now I get to pay for all the expenses for the house in the Gables AND the condo in Hollywood, which makes me the single largest job-creation program in South Florida, next to the FBI. I can now sleep well knowing that my taxes are paying for jail terms for politicians and bogus clinic operators in Miami-Dade and Broward. Not to mention my contributions to the mortgage industry, the employer of choice for people who escape from Raiford.

Condo associations help the economy in other ways. When the construction industry experiences a downturn, their lobbyists around the country fill the pockets of politicians with campaign contributions that translate into new safety regulations that result in, you guessed it, a new assessment. These regulations force you to replace elevators that worked perfectly well with new ones that break every other day, providing more job security for the folks in Germany who build 99 percent of all the elevators in the universe.

If it's not the builders' association pushing for some job creation program, it's the horticultural industry. When all of a sudden you see gardeners in your condo changing the plants, it's probably the result of some new law declaring that begonias must be replaced with blue daisies every other week to improve air quality. Don't complain; you are providing jobs to a lot of people who would otherwise go to law school and sue you.

Sense of Community

I have a confession to make. I'm a community psychologist, but I don't like people very much. I like the idea of people, but actual people is something else: they smell, talk too much, don't know how to spell, and wear Nike shirts with Adidas shorts.

For me, ideal encounters with other human beings are short, funny, and focused; except with my own family, of course, which are distressing, chaotic, and way too long (I love you, honey!). No, seriously, I love hanging out with my immediate family because it consists of only three more people (wife, son, daughter-in-law); big enough to qualify for a community, small enough to care. Four is a great number for a community—bigger than that and you risk distractions, solemnity, and overtime.

At home, our day consists of me making funny faces, singing made-up songs in various languages, some of which I actually speak, and talking about irreproducible topics leading to nowhere in particular. At work, my day consists of me making serious faces, suppressing my funny accent, and talking about reproducible topics leading also to nowhere in particular. I succeed pretty well at looking thoughtful, but I'm a total failure at suppressing my Argentinean-Israeli-Canadian-Australian-Nashvillean accent, which may prevent me from being president one day, although I do have good hair.

But despite my allergic reactions to certain smells and spelling mistakes, a sense of community is really a good thing. Take Colombia for example. In the 1990s, Colombians reported the highest level of happiness in the world. This was at the time that Colombia experienced the highest rate of random violence, kidnappings, and murders in the world. How do you explain that? Were they all high while answering the survey? No, the answer is that family cohesion and social support compensate for the violence around them.

Look at Mexico now. In the first decade of this century Mexicans reported the highest level of happiness in the world, at the same time that gang violence was rampant. What happened there? Too much tequila? No, as in Colombia, sense of community makes people happy, which is not to say that a little tequila doesn't help.

Incidentally, in the same survey where Colombians came first, Moldovans came last. Although I was personally offended at this finding, as my ancestors came from Moldova, this is not surprising, considering that Moldova is almost as corrupt as Miami.

My ancestors were very lucky; they escaped pogroms and the Cossacks in Kishinev to move to Argentina, which later became a haven for Nazis and a Fascist dictatorship. Don't get me wrong, Cossacks, Nazis, and Fascists had a great sense of community, but they had a very bad sense of humor, and a very bad genocidal streak—two things that we Jews don't really like. Besides, they had bad breath.

My fear of persecution is so big that I spent most of my adult life collecting passports from countries where, if needed, I could seek refuge. I know it doesn't sound like a big deal in Miami, but all my passports are legal. Let's say that one day Cossacks invade Miami; I could flee to Australia. Let's say that Australia is taken over by Vanuatu; I could go back to Canada. Let's say that Canada is repossessed by Queen Elizabeth; I could always go back to Nashville. The only problem in Nashville was that people made us feel more welcome than we really were. At first, I thought that we smelled bad, but I do remember changing my underwear.

You would have thought that all these multigenerational traumatic experiences would have made me into an antisocial, paranoid lunatic. Wrong. These experiences made me into a RABID antisocial, paranoid lunatic. But I want you to know that I'm in remission. After consulting with my doctor for side effects such as pancreatic cancer, fusobacterium, leprosy,

Fanconi anemia, fetal alcohol syndrome, and testicular evaporation, I decided to take *communophilicon*, by injection, in the eye, four times a day. I'm telling you, I'm a completely new person. Now I'm raising funds to rehabilitate homeless Nazis in Argentina, I'm creating a prison visiting program for former dictators, and I'm shipping forty thousand cases of Listerine to Moldova. It feels great to help the community. Thanks, *communophilicon!*

Beckhamania

David Beckham wanted to build a new soccer stadium near the Miami Port. I urged county commissioners to seal the deal in a hurry. There were many reasons to do so:

Local economy: This was our chance to rent a piece of land that soon will be under water. Who else but a clueless foreigner would want to rent it? I said that we should have given him huge tax breaks until the Miami Port and surrounding areas were under water, at which point the stadium would become a water polo venue.

Crime: This would have given us an opportunity to do something the British have known for a long time: it is easier to arrest hooligans and deport them when they are all in one place.

Community building: Next to Brazilian butt lifts and LeBron James, soccer is the only thing Miamians can agree on. If you don't believe me, just watch the Beckhamania going on around town. Whether you come from Haiti, Argentina, Colombia, or Jamaica, we are all crazy about soccer. All of us from Latin America and the Caribbean islands love the beautiful game. If we watch American football it's only because we are trying hard to acculturate. We want to be good sports. But truth be told, we are bored to tears with all the interruptions.

Health: Imagine, if we could all watch a game without breaks, there would be less time to go to the fridge, less drinking, and fewer cases of obesity, although getting up to go to the fridge is the most popular form of exercise in America.

Education: Beckham is the perfect role model for kids in Miami. He has a hot wife, plenty of tattoos, and his very own brand! He is also a model for his underwear line, something that many kids in Miami aspire to, after they get their Brazilian butt lift. Soccer lifted him from poverty to global fame. His dad was a plumber and his mom was a hairstylist, just like so many families in Miami. He has so much to share with our kids. He can convince them that education is a waste of time, freeing our schools from those who would rather be on the soccer field.

Focus: I credit soccer with my own success in life. Take concentration for example. As a youngster, all I could talk about from the age of eight to sixteen was soccer. Every Sunday I would wake up early to watch little league soccer on TV, followed by a trip with my uncle Saul to the local stadium to watch our beloved Talleres de Córdoba lose. After watching back-to-back two live matches, I would go home to watch another five hours of soccer on TV. I'd take my transistor to bed to listen to the latest soccer commentary before falling asleep. I memorized the names of all players of all the teams of all major leagues around the world. This was very valuable information that resulted in my failing several courses in high school.

Self-esteem: Playing soccer also helped my self-esteem, which academically was very low because of soccer. Above all, soccer helped me gain the respect of my son, who never cared about all my education, but was very impressed when I told him that I had a chance to play professionally when I was in university. I have to agree with my son that it was a stupid idea to go to graduate school instead. Today I could have been modeling my own line of underwear on billboards around the world.

Family relations: The opportunity for father-son bonding through soccer cannot be overstated. With nine out of ten fathers in Miami leaving their families for a younger Brazilian with you know what, we should seriously consider soccer as a family preservation strategy. A few years ago we were in Toronto for a wedding at the same time that the Argentinean Under-twenty team was playing the world championship match against the Czech Republic. We managed to get a second mortgage on our house and buy some ridiculously overpriced tickets through an agency in Texas. We watched Argentina beat the Czech Republic 2-1 in a dramatic game, and for one fleeting moment, I was proud to share with my son my Argentinean roots.

Despite all these compelling reasons, Marco Rubio, the senator from Florida, opposed the deal on grounds that the British are having a very bad influence on America. "First we made the mistake of giving Piers Morgan a visa, and see what he is doing now. He is making the NRA look terrible. He has even written a book promoting gun control. If we allow Beckham to bring more soccer, he will soon be talking to us about the merit of socialized medicine," said Rubio. "This is a very slippery slope. We better stop the Brits right now."

Rights, Rascals, Rats, and Retching

A recent look at the news brought to light the plight of three oppressed minorities: men, rats, and intoxicated drinkers. In an effort to claim their rights, these groups are fighting back through legal means. What's more, advocacy groups are popping up everywhere to make sure that their voices are heard. These communities deserve equal treatment under the law. To assert their legitimate rights, these groups are fighting phone companies, credit card monopolies, Morocco, women, inmates, and taxi drivers.

Rights of Rascals

A couple of years ago Mr. Anthony Weiner was defiant during a press conference about his continued sexting while he was running for mayor of New York City. He claimed that he was going to sue the mobile phone company responsible for his sexting. He asserted that "before this technology was available, I never used to sext." He argued that "it is time these companies took responsibility for putting in the hands of people weapons of self-destruction."

In their defense, makers of the "promisQ-E-T" phone told the media that Mr. Weiner should have activated the "savemyass" app that comes with the phone. The app, specifically designed for politicians, shuts off the phone every time the user is about to take a picture of flesh.

In a related development, Eliot Spitzer is about to retroactively sue credit card companies. Mr. Spitzer claimed that before there were credit cards, he never used to leave tracks of encounters with women in hotels.

Meanwhile, Silvio Berlusconi is suing Morocco for sending beautiful women to Italy, and Dominique Strauss-Kahn is filing papers to bring to court the entire female population of the world.

Rights of Rats

According to the August 23, 2013 edition of the *Miami Herald*, an inmate claimed that a rodent bit his genitals. This prompted the Society for the Protection of Rodents (SPR) to renew its campaign to protect rats. In a written statement SPR claimed that "it is a disgrace that rodents have nothing to eat and have to resort to biting genitals, exposing rats to venereal diseases. Rats deserve better. They are defenseless little creatures." County jail officials agree and promise to offer rats other body parts.

Officials with the county jail stated that "We know we should do better for our residents. We promise to work cooperatively with SPR." As for inmates, officials are asking them to bring a week's supply of rodent food to the county jail.

Rights to Retch

On September 2, 2013, the *Miami Herald* reported that a taxi company in Key West was planning to charge passengers who vomit in the backseat of their cars $50 (also true story). This is a flagrant violation of passengers who choose to get intoxicated. "Drinking is an act of freedom, and businesses have a duty to uphold this American value," said the Association for the Protection of Vomiting While Intoxicated. Besides, and this is a true statement, cabbie Jose Nascimento from Miami-Dade claimed that "a fee targeting vomiters could prevent people from coming to Miami-Dade."

It is obvious to all that men, rats, and intoxicated drinkers are victims of centuries of oppressive treatment by women, puritans, and county jail officials. Weiner, Spitzer, Berlusconi, and Strauss-Kahn are looking to form a broad coalition with rodents and intoxicated visitors to Key West. Their seven-point platform includes:

1. Women should take responsibility for their actions.
2. All county jails, here and abroad, should have rodent feeding stations.
3. Inmates should be forced to use underwear made of steel to protect rodents from venereal diseases.
4. Taxi cabs should be equipped with vomit sensors and self-cleaning sprinklers containing Chernobyl-grade detergent.
5. If #4 above fails, rodents from Miami-Dade County Jail should have the right of first refusal to feed on the leftovers.
6. Morocco should export only unattractive women to Italy.
7. Berlusconi should have the right to use Weiner's pictures when he becomes impotent.

The group, called the Coalition for the Liberation and Inclusion of Totally Ordinary Rodents, Individuals and Sympathizers, recently held a vigil in front of the White House. Members of the coalition carried placards in Washington, DC, claiming that "vomit is green," "men are people too," and "rats deserve rights." The group has already received endorsements from the former mayor of San Diego, Bob Filner, and from Miley Cyrus, who stated that "I do take responsibility for my actions."

THE LEARNING SIDE

We all want to belong to the community, and we all want to come across as competent. Language impediments are extremely frustrating for those of us who move to different countries, because they interfere with belonging and competency. To improve fit between person and environment, there is no doubt that the newcomer has to do some work; but the host community is not off the hook. In Nashville, I was made to feel more welcome than I really was. In Miami, they make you feel less welcome than you really are. Underneath discourteous behavior, however, Miamians are warm and welcoming. In the age of globalization, host and newcomer must come together to create true multiculturalism, the kind that respects diversity and fosters mattering. Good intentions are not enough, though. Skills, and the pursuit of justice, build thriving multicultural communities. Fitness and fairness improve the fit between newcomers and host societies.

Have you ever experienced being a minority? Do you have friends who have? What can you do to make sure that members of minority groups feel welcomed and accepted in your community?

People are attracted to in-groups and reject out-groups. Due to ignorance or stigma, people are afraid of others who look and sound different. We feel safer with people who look and sound like us. Ample evidence documents the deleterious effects of creating rigid in-groups and out-groups.[1] Some people are happy to commune, but only with people like them. This is what Robert Putnam, the Harvard political scientist, called bonding social capital. To foster a sense of community, we also need to foster bridging social capital, which is the practice of reaching out to people in other ethnic, linguistic, or socioeconomic groups.[2] The more we spend time with people perceived to belong to out-groups, the more we find commonalities with them. Nazis, Cossacks, and Fascists were the epitome of bonding and the nemesis of bridging.

We love celebrities. We admire and worship them. Beckham is the perfect celebrity for Miami. It may be sacrilegious to touch on the subject of celebrities, but think about it for a minute. They represent some very conventional values like wealth and sexiness that only a minuscule proportion of the population will ever achieve. Moreover, they represent commercial interests aimed at making you buy certain products that create the illusion that your life will be wonderful if you purchase a brand associated with Beckham.

Celebrities often espouse the narrowest definition of healthy, wealthy, and sexy and perpetuate images of happiness that are the province of the privileged few. Happiness and well-being must be democratized. We have to create images of well-being that most of us can attain. Women have been subjected to endless images of the unattainable perfect body, and an increasing number of men as well. How do you feel about your body? How accepting are you of your body? Do popular images have anything to do with how you feel about yourself and about others?

The last story shows the easiness with which we accept (a) norms of discrimination against women, (b) tolerance for excessive drinking, and (c) abuse of inmates. People often engage in stupid behavior because societal norms approve of them. Civil behavior requires rewards for dignified conduct and punishment for unethical demeanor. People in positions of power tend to abuse it. History is replete with examples of abusive behavior toward women, minorities, children, and inmates.[3] This is a question of fairness. Power and authority must be coupled with ethical behavior to prevent corruption and uncivil behavior.

Community Well-Being Defined

Community well-being refers to your level of satisfaction with the place and the people in your community. The more we feel like we belong, and the more we feel that we matter to our community, the higher our overall physical and emotional well-being.[4] Communities can also be helpful in overcoming challenges. When we work with people we love, we have a better chance of improving our well-being than if we work by ourselves or with a group of strangers.[5]

Despite the occasional annoyances of community living, a sense of community is really important to us. Think about it as the extension of interpersonal well-being. Our need for mattering goes beyond our immediate circle of friends and acquaintances. We light up when people in our neighborhood say good morning and when they offer unsolicited help. We get a warm feeling inside, a neighborly feeling. We take pride in good relationships with people in our community.

In some places, people develop long-standing bonds with their hairdresser, grocery store owner, or the mailman. Needless to say, we see less and less of these relationships in urban settings. Now you're more likely to bond with your yoga instructor than with the mailman. But the point remains that we cherish community relations. A sense of community builds on relating with caring and respect. A healthy community enables individuals to experience self-determination. A healthy community opens the door to all its members to pursue their goals and ambitions.

There was a time when neighbors took responsibility for all the kids in their community. Young people benefited from mentoring relations. Similarly, there was a time when friends in the community looked after all folks. These bonds have deteriorated greatly in the United States in the last fifty years, but people still yearn to have a sense of community. This is why we still see millions of people searching for a sense of belonging in faith-based communities.

Community Fit

A good fit is as helpful in communities as it is in relationships. The same goes for mattering. Our thirst for social interaction derives, in part, from our need to be acknowledged and eagerness to make a difference. The right fit between individual and community enables the former to experience recognition and efficacy. A poor fit may lead to marginalization and exclusion.

Think of people with disabilities and their struggles due to barriers in physical access. I know this only too well because Ora, my wife, uses a wheelchair. Some cities are more congenial to people in wheelchairs than others. We experienced friendly Toronto and inauspicious Rome; welcoming Oslo and inaccessible Puebla. When you are blocked from access to a building because it has no ramps, you get a distinct sense of invisibility. When your voice is not heard because you cannot access the darn building, you want to scream. On the other hand, when institutions make an effort to include everyone, recognition flows.

Ora and I visited Norway a few years ago for talks and a conference. I was giving some talks in Bergen, and Ora was presenting at a conference in Oslo. Ora called the organizers ahead of time to make arrangements to rent a scooter. Not only did they organize one for Oslo, where her conference was, but they also arranged for us to have one in Bergen, our first stop. When Ora was getting ready to give her credit card over the phone, she was told there would be no charge: courtesy of the Norwegian government. Sure enough, when we got to the hotel in Bergen, a scooter was waiting for us. When we arrived in Oslo, we realized the scooter they sent to the hotel was too big for the elevator. We made a phone call, and within a couple of hours a smaller one appeared; again, no charge. Communities like that make you feel valued.

In contrast, when Ora and I visited Rome last time, with our own scooter, we got quite a different welcome. Never mind there are no cuts in the curbs—I can lift the scooter, and Ora and I can maneuver pretty much any terrain—but one restaurant refused to seat us outdoors. Of course, they would never admit to it, but they did not want customers to be cursed by the presence of a wheelchair. They offered us a table inside, removed from public view. Ironically, in a country where laws are made to be broken, they told us that the scooter would interfere with passersby. I never heard such baloney. It was good I had been studying Italian for a while then, because I got to practice all my pugnacious vocabulary in the language of Dante.

The whole history of the disability, gay, women's, and civil rights movements is a history of mattering. It is a struggle for recognition and voice. Movement participants protested the lack of fit between their human rights and oppressive social norms.[6] Ironically, many communities don't provide a good fit even for the majority of the population. Exemplary communities are the exception rather than the rule.

Explorer Dan Buettner studied places where people live long and happy lives. In his search for the healthiest communities he discovered that they share a few characteristics. People thrive when they live in prosperous, accepting, healthy, walkable, and safe communities. These regions afford economic freedom. They have low unemployment, high tolerance for diversity, and good-quality government. To make people matter, they involve them in decision making.[7]

San Luis Obispo, a city in California, planned for years to become a healthy place. They invested time involving the residents in urban planning. This resulted in more green and walkable spaces, outdoor eateries, pedestrian malls, and a vibrant downtown. They made the city inviting and walkable. Public spaces now enable communication among residents. The effort was well worth it. San Luis Obispo enjoys the highest level of well-being in the United States. What happened there is that structures were put in place for people to feel recognized, engaged, and active. The landscape and the policies governing the city were transformed to foster meaning and mattering.

Unfortunately, few cities engage in deliberate planning to promote well-being. Many communities lack the safety and public spaces required for informal interactions. These connections build social capital and trust. Many cities require long commutes and experience pollution, which tend to make people very unhappy. My brother lives in Mexico City, which is neither safe nor walkable, by any stretch of the imagination. Commutes are long, insecurity keeps people from going out, and pollution is grave.

Within certain boundaries, you can make the most of the place where you live even if it's not perfect. Our son lives in New York City. The city offers him so many opportunities to study, play, and teach chess, that he can overlook some of the negative aspects of living in the Big Apple, such as the noise and the ridiculous cost of living.

I go crazy in Miami sometimes—traffic, incivility, texting and driving, crime. But the city has wonderful weather and I have a great job with friends and growth opportunities. There are awesome people here. When you have intellectual, financial, or social resources, you can compensate for some of the harmful qualities of the place.

However, some attributes, like corruption, are hard to get used to. Corruption erodes the social fabric of communities. In a study of sixty-eight countries, Margit Tavits of Washington University in St. Louis showed that people's well-being is inversely related to the level of corruption in the country—the higher the latter, the lower the former.[8] I lived in Argentina, where corruption was—and still is—rampant. Later I lived in Canada, which in comparison was moral paradise. I also spent a few years in Melbourne, Australia, which in comparison to Miami seemed totally utopian. Corruption is toxic because those with integrity feel tainted, and those without it feel encouraged.

Democracy and clean government, on the other hand, are salubrious. The more we practice democracy, the higher our well-being. A Swiss study demonstrated that citizens in cantons with frequent referenda report higher levels of well-being than those with fewer opportunities to vote. What happens is that people who vote often feel more in control, and higher levels of control lead to mattering and well-being.[9]

To protect themselves from bad government, pollution, crime, illness, isolation, or poverty, people form small communities. In Okinawa, Japan, a place with a high percentage of centenarians, citizens create moais—groups of friends with whom you travel through life. People in the moai help you in times of distress and celebrate with you in times of joy.[10] All over the world people join self-help groups to cope with adversity. These small communities fulfill the requirements of mattering: recognition and impact. You are acknowledged, heard, valued, and appreciated. At the same time, you offer help to others within the group, affording you an opportunity to make a difference in somebody's life.[11]

An interesting effect of both democracy and social support can be seen in Colombia and Mexico. In the first decade of this century, Mexicans reported the highest level of well-being in the world. In the previous decade, Colombians won the prize. Despite acute levels of crime, both countries reported good grades in happiness due to a surge in democracy and strong bonds of support. Renewed hopes for democracy, along with robust networks, managed to compensate for random violence.[12] One corollary of this phenomenon is that we should build on social networks not just to protect us against social ills and fragility, but also to build healthier and fairer communities.

We know that a sense of community is good for mental and physical health. We know that small groups of friends can make us more resilient. We know also that lack of safety, long commutes, as well as pollution and economic insecurity are deleterious to community well-being.[13] That much we know. The question is what type of skills can improve community well-being. What should we have in our toolbox to build healthier communities?

Community Fitness

Like it or not, we are surrounded by community, and the more we feel a part of it, the better off we are. As was the case with interpersonal well-being, to belong and to build a community require skills. One of the skills required is the promotion of social capital. Social capital refers to the density of the networks in which you participate. In other words, the more you engage in civic participation—parent-teacher association, church activities, volunteering, sporting events, political activism—the higher the level of social capital, and the higher the level of health, welfare, education, and overall community well-being. You can cultivate the skills required to engage in civic affairs. You can practice listening, cooperating, working in groups, and embracing a nonjudgmental attitude. In essence, it is about connecting and communicating with a wide variety of community members.

The research shows that the more you participate in civic affairs, the more you benefit from it personally, and the more you benefit the community. The research also demonstrates that some cities and states display more social capital than others. This is natural. Some places are friendlier than others. But this knowledge did nothing to convince my former students at Vanderbilt that it was not personal. Tennessee has a low level of social capital. In contrast, Minnesota, North and South Dakota, and Vermont have high levels. This offended my students in Nashville. They claimed that southern hospitality is all about social capital and friendliness. What the students did not know is that there are two kinds of social capital: bonding and bridging.[14] In the former, you are friendly to people who are like you. In the latter, you stretch yourself and engage with people who are not like you and who do not share your ethnic, religious, or socioeconomic background. Folks in Tennessee, where we used to live, have plenty of bonding but, according to research, not enough bridging social capital.

You may well be thinking that you don't need community interactions. I happen to be oversocialized at work. I interact with folks all day, so at night and on weekends, I like peace and quiet. That doesn't mean I don't need a sense of community. In my case, I get a lot of it at work, where I have wonderful colleagues. Each individual is unique, but what we do know is that you need to get a sense of belonging and affiliation from somewhere.

Regardless of our personality profile, we all end up interacting with the community around us, so we better learn a few skills to be effective community builders, even if our community is our family, work, a small faith-based congregation, or a self-help group. The mattering principle is a useful guide. To uphold the values of recognition and impact, I devised a simple method called I VALUE IT.[15] It stands for

- Inclusive host
- Visionary
- Asset seeker
- Listener
- Unique solution finder
- Evaluator
- Implementer
- Trendsetter

If you are a leader or a member of a group, the first order of business is to behave like an inclusive host. You want to display hospitality. Good hosts make people feel welcome and comfortable. When you invite people over for Thanksgiving, you ask them how they are doing, you acknowledge their presence, introduce them to other guests, and make sure they feel at home. Well, at least this is what you should do. This is what inclusive hosts do, anyway. This is why it's important at the beginning of any group activity to make sure people know each other.

We all need an opportunity to be heard. Whether you are the group leader or merely a member of the group, you need everyone to feel at ease. If the host doesn't fulfill this role, people spend time in their heads feeling invisible as opposed to concentrating on the task at hand. Plain courtesy goes a long way. Ignoring the relationship dimension of a group can interfere with its task dimension, whereas attending to relationships can contribute to great productivity. Notice how good leaders behave and you will see that they act like inclusive hosts.

That was step one. Next you want to make sure that this group or community is clear about its vision. What are you all going to do together? What is the better state of affairs that will be accomplished if the group does its work effectively? Will people overcome an addiction? Will members enjoy reading books together? Will they fight isolation? Will they complete an important task at work? Will they improve their local school? Will they eradicate poverty or discrimination? The sky is the limit, but whatever the goal is, it is important to be clear and focused as to what you are after. From small groups to large communities and social movements, a vision is a must.

The vision, however, pertains not only to the end, but also to the means. It is not just about creating a better world through social action, or making the planet greener; it is also about the *how*. There are thousands of worthy causes to pursue, and you will likely get involved in something that you are passionate about. No shortage of causes, but there is often a shortage of skills for how to get there.

A complete visionary doesn't just point to a better future, but also lives by values that make her credible—respect, inclusion, self-determination, cooperation, caring, compassion, and fairness. So you have to be visionary about the goal and about the means. If mattering is largely about making a difference, the visionary must articulate the goal and the path. If self-determination is important, the leader will make sure people are not coerced to do something they object to. If diversity is valued, they will strive to be inclusive. If compassion is a value, empathy will be practiced.

At the University of Miami, we have embraced the following purpose statement: *At the U, we transform lives through teaching, research, and service.* This is our goal and aspiration. To get there, we committed to live by certain values: *diversity, integrity, responsibility, excellence, creativity, compassion,* and *teamwork* (DIRECCT). Each value is accompanied by a set of expected behaviors.

You are now familiar with the first two skills of community well-being: inclusive host and visionary. The third one is asset seeker. This also fits right in with mattering. Community members need to feel they can make a difference, and the best way to do so is to use their strengths. People have gifts of the head, the hand, or the heart. You can offer good ideas, practical or emotional support, respectively. Anyone can contribute to a process of change. The sooner you give folks a task that is well-aligned with their strengths, the better they'll feel.

The complement to asset seeker is being a good listener. The first part of mattering is recognition, which comes through listening. Spend time to let people tell you who they are, what they think, and how they can help. In the previous chapter we offered the *need, feel, believe* model of listening. You can practice your listening in group and community settings alike. Community members, like your friends and colleagues, are expressing needs, feelings, and beliefs. You have to pay attention to them.

Unique solution finder is an important attribute of community leaders; they don't just replicate whatever other people have done. These leaders don't assume that what worked elsewhere will necessarily work in their community. They adjust to local realities solutions that may have proven useful elsewhere. Making a difference involves being creative and devising innovations. This is what gives people a sense of meaning and uniqueness.

Evaluating what groups and communities do is an essential part of community building. Are you achieving the goals you set for yourself and the group? Implementing actions and changes is also a part of making a difference. The second branch of mattering is being effective. Without implementation, it is all talk and no action.

The final ingredient of I VALUE IT is trendsetter. This goes along with mattering and making an impact. Human beings crave innovation. All forms of art are expressions of individuality. We don't get excited about copying what somebody else created. Rather, we get energized by inventing something useful and beautiful ourselves. Trendsetting gives expression to originality. We want to create solutions that reflect our signature strengths.

Condo associations are a microcosm of community. Without participation by people with skills and a sense of fairness, these communities can become a playground for control freaks, as we saw in one of the stories in the *Laughing Side*. I VALUE IT competencies can help in community organizing as well as in running a not-for-profit association.

To run a condo association, or any not-for-profit, you must be an inclusive host, a person who makes everyone feel welcome and comfortable. If you are running a meeting, you want to make sure all participants feel at home. Feeling recognized is rule number one in mattering. To achieve this goal, you ask people their names and solicit their ideas. You monitor how much you talk compared to how much they talk.

You must also be a visionary. But don't get me wrong. I'm not talking about a visionary like Mandela, or Gandhi. You don't have to be a giant. I'm talking about the ability to put forth a better future for the residents of your condo association or your community. Without a vision of a better future nobody will follow your lead. If you do your homework right as an inclusive host, your vision will include the needs of your constituents.

Asset seeker is the third role you need to assume as a leader. To matter, people need to feel valued. To feel valued, they need to make a contribution to the community. To make a contribution, you, as leader, need to recognize their talents. Some people are good with accounting, some are good with their hands, and some are good with social events. Whatever organization you run, for profit or not-for-profit, you need a wide array of jobs to be done. For that, it is your job to identify people's talents.

Listening is the fourth role you must perform when you are in a position of authority. In the incident with the hard-of-hearing woman in my condo association, she was not the only one having trouble hearing. The board was not willing to listen to dissenting opinions. They had decided that there was no room for dogs in the building, and that no exceptions would be allowed. Despite the fact that their auditory systems were intact, they were terrible listeners.

If you want to improve the lot of people in your community, you must be creative. This is the role of the unique solution finder. Members of my condo association saw absolutely no way to reconcile the fact that there was a no-animal rule and a person in need of a service animal. They were petrified that the building would become a zoo. It is not all or none. Rigidity is a recipe for exclusionary practices. Think diversity of needs and diversity of solutions.

If you want to be a leader, you need to be an evaluator. You must challenge the status quo and ask questions such as:

- Are our policies and practices working?
- What are we doing well and what are doing wrong?
- How can we change?

Some leaders are very good listeners and great visionaries but poor implementers. Want to have a better condo association? Better have a plan of action with concrete goals and specific actions to achieve them. This is the role of the implementer. Tired of your condo being run like a dictatorship? Get involved, perfect your community fitness skills, and practice fairness. As a community builder, your job is to make people feel like they matter, and that their voices count. If they feel recognized and empowered by your actions, you will too. Can you think of ways to use these skills at your next meeting at work?

The most rewarding outcome of becoming an effective agent of change is helping yourself while you help others. You replenish your own mattering batteries while you help others do the same. This is not a zero-sum game. The more you give, the more you enjoy it. This is called the helper therapy principle.[16] Help yourself as you help others. One of the greatest contributions any of us can make is to promote fairness in the community.

Community Fairness

If you are lucky, you live in a community that is built to foster well-being, or you can move to one that does. Perhaps you want to move to San Luis Obispo. But what if you can't, or don't want to? What if you want to stay where you are? You have the right to choose where to live. You may be passionate about making a difference in your own community.

To make a difference you have to master the elements of community fitness and community fairness. Community fitness is about knowing how to start a conversation with somebody from another culture, how to run a board, how to start a letter-writing campaign, and how to use I VALUE IT. Community fairness is mainly about two things: fair distribution and fair processes. The former is called distributive justice and the latter procedural justice. A fair distribution is about providing people what they need to thrive.

Is it fair to marginalize people with disabilities with inaccessible buildings and lack of transportation? Is it fair to have well-endowed schools only in the wealthier parts of town? Is it fair to deprive children of medical care? As we started 2015, the January 1 issue of the *Miami Herald* reported that a federal judge ruled Florida's health care system for needy and disabled children in violation of several federal rules, in effect depriving kids of required and legitimate treatment. These are questions of fairness. All children, not just kids from wealthy families, deserve excellent care. You can extend the example to proper nutrition, safe streets, and enrichment opportunities. No shortage of challenges for poor children.[17] In late June of 2015 the *Miami Herald* reported that fully one-third of kids in Miami live below the poverty line.

To realize distributive justice, certain criteria must be present. The three most important are merit, need, and effort.[18] If we are to distribute an educational good, such as a scholarship, we need to consider the three criteria. Other things being equal, it is fair to give a scholarship to the student who was the most accomplished (merit consideration). However, if other things are not equal, such as opportunities for educational enrichment or socioeconomic situation, the picture changes dramatically. It would be unfair to penalize some students for something they are not responsible for, such as poverty. It is entirely possible that two students worked equally hard in school (effort consideration), but that some did not have the resources to obtain enrichment or medical care (need consideration), and therefore did not perform as well (merit consideration). To consider only merit would be making a decision out of context.

With regard to procedural justice, a different set of criteria applies. To achieve procedural justice, we must take into account whether people affected by decisions have been consulted (participation consideration) and whether the process has been fair to all (impartiality consideration). Procedural justice is not just about implementing rules but about a proactive process of meaningful engagement.[19]

Questions of distributive and procedural justice take place in community settings such as schools, churches, health care facilities, and government. In schools, distributive and procedural dilemmas abound, but so do opportunities to practice fairness. Hundreds of decisions are made in classrooms every day. Do students participate in them? Do teachers have a say about a new curriculum, or is it foisted upon them by school boards?

Community justice gets enacted in different contexts. Cultural justice, for example, refers to the treatment of minority groups in society with respect (procedural justice), and affording them equal opportunities, such as access to jobs and health care (distributive justice). Another type is retributive justice, which deals with accountability for transgressions, or paying the price for a crime (distributive concern). Corruption is a particular case of community injustice, in which a particular group violates distributive (e.g., not paying taxes) and procedural principles (e.g., disrespect for norms of coexistence).

For the process of change to foster mattering, residents have to be consulted and their strengths have to be employed.[20] Outside help without local ownership does not work. An empowering journey starts with exercising control over your future. Healthy communities do not relinquish control of their fate to outsiders, however well-intentioned they might be. A principle of community building is to never do for others what they can do for themselves. The more people participate in the building of their own community, the prouder they'll be.

Distributive and procedural justice in communities sometimes requires changing policies. Social change goes beyond particular communities. From time to time, it's the only change that will bring distributive and procedural fairness to communities. What Rosa Parks, Martin Luther King, and Nelson Mandela did was not just to change attitudes and practices within their communities, but in society at large. They knew that without social change, their communities would not know fairness.

Know Yourself, Help Yourself

To improve your community well-being you need to know if the community where you live works for you. There are basically three possible answers to this question. First, I like it and it's good for me. Second, I like it but it's not working for me very well, so I'll try to do something to improve it. Third, I don't like it, it's not working for me, and I doubt I can change it. A lot of folks fall into the third category.

If you have any doubts about how serious people are in their search for the best community fit, just remember that every year millions of people pack up and move. And they don't just move to get a better job in another city. They leave their countries. Sometimes as refugees, sometimes as legal, and sometimes as illegal immigrants. People are willing to leave their past behind in the search of a better future. In other cases, people fight with their lives to create fairer communities. This is how important the right fit with community is.

How good is your community fit? Do you live in a place that makes you feel like you matter? Do you feel appreciated and valued? Is this community the best place for you to thrive? I'm probably an extreme example, but for different reasons, across different periods of life, I packed up and moved. By age fifty-six I've lived in five countries in four different continents (Latin America, Middle East, Oceania, and North America). Argentina was and remains an anti-Semitic country. Poor fit for a Jew. Canada was and remains a great country, but it was too cold for a family with a physical disability. Admittedly, leaving a country is a very difficult proposition, but leaving a town is something people often do. Mobility is great in some respects, as people improve their occupational and financial well-being, but it is not so great in others, as people lose their sense of belonging to place.

Within geographical communities there are relational communities, such as schools or churches. Do you feel accepted and welcome in these communities? Do they value your identity? If you are gay or lesbian or transgendered, is the place where you live accepting of your sexual orientation? I'm certainly not a proponent of leaving friends and family behind, but for some folks, some places are more welcoming than others. Miami, for example, seems to be very welcoming of people with diverse sexual orientations. I could not say the same thing about Nashville, or Córdoba, my place of birth in Argentina.

If you like where you live, and you want to make it better, which is what many people do, you try to improve it, for your own sake and for the sake of others. If you choose to make your community better, you can use the I VALUE IT skills you learned in this chapter. If you choose to get involved in the community, but feel somewhat reluctant, you can use the GREASE method of change. After you choose a cause in which to get involved (accessibility for people with disabilities, environmental protection, refugee settlement, mentoring of youth, etc.), you can become involved gradually to make it easier.

You can go to a meeting, learn about the issue, join an association, and make your interest known. Reward yourself for getting involved, and make it easy to stay involved. Don't pick a cause for which you have to travel many hours a week, because you're unlikely to keep it up. Finding an alternative to the problem community is also an option. When the community where you live rejects who you are, and what you stand for, you have the option of leaving. I exercise my option not to go with my wife to cities that are not wheelchair accessible. Get support for your decision, and most definitely educate yourself. Don't pack up and leave before you know where you're going!

Consistent with the helper-therapy principle, the more you volunteer to help the community, the more you'll help yourself. Getting involved in social issues can provide many personal benefits. You gain a feeling of mattering and a sense of belonging. You feel recognized and you take pride in making a difference. The journey to community change can be as meaningful as the change itself. People bond when they fight for a good cause. You feel embraced and valued and gain strength to embrace and value others as well.

Know Others, Help Others

You may find the community very welcoming of you, personally, but not very welcoming of others. If that is the case, you may wish to get involved to improve a sense of community and a sense of fairness for everybody. There is no shortage of social issues to tackle, from poverty to inequality to teen pregnancy to school dropouts to animal rights to climate change. It all depends on your passion. The beauty of helping the community is the boomerang effect. What goes around comes around. You help the community, but first and foremost you're increasing your personal sense of mattering and meaning.

If you're already involved in a community cause, you may wish to think about the I VALUE IT principles. When you organize community events, are you an inclusive host? Do you make sure that everyone feels at home? Do you help your group come up with a compelling vision for the future? Are your strengths maximized? Perhaps you need to tell someone what you're good at. Stepping up means taking leadership roles, but perhaps you're a little shy. If that is the case, use the GREASE method. You don't have to assume a big leadership role. You can assume responsibilities in your group gradually. If you do so, don't forget to reinforce yourself for doing so. Chances are people will really value your input. Make it easy to get involved. Don't choose a huge task at first.

There are many ways to help community organizations. If someone asks you to do a big job you're not ready for, such as talking to city council about recycling, or the state of education, choose an alternative. You don't have to become a community hero overnight. Pick an alternative that suits you. Whatever you do, get support from others. It's fun to work on projects together with others, and finally, educate yourself about your cause. The more informed you are, the more helpful you'll be.

4

Occupational Well-Being

THE LAUGHING SIDE

So far you've learned about interpersonal and community well-being. In a sense, occupational well-being is a blend of the two, with some additional features, like measurement, efficiency, and organizational skills; all parts of work culture, and all very funny. Following several humor stories, we will get to the serious part of well-being at work. But first, some parody.

Managed by Metrics

As every self-respected manager knows (I know because I'm UPPER management), you have to have metrics to measure your goals and assess your progress. You have to have metrics to measure your goals, achievements, wellness, productivity, savings, and laundry habits. Let's say you've worn the same pair of socks for the last three weeks; a reasonable goal would be to wash it at least once a week.

All over the world, corporations and incompetent people alike pay thousands of dollars for coaches—usually high school dropouts—who tell their clients that they need metrics. I was very skeptical, so I did some research on these coaches. I discovered that the only experience they have is telling other people how to achieve their goals; the only goal they've ever achieved is getting a website, and the only metric they count is the number of fools who hire them.

I found my solution right here on my Outlook program. I decided to use the Tasks tab to record my goals and to color code them. After typing furiously for seven hours I recorded 257 goals with all the colors of the rainbow:

Blue: get rich
Purple: look like Hugh Jackman
Green: get hired as a coach

I tried them for a week and it didn't work, so I hired a coach: Fernando Menendez Gutierrez de la Sabiola Junior. At least mine was a student. He was studying to become a chef, and he had a really nice website. There were lots of pictures of him surrounded by beautiful women.

The website also said that he belonged to the "Latin Kings," which I'm sure was some kind of charitable organization. With such credentials I hired him right away. He told me I had to be more specific, and more gradual. I revised:

Blue: make $5,763,112 in seven years
Purple: get Hugh Jackman's muscles
Green: get four people to visit my website

He told me I needed to choose. Three goals are way too many. I chose the first two. He made me a plan to get Hugh Jackman's muscles. He told me that if I ate meat three times a day, put on about another one hundred pounds, lifted more weights, and went to Butts and Biceps on US 1, the plastic surgeon might be able to extract some flesh from my big nose and implant it into my biceps.

What about my blue goal? He said that if I started saving, invested wisely, opened a clinic, and defrauded Medicare like every other human being in Miami, I would have a chance. "You are a doctor, aren't you?" he said. I tried to explain that I was a PhD, not an MD, but he wouldn't listen.

The importance of metrics was driven home again when I watched *60 Minutes* the next day. Turns out, true story, that a certain health care company, let's call it "From Your Sickness to My Wealth," set metrics for its emergency room physicians in hospitals around the country. At least 20 percent of patients seen in the emergency room had to be hospitalized to generate revenue for the hospital. No matter what the patient had—bleeding nose, periorificial dermatitis, gestational trophoblastic tumor, evil eye, flatulence—it was all the same, a metric is a metric. If the doctor needed to meet a quota, somebody was going to get the stretcher.

After a few days, Fernando left me. He had to flee the country suddenly. Too bad; I had grown fond of him.

Next I hired the former CEO of From Your Sickness to My Wealth, but he also had to flee the country. I was on my own again, so I went to the website of his company to learn as much as I could about management.

I learned that you have to plan your day, your week, your month, your year. They tell you to track everything, to color code your activities, and to take note of any obstacles. They ask you to download tracking apps and keep meticulous records of your hourly achievements. When you get home, they ask you to log in to a special website and check a bunch of little boxes to document your progress, minute by minute. By the time you are done with all this, you have exactly three minutes left in the day to do any work, or admit 3,462 bogus cases into the hospital.

Efficiency

Big, it must be big, very big, and red, and round, like the "easy" button from Staples, and I want it on my desktop, flashing, with a big inscription, in neon letters: UNSUBSCRIBE. With all the latest technology and whatnot, I'm surprised that nobody has invented yet the UNSUBSCRIBE app. I want to be able to click on that icon and unsubscribe in one fell swoop from all the intrusive and irritating email lists that are making my life miserable. Until such invention comes along—and I do want a commission for giving all you hackers the idea—I must go over thousands of emails manually to find the annoyingly small print where it says "unsubscribe," which is usually buried deep in the body of the email, among a pile of legal junk.

Not only is it difficult to find the stupid link, but once you click on it, you land on a page asking you three times to reconsider. This is especially true of political causes, where the politician in question, all the way from the president to the most obscure Democratic candidate for school board in North Dakota, begs you to stay. For some reason, I never get emails from the Republican Party asking me for money, or from the National Rifle Association. They respect my privacy. I value that. The Democratic Party, in contrast, is way too promiscuous with emails.

I fantasize about having this big red icon on my desktop and being able to press it and all of sudden reduce the number of daily emails from unwanted sources from about sixteen thousand to two. In fact, I will pay a handsome reward for the computer programmer able to devise the object of my fantasy. It must be big, and red, and require just one click. No questions asked, no options to reconsider, no text boxes explaining why you are leaving. Zero, zilch, good-bye. That will constitute my liberation.

Until such time, I have to contend with emails from the likes of Cyagen Biosciences, which can't distinguish between a doctor in psychology and one in ratology. Word for word, here's their latest email dated July 2, 2014, 10:49 a.m.:

Dear researcher,

Outsource your transgenic or knockout mouse projects to Cyagen this summer and pile on the savings! Invite your friends or colleagues to take advantage of our group buy on transgenic, knockout & knockin mice—get up to 20% off of multiple mouse lines when you or anyone in your group places an order:

- *10% off 1 mouse line*
- *15% off 2 mouse lines*
- *20% off 3 or more mouse lines*

Cyagen's animal model generation service gets you the knockout, knockin, or transgenic mice you need guaranteed, at the industry's lowest price.
   Hyperlink: >>>Learn about our animal model expertise
   Hyperlink: >>>View our transgenics & gene targeting mouse offerings
   Were you referred by one of our existing customers? Let us know through our Mouse Service Referral Program and enjoy an additional $500 discount or 5% off (whichever is greater)!
   Cyagen's mouse service team provides technical support throughout your project and was rated "very technically capable" by 9 out of 10 recent clients. Use our service to boost the impact of your basic research: Cyagen animal models have been published in top journals such as Nature and Cell. It's easy to get started: just reply to this email or tell us about your research goals in the comments field of the groupbuy webform. You may also call us at 800-921-8930. Our mouse experts will be happy to discuss your research goals.
   *All customer inquiries are strictly confidential.

Best regards,
Cyagen Client Relations Team
2255 Martin Avenue, Suite E
Santa Clara, CA 95050
Tel.: 800-921-8930

Transgenic? Knockin? Knockout? That sounds like a boxing match between sexually diverse genes. I do have a PhD, and some psychologists do experiment with mice, but the only time I see rats is in nightmares, which have only increased since the Cyagen offers.

Apparently somebody really wants me to switch careers. The following email, received from Dr. Sam Wang, on the same day, reads as follows:

Dear Dr. Isaac Prilleltensky,

Have you ever spent much time and energy to generate an antibody, which unfortunately fails to perform in your experiments? We understand your struggles very well, and would like to offer you a working alternative.

We believe for most proteins, there are a certain number of regions that could be used as promising antigens to produce high-quality antibodies. To maximize the chance of success, we usually apply a number of antigens (up to 20 protein fragments and/or peptides) instead of just one or two; the diverse antigens could map all the best possible regions of the target protein.

Ordering is simple, just email me the target protein (accession number or sequence). We will provide a detailed evaluation and quote in two business days. If you have any questions, please feel free to contact me.

Hundreds of scientists have published papers which cite the use of our custom monoclonal antibodies. See table 4.1 on following page.

You know what you can do with your monoclonal antibodies, Dr. Wang? You can shove them up your associated autophagy, past your coiled-coil myosin, all the way to your epitopes. And if that doesn't work, use the Enhancer Binding Protein Alpha and the related key regulator to push it upstream to the open reading frame. I can only hope that the Retinaldehyde of your eyes will look like zebrafish. If you get dehydrogenase in the process, make sure the human hairless gene does not fall off your head. For further instructions refer to the table above, which you sent me.

What a waste of my time to have to go through all this junk. Forget Iraq, Ukraine, Obamacare, Donald Trump, tar sands, pot, and the Middle East; we need to invest in unsubscribe technology.

I see inefficiencies everywhere. When it's not email, it's government services.

I recently flew from Manchester, England, to Philadelphia. As it was the port of entry into the United States, all passengers had to go through customs. There were two lines, one for visitors and another one for US citizens and green-card holders. The lines went from Philadelphia to Kansas City and back. It took me seventy-eight minutes to get to the customs officer. There were sixty border patrol booths, fifty-six of which were totally empty, leaving just four officers to contend with tons of smelly, cranky, unkempt, constipated passengers. Thousands of people had to wait for over an hour when the entire process could have been done, seamlessly, ON THE PLANE, where passengers usually waste time, snore, fart, and make a total mess of the aircraft.

The flight from Manchester took approximately seven hours. If we would have had two customs officers checking passports of two hundred passengers at a rate of two minutes per passenger, in a little over three hours we would have been done, giving customs officials enough time to enjoy reruns of *Parks and Recreation*, not to mention the free pretzels and the opportunity to know some of the countries from which they incarcerate illegal aliens.

If you assign a monetary value to the time wasted by thousands of people in the Philadelphia airport—who could have been stimulating the economy by gorging on Big Macs and

Table 4.1. Monoclonal Antibodies and Me

Journal	Antigen	Description of the Antigen	Application	SEAL Service Package
PLOS Genetics 6,11	TnI	troponin I	IF	4 epitopes + 1 protein 15 antibodies
Blood 117,7014–20	C/ebp Alpha	CCAAT/Enhancer Binding Protein Alpha	WB; IP	6 epitopes 15 antibodies
Nature 464,601–5	zf Raldh2	zebrafish Retinaldehyde dehydrogenase 2	IF	3 epitopes + 1 protein 11 antibodies
Nature Genetics 41,228–33	U2HR	an inhibitory upstream open reading frame (ORF) in the human hairless gene (HR)	WB	8 epitopes 22 antibodies
PNAS 105,19211–6	Barkor; Beclin 1	Barkor: Beclin 1-associated autophagy-related key regulator; Beclin 1: Coiled-coil myosin-like BCL2-interacting protein	WB	5 epitopes 13 antibodies

buying laxatives—plus the cost of Febreze to eliminate unwanted passenger odors, sending two officers on every plane coming from overseas more than pays for itself. I got the inspiration for this brilliant idea from none other than American Airlines, which is trying to be a model of efficiency and recycling.

Flying to New York with my wife to visit our son, I discovered, and this is true, that the airline uses coffee bags as air fresheners in toilets. At first I thought I was mistaken, so I went to a second toilet, and sure enough, there it was, sitting on the counter, next to the tiny lavatory, another coffee bag, the kind you put in airplane percolators. If you don't believe me, have a look at the picture I took (see figure 4.1). That was American Airlines.

I flew back from England with US Airways, now part of the "new American Airlines," and what do you know, there it was, the coffee bag in the toilet. Thank God I don't drink coffee, but I could not help thinking who was going to drink the half-urinated coffee after the flight attendant recycled the coffee bag from the toilet. I'm sure flight attendants keep a list of difficult passengers. We need more companies like American Airlines that know how to recycle, how to be efficient, and how to punish difficult customers.

Traveling is indeed a great opportunity to sharpen my efficiency skill set. Prior to every flight I ponder for hours which book I will read during the three-hour flight. It usually takes me five hours of browsing a mountain of books at home to decide which one I will read on the plane. But don't get me wrong; the contents of the books are only marginally influential in my decision. More importantly, I have to see how much they weigh, whether they are soft- or hardcover, whether they fit into the backpack I chose for this trip, and crucially, whether the cover matches the color of my backpack.

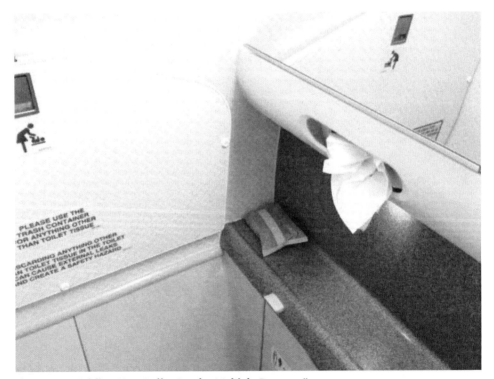

Figure 4.1. "Airline Uses Coffee Bag for Multiple Purposes"

I have a collection of backpacks and briefcases, and it usually takes me days to go through all of them to decide which one to take. Some are bulkier, for longer trips with possibility of airline losing my suitcase; some are lighter, for overnight getaways. Some are professional looking, and some are just cool, for the hip crowd at progressive conferences. Thank God they are all either brown or gray, which makes for efficient decision making. So the book I carry must fit into the chosen bag, which depends on what other transitional objects I will carry with me, such as almonds, Sudafed, travel pillows (inflatable around the neck, cotton for the lower back), earplugs, shredded wheat, eyedrops, reading glasses, laptop, iPad, Kindle, chargers, two legal passports (in case one gets lost, or stolen, you never know; don't get excited, border patrol, I have dual citizenship), neutral-tone light-foldable-wrinkle-free jacket, notepad, random piles of papers from work to assuage guilt, and an extra pair of underwear.

I thought that buying a Kindle would solve my problem—easy to carry and lots to choose from—but what about the first fifteen minutes of the flight, when you are not supposed to use electronic devices? To maximize the use of that time I invest another three hours at home deciding what I will read during the first few minutes of the flight. When I'm finally allowed to use my Kindle, I peruse the 268 books I started. After about an hour I finally settle on the one I will read, for about fifteen minutes, until the feature film starts. Not that I ever intend to watch it—after all, this is my chance to read without interruptions—but I see this as an opportunity to practice my lip reading, so from time to time I look at the screen and try to figure out what the heck is going on, without listening to a word of it. There are movies I have seen three or four times, like *The Hunger Games*, but I never heard a word of it. At this rate, I calculated that I will finish reading my first Kindle book in 2028.

I notice that some passengers are much more efficient than me, which is a source of great envy. They never move from their seats. I've been on very long flights (Atlanta to Cape Town, Los Angeles to Melbourne) and have seen people not move for fifteen hours! They must be doing something really important not to move for that long. They are not reading or playing with the touch screens; they just sit there, staring into space. I, in turn, waste a lot of time. I get up to stretch my legs, go to the toilet, do pushups at the back of the plane (source of great embarrassment for my family), and request cranberry juice mixed with sparkling water—no ice, please—to stay hydrated.

Watching our cleaning lady at home is another source of inspiration for efficiency. She manages the entire country of Honduras on the phone from our kitchen, while cleaning, cooking, ironing, and watching the telenovela, with a big smile. I'm so glad she is efficient, because our other cleaning lady, who is equally adorable, is so much into mindful cooking that it takes her three hours to prepare a salad. "Soy lenta, que le voy a hacer," she says (I'm slow, what I can do?). In Cuba there was no need to rush.

I noticed that the tourism industry in South Florida is also very efficient. Against my best judgment, we recently visited the Everglades, where my sister and her partner wanted to have a ride on an airboat. It was the middle of June, and muggy as hell, but they had come all the way from Israel, and we did not want to deprive the mosquitoes of some fresh blood. Of course the captain's tip depends on how much excitement he generates among passengers, so no sooner did we get on the boat than the captain spotted a crocodile. While everyone was taking pictures and getting all excited, I could swear it was a plastic crocodile; the most efficient way to generate buzz on the boat. In support of my hypothesis, I can say that we did not see a single reptile other than the one near the dock for the entire miserable hour on the boat. As far as I can tell, it was a total fake.

To compensate for the lack of crocodile sightings, the captain engaged in all kinds of naval pirouettes that made you want to vomit. The sickness, insufferable motor noise, mosquitoes, and heat made the whole experience very memorable. As I told my sister, it would have been much more efficient to watch some crocs on YouTube. Not only did I suffer from heat, insects, exhaustion, and noise pollution, but there was also so much mud in the Everglades that the car itself looked like a swamp. Sister, next time, you rent a car and go on your own. I will provide the GPS; much more efficient. Until then, I will be busy clicking on unsubscribe links.

Professional Conduct

Professionals adhere to the strictest standards of ethics in order to enhance the well-being of the population. I know because I belong to the American Psychological Association, the Canadian Psychological Association, the American Educational Research Association, and the Global Association of Deranged Writers. They all have rigorous codes of ethics that professionals must abide by. I also know that bankers, lawyers, teachers, accountants, firefighters, Edward Snowden, and Lance Armstrong have codes of ethics. Even the Miami-Dade City Commission has a code of ethics, but unfortunately nobody can find it since the FBI left a mess in its last raid. They do have it, though, and it is in three traditional languages: Tonkawa, Etchemin, and Hialeahan.

This ethics business can be very tiring, especially when you work in stressful jobs like Firefighting, Law, Medicine, Teaching, and Lance Armstrong, with all the lying he had to do for so many years and whatnot. It is exhausting to cope with danger (firefighter), unruly children (teacher), difficult patients (doctors), crooks (lawyers), and Oprah (Lance Armstrong). Still, professionals remain stoic. This is why Lance Armstrong kept lying and lying for so many years about taking drugs during the Tour de France. He was the epitome of stoicism. No matter what you threw at him, he remained stoic. This is what professionals are made of. You remain true to your truth, even if it's the biggest fabrication of the century.

Codes of ethics demand respectful treatment of your clients at all times, and under all circumstances. Accountants, for example, would never tell a client, "You are running the biggest scheme in the history of forensic accounting." Instead, they are going to write a report to the board stating that "a fiduciary audit revealed a larger than expected shrinkage in the accrued income collateralized with tangible assets which has resulted in a smaller than expected WACC (weighted average costs of capital), leading to large sums of money deposited in suspense accounts which were securitized against promissory notes and future taxation used to defray costs of doing business in certain parts of South Florida. Computer models based on SWOT analyses predict that outside agencies will show interest in your business."

TRANSLATION: You should stop bribing city commissioners and start paying taxes or you will be in jail in three to five months.

Teachers are also very respectful professionals. They prepare for months for parent-teacher interviews. Some excerpts:

GRADE 11 TEACHER: Jordan's performance in the SMRT-VII has remained stable since the last time he was evaluated.

TRANSLATION: He is still as dumb as he was in grade 2.

GRADE 3 TEACHER: Suzie is extremely peripatetic and shows great curiosity toward people and events unrelated to the subject matter at hand.

TRANSLATION: If you don't put her on Ritalin, I will.

GRADE 7 TEACHER: Due to hormonal changes, it is not uncommon for children at this age to show interest in the anatomy of the opposite sex.

TRANSLATION: Your son has a collection of *Playboy* magazines under his desk, distracting most male teachers from their duties and endangering the standing of our school in the state ranking. Please tell him to obtain a digital subscription instead of bringing hard copies to school. Failure to do so will result in disciplinary hearings and confiscation of all the magazines, including the special double edition of December 1998 with black-and-white photos of Pamela Anderson and Anna Nicole Smith. And by the way, your son is missing the January 1987 edition with never-before-revealed photos of Marilyn Monroe at the White House.

This is how serious teachers are.

Predictably, lawyers have the strictest code of ethics. This is why they reassure you that if they sue 734 innocent people on your behalf and by random chance the judge falls asleep during the proceedings and they win three cases, they will share with you 0.0000001 percent of the money. After taxes, photocopying, paper clips, faxes, office parties, late-night pizza dinners, and courier expenses, they guarantee to pay you 0.00000000000001 percent of the net profits. This is the only profession that guarantees 0.000000000001 percent of anything. No questions or medical exams required. In contrast, most other professions require you to pay them.

Take doctors for example. Before you even say what is wrong with you, a smiling assistant will invite you to a little booth, take an x-ray of all your bank accounts, conduct a physical examination of all your credit cards, insert a finger in your wallet to extract your driver's license and your health insurance card, and review the chart of payments on your mortgage. She will also perform a stress test on your 401(k) account and check the pressure in the tires of your car, just to be sure there is something of worth in case the insurance company denies your claim, which happens 99 percent of the time.

By the time you see the doctor your blood pressure is so high that the insurance company is bound to reject your claim, leaving the smiling clerk with no choice but to impound your car and clean up your 401(k). The American Medical Association is very explicit in its insistence on equality: all patients will be treated the same. No matter what the ailment is, your ability to pay, or the insurance you have. Before the doctor sees you, everyone must sign twenty-nine forms with very small font relinquishing to the doctor all your possessions, for generations to come. They don't pressure you to sign the form, however. You can take your time.

At an average speed of three minutes per page, it will take you five hours to read the forms they give you. Allowing for lunch and bathroom breaks, you are lucky if you see the doctor at 5 p.m., provided you got there at 6 a.m. Doctors will never pressure anybody to sign anything they don't understand. The AMA is very explicit about that. You don't have to sign anything you don't feel comfortable with. But if you read the whole thing, you will never see a doctor in your life.

Doctors do all of that to prevent any harm, to their pocketbook. They will do whatever they can to keep you as a patient and to run all the possible unnecessary exams that insurance companies will cover in order to pay their overheads. They also scare you into not buying prescription drugs from Canada or going to India to receive medical treatment. The AMA is against medical tourism. I do have to agree with them on the India thing. A friend of mine went to India to have a heart operation and returned without testicles. Doctors are obliged to warn you against things like that.

The pharmaceutical industry also has very high standards of professional conduct. They are so strict that instead of drafting their own, they copied the code of ethics from the tobacco industry, which used Lance Armstrong as a consultant.

Pharmaceutical representatives also adhere to principles of equality. They reward all doctors the same for pushing their pills, regardless of nationality, ethnicity, or place of origin. It is inconceivable to them to discriminate on the basis of anything other than ability to increase sales of Obliviontix and Peacequility.

In the latest round of the ethics bowl, the Food and Drug Administration decided to become the toughest. As of 2014, no more than eleven out of the twelve-person panel reviewing new medications will be allowed to serve on the committee if they have any sort of conflict of interest. This is seen as a blow to the pharmaceuticals that lobbied hard to keep the number at twelve.

The National Security Administration remains the paragon of ethicality among government offices. When listening to Angela Merkel's conversations, they delete all references to her views on Greece, Portugal, and Spain.

The North American League of Mayors imposes strict penalties on violations of professional conduct of the smallest kind. This is why Mayor Rob Ford of Toronto was suspended from duties for a day for drug dealing. In his defense, he said that he was doing drugs while he was in a drunken stupor. The League of Mayors said that his thinking was in line with the legal arguments that George Zimmerman used in his defense. A repentant Rob Ford returned to duties after his day suspension and promised to call Zimmerman for ethical guidance.

Meanwhile, the former mayor of San Diego, Bob Filner, complained that he was also willing to seek Zimmerman's counsel but was fined $1,500 nonetheless. After sexually harassing the entire female population of City Hall, justice was served, and poor Filner had to be on probation for ninety days and keep his hands to himself. The North American League of Mayors interceded on his behalf, claiming that a day's suspension would have been harsh enough. "We are all for equal treatment under the law," a spokesman for the organization said. They said that Filner never sent pictures of his anatomy via Twitter like Anthony Weiner, a mayoral candidate in New York City, and therefore a more lenient punishment would have sufficed. In a show of force, the League of Mayors demanded that any future pornographic pictures sent by Weiner be done anonymously.

The National Football League proved once again that ethics is second nature to the profession. After twenty-five years of conclusive evidence that concussions cause irreparable brain damage in players, the NFL appointed Richard Incognito to chair a committee on bullying players who complain about headaches and dizziness. "We will make sure that no current or former player, or their families, now or in the future, ever complain about concussions without a personal visit by me. We know how to take care of complainers," Incognito said.

Granted, some groups, such as bankers and mortgage lenders, are morally challenged, but not to worry. Many repentant souls have seen the light and are ready to help. For sexual perversions call the Law Offices of Spitzer Weiner Filner Berlusconi Strauss-Kahn. For pathological lying call Armstrong Incognito Ford Zimmerman and Associates. Professional conduct guaranteed.

Graduation

Education is essential for well-being. College graduates earn more money, live longer, and are healthier than school dropouts. This is why graduation ceremonies are such a big deal. It is really important to celebrate this great educational achievement.

In a rapidly changing world, graduation ceremonies around the country remain a well-established tradition. Some things never change in college graduations:

1. 99 percent of the graduating girls will have to see a podiatrist after wearing high heels designed for masochists.
2. 100 percent of 7-Eleven stores will run out of beer.
3. 99 percent of commencement speakers will say one or more of the following:
   a. I had to go to school uphill both ways;
   b. When I went to school, "cut and paste" hadn't been invented;
   c. Turn off your cell phone and smell the roses;
   d. Steve Jobs, Bill Gates, Warren Buffett;
   e. Change, change, change;
   f. Change the world;
   g. Inspiration;
   h. Entrepreneurship, technology, start-up;
   i. Within you;
   j. Never ever ever ever ever ever ever ever ever ever ever ever give up; and
   k. Integrity, serenity, sorority, fraternity, liberty, plasticity, creativity, identity, solemnity, curiosity, and many other words ending in "ity."
4. 99 percent of the graduating students will not hear a word said by the commencement speaker because they will be changing their Facebook status from Single to Graduate.
5. The announcer will butcher the names of 99 percent of the graduating students from engineering.

A typical graduation speech goes something like this: "Steve Jobs went to school uphill, both ways, until he met Bill Gates and then quit school because he had a huge inferiority complex and decided to use his brain plasticity to invent time-wasting technologies so that all the students graduating from engineering schools around the country would have a job and show Bill Gates that he also could do something good for humanity that did not involve malaria, Africa, or Warren Buffett."

Nowadays, of course, no graduation speech would be complete without reference to Nelson Mandela or Rosa Parks, who all of a sudden has become an iconic figure among Republicans, who liken her to Ted Cruz. A typical sentence in a graduation speech today goes like this: "Rosa Parks did not have a Twitter account, but Nelson Mandela could have used one—entrepreneurship technology entrepreneurship technology entrepreneurship technology Bill Gates start-up change technology change neuroscience start-up change Warren Buffett start up entrepreneurial spirit don't forget to thank your parents."

When it comes to the student speaker, a typical speech goes like this: "Remember during orientation when all we cared about was sex. . . . education and they told us to refrain from alcohol and we went to the football game and what's-his-name and the cheerleader—fidelity, integrity, validity, reliability—and all of us went straight to the bar—values, ethics, don't drink and drive—and during sophomore year when the school newspaper published photos of the girls in Gamma Lama Mamma in—integrity, modesty, values, ethics, loyalty, start-up, fidelity—and remember Mrs. Fields from the cafeteria who used to let us in late after midnight? Too bad she was fired for smoking pot with us."

Another common graduating speech is: "When I came here I was a complete degenerate. I spent the entire first year of college playing poker and smoking pot. I used to spend a lot of money until Professor Smith joined us for poker and started bringing free pot from the biology lab. He showed us how to get into the biology lab through the rear entrance of the chemistry building. Professor Smith was a real friend. It was too bad the administration got rid of him. Luckily, no sooner did they fire him than Professor Pothead became the head of the oxycodone research program and we were able to find new ways to pursue meaning in life. Too bad he was fired for sexual harassment. But I'm here to tell you that after seventeen years and three expulsions, I'm finally getting my bachelor degree in pottery. I have a bright future ahead of me, and I could not have done it without Professors Smith and Pothead. I owe a lot to this institution of higher education. In fact, I owe it in excess of $85,000 in tuition and $5,398 in library fees for overdue books. When you add my student loans to the federal government, I'm looking at something like $357,999.00, which I plan to pay playing poker using some tricks that Professor Smith taught me and never forget integrity, loyalty, fidelity, voluntarism, alma mater, football, football, football, Katie Gotfrendsen, and God bless America."

Unlock the Secret to Leadership and Managerial Excellence with MI MA MO

Amanda is brilliant but doesn't do squat. George produces but he is no genius. Beatrice blathers all day. That's all you can think of when you meet with your employees. At this rate, instead of a raise you will get a demotion; and that is all you can think of, meeting after meeting. When you snap out of your trance, you realize that you're not very productive yourself and that you may have to rely on some serious sucking up to keep your job.

Life is hard as a LEADER. There is only so much sucking up you can do, especially when they keep changing SENIOR LEADERSHIP. But you know that they expect EXCELLENCE from you, so you have to produce. To produce, you need good people. To get good people, you need to screen them. To screen them, you need MI MA MO. I developed MI MA MO for people like you, who like to daydream when they should be working, who are tired of sucking up, and who like to delegate instead of lifting a finger. If you are that kind of LEADER—and let's face it, who isn't?—try MI MA MO.

After years of serious daydreaming, delegating, and fears of demotion, I've come to the conclusion that all of us, LEADERS, need better ways to hire for EXCELLENCE. Otherwise, our ass is on the line. We've all been administered the Myers-Briggs, the engagement assessment, the EQ test, and the sexual perversions diagnostic before we were hired, but none of them help hire for EXCELLENCE. This is why I developed the MI MA MO test. MI stands for *mind work*, MA stands for *manual work*, and MO for *mouth work*. Mind, manual, and mouth work. When you think about it, all you need to know about your employees is how well they perform on the various dimensions of MI MA MO.

To illustrate what the various types do, let's look at our own Miami. Examples of high-level MA (manual work) include:

- Take bribes
- Take drugs
- Push drugs
- Insert silicon
- Shoot guns
- Shoot baskets
- Build stadiums

These are all manual occupations that define South Florida. Not surprisingly, there are also some cases of MI (mind work):

- Ponzi schemer
- Medicare defrauder

We also have our share of MO (mouth work):

- Politicians evading prosecution
- Lawyers helping politicians
- Anchorwomen reporting on politicians and their lawyers
- Anchormen filling the air with nonsense and inane jokes
- Reporters talking about the latest shooting
- Silicon lips

Mouth types tend to talk a lot. Mind types tend to think a lot, and manual types just do whatever the other two didn't have time for because they were too busy talking or daydreaming. It's a terrible thing when you need someone to DO STUFF and all they can do is TALK instead of PERFORMING FOR EXCELLENCE. Generally, you want people who are low on mouth work and high on mind work. Of course, if they are good on manual work, you want them to have an IQ of at least 100 so they don't screw up whatever it is they're doing. Needless to say, a high IQ does not hurt, unless it is accompanied by verbal diarrhea, which is often the case in law firms, universities, government, and the Chris Matthews show.

To help you hire for EXCELLENCE and PERFORMANCE, I have developed an easy-to-remember, simple classification system. If you commit it to memory, you will never have to suck up again to your bosses. What's more, they will start sucking up to you. To help you internalize the various occupational profiles, and help you achieve the NEXT LEVEL, I created a little chart (see table 4.2).

My friends in the math department tell me that this little chart can result in twenty-seven unique occupational profiles. You can be a high-mind, medium-mouth, low-manual, like me, or a high-mouth, high-mind, medium-manual, like Chris Matthews. Not only can you classify your existing employees with this methodology, but you can hire for specific jobs. This approach can also fuel endless gossip by formulating a typology of celebrities, increasing your popularity in the firm. Is Kim Kardashian lo-mi hi-ma me-mo, or lo-mi lo-ma lo-mo? What about Maks Chmerkovskiy from *Dancing with the Stars*? We know he is hi-ma and hi-mo, but is he me-mi or lo-mi? If he goes out with J.Lo, does that make him hi-mi, lo-mi, or just lo-co?

You can also use the MI MA MO approach to identify strengths and weaknesses in the organization. Let's say you LEAD a news organization. You need reporters that will be well

Table 4.2. MI MA MO Occupational Profiles

	Level		
Occupational Strength	*High*	*Medium*	*Low*
MI (mind work)	hi-mi	me-mi	lo-mi
MA (manual work)	hi-ma	me-ma	lo-ma
MO (mouth work)	hi-mo	me-mo	lo-mo

aligned with emerging technologies. Look at John King from CNN as an example. He is hi-ma hi-mi hi-mo, and if you don't believe me, just watch him gesticulate in front of the ninety-eight-inch interactive monitor on election night. Wolf Blitzer, in turn, is hi-mo lo-ma hi-mi. With this approach, cable networks can hire reporters based on the size of their interactive electoral map: the bigger the touchscreen the greater the need for hi-ma reporters.

Say you need to hire consultants, who tend to be hi-mo me-mi lo-ma. They talk forever, think they are the smartest, and do very little. Next time you interview one of them you can start by asking them not who they have consulted with, but rather what they have DONE, like, actually running something. Real stuff, you know, and if you disagree with me you can start your own Twitter account @memihimoloma and use #myhimo.

THE LEARNING SIDE

The last story captures a great deal about people at work. Some are great talkers but not very good listeners. Some are very smart but do very little, while others pick up the slack for the rest of us. Of all the sins I've observed in the workplace, poor listening is by far the major one. Many people love to hear themselves talk. Meanwhile, they exhibit fitness and fairness deficits. They lack listening skills, undermining mattering and recognition, and they lack a sense of fairness, robbing others of time to express their views.

Talking too much instead of listening violates the principle of procedural fairness. This is because the process is neither inclusive nor participatory. Many people quit their jobs because management does not listen to them. But poor listening is only one of the problems in the workplace. Some people confuse metrics with meaning.

The first story revealed the virtues and vices of goals and metrics. Needless to say, some businesses, like the health care company exposed in *60 Minutes*, use metrics to make sure their corrupt practices are profitable! Some others use metrics to create the impression of progress and growth. But without metrics, it is hard to see whether you are making any progress at all. The key is to identify meaningful metrics that align well with your goals. Metrics should not replace meaning. The most important task in any organization is not to find the right metric, but the right meaning. Metrics should follow meaning, and not the other way around.

The story on professional conduct teaches us to be cautious around professionals. The word *professional* conjures up images of ethical behavior. The examples provided in the story show that personal interests often interfere with the social good. There is often a deceptive common narrative that becomes received wisdom, such as the one by pharmaceuticals: "we need to charge exorbitant amounts of money for medications to support research." Organizations often become so self-centered that self-preservation supersedes the common good. In the Hoffman report in July 2015, my own professional association, the American Psychological Association, was found to have colluded with the Department of Defense in aiding and abetting torture. Needless to say, professionals do a lot of good, and many professional associations protect the public, but caution is warranted.

Professionals often form in-groups that protect their own interests before the interest of the public. This is not to vilify professionals (I'm one of them), but rather to make the point that slowly and gradually, some of these groups create norms that make it okay to charge patients for needless tests, or bill insurance companies for frivolous procedures. To their defense, one group, the medical doctors, will say that the lawyers will sue them if they don't conduct all these tests, but in all of this there is a clear loser, and that is the patient. All these problems with work beg the question: what is occupational well-being?

Occupational Well-Being Defined

Occupational well-being refers to the level of satisfaction we derive from our main occupation. This can be a paid or a volunteer job. It can be done at home, at a workplace, or in the community. Not all people have paid employment, but many people volunteer and are active in other ways. Stay-at-home parents are plenty busy, no doubt. Therefore, I choose to refer to occupational well-being as satisfaction with your main job, vocation, or avocation. For many people occupation will in fact connote paid work, but not for all.

To achieve high levels of occupational well-being you must meet four conditions:[1]

- Be organized
- Use your strengths
- Feel engaged
- Feel appreciated

These conditions meet our needs for recognition and impact, the essentials of mattering. By being organized, using our strengths, and feeling engaged, we are likely to do a good job and gain the respect of peers and superiors. Feeling appreciated is a hallmark of healthy workplaces. If you meet the four conditions above, you will also feel that you are making a difference. Since we spend so much time around our main occupation, it is natural that this would be a significant source of mattering. Unfortunately, workplaces are not always in tune with mattering, to their own detriment.

To feel that what we do matters, we must be acknowledged. Some people are pleased with self-reward, and that is wonderful, but our social nature demands that most of us get a good word here and there. Developing apps, saving lives, teaching children, or building houses, whatever your profession is, you want to feel that you are making a difference. This is at the heart of mattering. A job with a great fit will make you feel like you matter because you are valued.

Occupational Fit

Great places to work for make sure your contributions are acknowledged.[2] They also provide opportunities for growth and flow. They worry about person-environment fit. They want to make sure that you use your strengths and that the job you occupy is right for your talents and personality.

When you are at your best, you are organized, committed, and creative. Organization is fundamental to self-efficacy, which is related to psychological wellness. Engagement, in turn, is associated with both psychological and physical health. Studies show that men who live to ninety-five usually stay in the workforce until they are eighty years of age. The more you feel engaged at work, the healthier you become, and the more your cholesterol and triglycerides go down. On the other hand, when engagement goes down, through unemployment, for example, depression and illnesses go up.[3]

Unemployment affects mattering in very negative ways.[4] Individuals who build their identity around their job feel deprived when they are laid off. This is why it's crucial for retirees and the unemployed to find meaningful alternatives. Work provides a steady supply of affirmation and efficacy that vanish with a pink slip. Unless we plan for meaningful ways of engagement, feelings of depression can unleash a negative chain reaction: we don't get out of bed, we don't exercise, we don't eat well, and we don't get along well. This is why developing a sense of purpose outside of work is important. It is one of the most preventive actions any of us can take. Unfortunately, workplaces, schools, and families often neglect to train for purpose. Workplaces often train for profit, but not for purpose, much to their own financial detriment.

Institutions do not invest nearly enough to create a culture of meaning and mattering. They usually leave it up to the employee to "find meaning." This is a mistake. While many workers bring with them a sense of purpose and mission, the organization must make a conscious effort to be explicit and deliberate about the social value of the enterprise. Once the common purpose is clear, an effort should be made to help workers see how they fit in the larger mission of the organization. Hospitals are not just about doctors, and construction is not just about the chief developer. Nurses, cleaners, plumbers, and welders are part of these companies. But whatever the social mission is, healing patients or building public housing, the purpose better be authentic. There is nothing worse than a phony mission statement that nobody abides by. It is very demoralizing to have a mission statement that talks about caring and respect when your boss treats you with disdain. Empty words do not make for a great fit. On the contrary, they make for a cynic fit.

A poor fit often derives from a culture of blame. Blaming poor organizational performance on individual deficits is the easiest thing. The hardest thing is to reflect on institutional habits that lead to disengagement. This is not to say that individuals do not need to improve performance. That is always the case. We can all do better. But the problem is that an exclusive focus on what Frank is doing wrong prevents the management team from contemplating what it's doing wrong.

A great fit comes down to creating an environment where everyone matters. A sense of meaning is related to a sense of belonging; and you cannot feel a sense of belonging unless you feel recognized by your peers and superiors. Similarly, you cannot experience meaning and purpose unless your actions make a difference. Mattering is ubiquitous and universal. Caring parents make their infants feel loved and help them grow. Caring teachers welcome their students and promote self-efficacy. Caring managers make employees feel part of the team and nurture mastery. As we mature and develop, we become responsible for enabling mattering experiences in others.

The greatest places to work for are learning organizations. They invest in becoming more *effective, reflective,* and *supportive.*[5] They study their processes, reflect on their mission, and offer instrumental and emotional support. Note that some places can be highly effective but highly unreflective. Others can be supportive but highly ineffective. To be a winner you need the three of them. It is like a three-legged stool. Not enough to have only two attributes.

As a young school psychologist I worked at a very effective and supportive child guidance clinic. The team was very professional and the atmosphere pleasant. There were wonderful and committed colleagues who cared deeply about children, families, and teachers. Still, it was not very reflective. We spent considerable time conducting assessments for special-education placement. The balance of the time was used consulting on behavioral problems. Most of our time was used reacting to problems, as opposed to preventing them. We were the equivalent of a mental health firefighter squad.

We were very good at doing what we were told, but what we were told to do was not always the best thing to do. We completed many assessments dutifully. We met with parents and teachers to explain the cognitive and emotional profile of their children. We rushed to schools when there was a suicidal kid. Unfortunately, we did not use all our knowledge to prevent any of these problems. We were constantly in reactive mode. When I suggested that we reconsider our mission and rebalance our portfolio more toward prevention, I was told to keep doing what I was doing: putting out psychological fires. I argued that tackling the risk factors associated with these learning and behavioral problems early on would make for a more humane and effective approach, but lack of reflection stopped our efforts. It was ironic that a clinic full of psychologists and learning specialists was not a learning organization.

We were not unique, however, by any stretch of the imagination. Many organizations do not stop to think whether the mission they adopted thirty or fifty years ago is still relevant. A learning organization stops and asks the big questions: Are we doing what we are supposed to do? Are there more efficient ways to accomplish our vision? Part of occupational fitness is training employees to ask these questions, and supporting them in the pursuit of answers.

Some workplaces are effective, and can even be reflective, but insensitive to people's needs. The supportive leg is broken. These corporations suffer from increased turnover, attrition, and brain drain. Without recognition and affirmation, the sense of mattering evaporates. To be sure, some people can enjoy the technical work immensely, and manage to go on for a while without emotional support, but in the long term, organizations do not survive without human warmth.

Occupational Fitness

We need competencies for being employed and unemployed. In some respects, being unemployed is harder than being employed because nobody trains us for it. We have to develop our occupational fitness to succeed on the job and off the job.

It is extremely difficult to get a job without a college degree.[6] The income gap between college and high school graduates continues to increase. College graduates not only make more money, but they also live longer and happier lives. In part, this has to do with the level of occupational control that a college degree affords. The more education you have, the more control you command over your environment, and the more respect you get. Control and respect are essential ingredients of occupational well-being.

Two sets of skills are required for success in any vocation: attitude and aptitude. The former refers to your social intelligence, the latter to your technical capacity. It is entirely possible to be gifted in the technical domain and a complete jerk in the interpersonal terrain. Some people claim that it is easier to train for aptitude than attitude. If you are arrogant, defiant, insolent, and uncooperative, chances are you will be fired soon. In contrast, if your job-specific skills are not great, you can probably learn. In an ideal world, we want people who are highly trained and skilled in both attitude and aptitude. They should know how to cooperate with others and how to fulfill their specific role with dexterity.

Unfortunately, many schools and universities train only for technical skills, resulting in a workforce that is devoid of social and emotional acumen. The technical skills are up to you, the school you attended, and the company you work for. But the good news is that you can also enhance your social and emotional intelligence. To do that, you need to become an agent of mattering. The two pillars of mattering are recognition and impact. For you to foster recognition of your colleagues, and to help them become more impactful in the world, you have to be able to *listen* and *empower*. For you to synergize your efforts with theirs, you need to *cooperate*.

As noted in chapter 2, the art of listening is about recognizing the needs, feelings, or beliefs inherent in verbal or nonverbal communication. When you listen to your colleagues, you have an opportunity to make them feel that they matter by recognizing their needs, feelings, or beliefs. To do that, remember that sometimes you need to park your intrusive thoughts. Affording a sense of recognition is about the other, not about you. This requires a fair bit of self-regulation.[7]

If you are invested in validating the experience of your colleague, you need to delay gratification and put your own needs on hold, at least for a while. You have to tell yourself that "now my job is to listen to Robert, not to tell him all that is crossing my mind." You will have time to share with Robert your thoughts, but keep in mind that to build a sense of belonging, you have to make him feel understood. Some people feel that to make their mark they have to talk a lot and show how smart they are. It is true that unless you speak up and voice your opinion, nobody will know that you have one, but you have to discern what is the best time, for how long you're going to talk, and how frequently you're going to do so. We will get to that, but for now, let's stick to your role as listener.

Listening is both intrinsically and extrinsically good. It is intrinsically good because you are creating a sense of acceptance and belonging, and it is extrinsically good because you are building the foundation of dialogue. By role modeling how to be a good listener, you are establishing rules of cooperation that will allow you to build a great team. After you listen for a while, people will feel comfortable around you. Listening is a powerful tool to enact the values of relating with care, relating with respect, and building a sense of community. Thus far we have talked about listening for recognition, the first pillar of mattering. Let's talk now about empowerment and how it can foster a sense of control.

Feeling like we're making an impact is the second pillar of mattering. To reach that feeling, we must experience control over our environment. We can facilitate that experience by empowering others. In the context of occupational well-being, empowerment is about working with others in a way that enhances their control. This can be accomplished by giving employees a say in decisions, training them in all aspects of the job, and creating leadership opportunities. Promoting voice and choice gives expression to the value of self-determination, which is the moral imperative behind making an impact. Self-determination is about expressing our uniqueness and our wishes. This is how we feel authentic and effective in the world. When others enable in us that feeling, they are empowering us to be authentic and effective. In short, listening is about affording recognition, and empowerment is about affording control. Without them, mattering cannot flourish.

If you've mastered listening and empowerment, you've conquered the first two essentials of social intelligence at work. The third basic component is cooperation. Listening and empowerment are about the well-being of the other person. Cooperation is about the well-being of everybody, including yours. After all, you have the right to self-determination as well. In chapter 2 we learned about *responding to others*, of which listening is a big part, and also about *expressing yourself* and *creating together*. In the context of work, the last two are part of cooperation. To achieve great outcomes at work, you have to be able to express your ideas and work together in productive ways.

What works for interpersonal fitness also works for occupational fitness. First, you have to express yourself in ways that are appropriate in terms of *content*, *tone*, and *length*. Of course, the content of what you say must relate to the conversation at hand, and hopefully will reflect your aptitudes and technical knowledge. Ideally, you are talented and your ideas make sense. But it is not only *what* you say, but also *how* you say it and *when* you say it that matters. If your tone is self-aggrandizing and dismissive, your listeners will not pay as much attention to your ideas as if you presented them with humility. The timing is also important. Monitor how often you talk, and for how long you talk. Hogging the microphone sends a message that "I'm the most important speaker in the room." Great team players build on other's ideas, look for common ground, create actionable plans, and support team spirit. For them, the "we" is more important than the "I." This is when their occupational fitness fosters fairness.

To summarize, people can foster occupational satisfaction by refining their attitude and aptitude. To become an agent of mattering, you have to foster a sense of recognition and control in your colleagues. To do that, you have to refine your ability to listen, empower, and cooperate.

Occupational Fairness

Workers who feel respected and treated with dignity report better physical and emotional health.[8] It is often said that your boss can be your best healer or your worst killer. When your superior treats you with respect, values your contributions, and gives you a sense of control, your health goes up. When control is withdrawn and appreciation replaced with domination, your psychological and biological well-being go down.

Lack of respect at work is perceived as a form of *interpersonal injustice*. This is well documented. Bullying, harassment, and psychological intimidation make the workplace hell. These toxic behaviors need not come only from your boss. Horizontal aggression among peers is not uncommon. As every human being is entitled to respectful and dignified treatment, fear-inducing climates violate basic rights. Burnout is often the result of interpersonal injustice.

A second type of injustice at work is *informational injustice*. Lack of transparency creates resentment. Professionals feel infantilized when information is withheld. They are made to feel that they cannot handle decisions. In terms of mattering, this is an assault on both recognition and impact. If you don't know what is going on, you can't have input and you can't make a difference.[9]

This is related to *procedural injustice*, which refers to fair processes. A fair process involves people affected by decisions. Participation in decision making is a definitional element of procedural justice. No voice, no choice.

Finally, *distributive justice* deals with the fair and equitable allocation of pains and gains, benefits and burdens. In simple terms, employees are to receive rewards and carry out obligations in a manner corresponding to their effort and talent, without favoritism or nepotism. Free riders are a common phenomenon. Few people do the work, but many get recognition. In some cases, graver forms of injustice take place—making people work in unhealthy conditions, withholding benefits, and creating intimidation. Lack of fairness at work diminishes your sense of mattering. Lack of fit and lack of fitness reduce your chances of occupational success.

Know Yourself, Help Yourself

Occupational well-being has a lot to do with being organized, using your strengths, feeling engaged, and feeling appreciated. How are you doing in these four dimensions of work? Getting organized is the subject of one of our humor stories and a source of concern for millions. Many people struggle with organization, either because they have a form of attention deficit disorder, or they were never taught. Indeed, clutter is the subject of books, coaching, and misery for many people. Let's say you want to become more tidy and timely. You can use the GREASE method reviewed in the first chapter of this book.

If your overall goal is to be more organized, you need to take gradual steps. Right now, you may be staring at a pile of papers that cover your desk from corner to corner, or you may be looking at an inbox with hundreds of emails. You may have a few deadlines looming, but you don't even remember the due dates. At home, you may have a drawer where you stuff bills, receipts, mortgage documents, batteries, paper clips, old movie tickets, chewing gum, and condoms. If you experience any of these symptoms, don't worry. There are thousands like you.

To become organized, don't try to tackle the desk, the inbox, and the drawer all at once. Pick something that is a priority. It may well be that the approaching deadlines at work are your main priority. If you don't meet them, you may not have a desk or a free email account anymore. Settled: you want to start by developing a system to keep track of deadlines and to stop procrastination. To do that, you can have either an electronic or a paper calendar with deadlines and major milestones. No project is completed overnight, not well anyway, so you better break down projects into small chunks.

If you have to write a report, it helps to break it down into small pieces. Let's say your report has five parts. Write an outline and decide how long each section needs to be, then budget appropriate time for each segment. Make it a habit to check your schedule periodically to see how you're doing. Are you on track to finish the report on time? Are you behind schedule? When I was writing my doctoral dissertation, I had a cue card with the various chapters and a timeline for completing each one of them. I used to reward myself for beating my own deadlines, which leads us to the second component of GREASE the plan: reinforcements.

No matter how small the first step is, make a point of celebrating your accomplishment. This can take the form of self-praise, or a check mark on the calendar. What you're doing is creating a new narrative about yourself. The story line says a few things:

- I can be in charge of my projects.
- I can change.
- I used to be disorganized but am taking steps to overcome this challenge.
- If I can change this about my work habits, I'm sure there are other things I can also change.

With every statement you're improving your self-efficacy, which is the engine behind impact, the second leg of mattering. If I can redefine myself as a competent person in this one domain of my life, I can gradually gain control over my affairs. This positive chain reaction gives expression to the value of self-determination. This is how important it is to celebrate small wins. To make sure you have small wins, you have to set easy targets at first, which is why you're not about to conquer the drawer, your email, your desk, and your deadlines all at the same time. Remember, the E in GREASE stands for *easy*.

The A is for *alternatives*. The key to replace a poor habit is to find a suitable alternative. You might have managed to submit reports on time, but with all-nighters and with a great amount of stress. If you find yourself sweating every time you need to meet a deadline, it is time to find an alternative to the madness. I suggested creating a calendar with clear milestones, drafting an outline with approximate length for each section of the report, and rewarding yourself for sticking to the plan. This may not work for you. Fine, I won't take it personally, but do yourself a favor and find another alternative to the mad rush.

So far you've relied on your own efforts to cope with deadlines. It is time to get some support: the S in GREASE. Help from others can take many forms: make a commitment to your boss to submit things on time, get your colleague to partner with you, share with your wife your new goal, and ask her to nudge you to completion. Ask your support team to cheer you on. Ask them to review drafts. Leverage their expertise. Set up regular times to meet with your colleagues until the report is done. Research supports the notion that working with friends or relatives facilitates goal achievement.[10] Finally, if you want to get organized, educate yourself about effective strategies, but whatever you do to get informed, don't spend eight hours on the app store trying to find the miracle app. This is time you could have used to finish your report on time.

You can use the GREASE method to improve other aspects of occupational well-being too. Our MI MA MO story depicts characters we've all come across in the workplace: some who talk too much, some who are quite smart, and some who are pretty handy. Of course, some are brilliant, but do very little, probably because they talk too much. Let's imagine that after some reflection you come to the conclusion that you talk too much and listen too little. You may set a gradual goal to talk a little less and listen a little more. You need to be better at parking your intrusive thoughts.

You can set a goal to stop one intrusive thought from coming out of your mouth for each of the next three conversations. You can catch yourself and stop these thoughts from coming out of your mouth. Next, you can try to spend more time listening without talking. That may be hard, but try it, even for a few seconds. This is like yoga for your mouth. Hold it shut for a little longer. Be quiet for a little longer. As you exhale, reward yourself for becoming a better listener, one breath at a time. Like yoga, start easy. You can gradually increase the length of time you keep quiet.

When you're used to blurting out whatever comes to mind, it may be a challenge to find a suitable alternative. After all, listening attentively is the opposite of impulsive talk. One option may be to write down your thoughts. If you're in a meeting, and you feel the urge to talk, for the tenth time, put it on paper instead.

Controlling your need for self-expression may require a little help from your friends. How about asking them to give you a surreptitious signal when you're talking too much? If you need further help, learn about the impact of incessant yakking on relationships.

As you can see, GREASE can help with organization and with too much talking, but it can also be useful with cooperation, empowerment, and engagement. The more organized and cooperative you are, the more recognition you will get at work. The more you empower others, and the more effective you become, the stronger your organizational impact will be.

Know Others, Help Others

You always wear two hats at work. With one, you try to improve your occupational well-being. With the other, no matter how high or low you are on the occupational food chain, you strive to help others. Whether you're appointed as a formal leader or not, as part of a team you have an opportunity to make a difference. In the previous chapter we learned about I VALUE IT roles. These are functions that professionals fulfill to work effectively with teams. To illustrate their applicability, let's choose a typical problem at work: negative culture.[11] If you are like most people, chances are you often feel disengaged at work. In some cases, lack of engagement may have to do with your preoccupations, but in most cases, it has to do with the culture of the place.

Many workplaces fail to appreciate employees and miss opportunities to engage them in a common purpose. They use threats to motivate. Instead of fairness, they instill fear. Listening, empowerment, and cooperation are nowhere to be found. The fit between person and organization is terrible. People are too busy protecting themselves as opposed to appreciating others. Mental energies go toward survival instead of building a better place. Your boss makes you feel like you don't matter. Your voice does not count. You don't have many opportunities to practice choice either. The main skill you practice in such an environment is self-protection.

With a culture like this, no wonder the vast majority of workers in the United States report feeling disengaged. A study by Gallup found that in 2014 51 percent of the workforce was "not engaged" and another 17.5 percent was "actively disengaged."[12] This is a major challenge for the workplace. If getting organized or becoming a better listener looked hard, wait till you try to improve organizational culture. But given that this is such a huge barrier to occupational well-being, let's figure out how to tackle it by trying I VALUE IT roles.

Your first job is to act like an inclusive host. If you've identified a poor culture at work, and you want to change it, the first thing you need to do is to convene a group of people to devise a plan. Depending on your level of influence in the organization, you may invite senior managers, line workers, or anybody else who can help, but it's clear that you cannot effect change by yourself. Once your colleagues come to your meeting to discuss culture, you must embrace the role of an inclusive host. You need to make them feel comfortable and safe. You may need to establish some ground rules, such as mutual respect and confidentiality. The goal is to create a climate of trust where peers can discuss freely the good, the bad, and the ugly.

As the host, it's your job to make sure that people are heard, and that no single person monopolizes the conversation. At this initial stage, the goal may be to elicit comments about culture. Depending on how far you are in the process, you can move from diagnosis to planning to action, but before you get to that, you need to create a vision of a better state of affairs. This is when you assume the role of visionary, the V in I VALUE IT.

A visionary facilitates a process of imagining a better future, a greater fit between person and environment. Your job is to create with the group a vision of a healthier culture. But a good visionary encourages the group to imagine not just a better outcome, but also a good process to get there. A good process is focused, respectful of diverse opinions, and accountable to its constituencies. In other words, it affords voice and choice to participants, and it ensures the delivery of a concrete plan. If you want to improve the culture, you need to model a better one in your process.

Since you cannot accomplish the vision by yourself, you need allies. Your colleagues have a wide array of strengths: information, access to resources, skills, experience, personal interest, passion. These are all assets that you need to leverage. In building on their strengths, you are enacting recognition. You are telling your colleagues:

- You are a valued member of this organization.
- You can help with the process of improving our culture.
- I'm so glad you decided to join our group, because you have a lot to contribute.
- I appreciate your willingness to help me.

Building on assets is in the best interest of everybody. People usually operate from a place of interest. They are interested in not only feeling recognized, but also in making a difference, the second pillar of mattering. By identifying their unique talents, you are opening a door for them to experience self-efficacy. To become a good asset seeker, you have to get to know your colleagues. You can then foster a good fit between their capacities and organizational needs.

The L in I VALUE IT is for *listener* and sense maker. We reviewed the essentials of listening already. Let's review the role of sense maker now. After you listen and attend to organizational dynamics, risks, challenges, and opportunities, it is your job to try and make sense of it all. Can you discern some patterns? What are people saying about workplace culture? If you listen carefully, in all likelihood, they will be talking about recognition and impact. If the culture is deficient in some way, you will likely hear one of four things:

- Some people feel invisible.
- Some people feel entitled.
- Some people feel helpless.
- Some people, usually those who feel entitled, make others feel invisible and helpless.

The first two bullets threaten a culture of recognition. The second two undermine a culture of impact. If the culture is constructive, you'll likely hear that people feel engaged, appreciated, valued, and useful. In most cases, it's not all or none, and in some pockets of the organization there is likely to be a better climate than in others. Your job is to discern where things are working, where they are not, and why. This is the role of the sense maker. It is detective work. You should try to ascertain the source of the problem and the unique contextual dynamics affecting culture.

Unique dynamics require unique solutions. Is it a leadership problem? Do you have people in senior management positions that are dismissive or disrespectful? Do you have communication problems? Culture is usually a combination of people, places, and processes. Are people disengaged? Are they demoralized? Does the place look professional and clean? Is it an inviting place? Are the processes clear? Is there a good fit between person and environment? Is the workplace fair? Are there processes to promote aptitude and attitude? Making sense of organizational culture is a difficult task. You should take your time before you offer unique solutions to your distinctive culture. Listening is a great place to start. Having the right diagnosis is the major part of the cure.

The E is for *evaluator*. To be accountable, you have to evaluate previous, current, and future efforts. Unless you measure what you are doing, you are not going to know if you are making things better or worse. Adopt a curious attitude. Learn about what worked and what didn't in the past. What are some of the barriers to change? What elements of your intervention are making the biggest difference? You don't need to have the skills of a program evaluator yourself, but you can bring this to the attention of your team as an essential part of change.

Once you've listened, evaluated, and made sense of the situation, you need to implement an action plan. Talk must be followed by action if you are going to be a credible agent of change. Either as leader or follower, nothing builds your reputation as much as follow-up and follow-through. Implementation requires organization and planning. Without specific tasks, roles, timelines, and measures, it's hard to carry out culture change. If you succeeded as inclusive host and asset seeker, you would have a team of supporters. If you managed to listen well and to make sense of the situation, you would have some clarity about the diagnosis and the correct prescription.

Being useful to your colleagues and the institution requires more than implementation of borrowed ideas. The T in I VALUE IT is for *trendsetter*. This means creating an innovative path forward. It is hard to get inspired by copying other people's solutions. Creativity leads to meaning and mattering. You are using your signature strengths to tackle a major problem. Actors and musicians, like writers, touch lives through their performance. They derive meaning from their distinctive interpretation and treatment of human concerns. In workplaces, you are the actor. You are the agent of change. You can project your singularity to any of the I VALUE IT roles. In doing so you will grow your self-efficacy and make meaning of your efforts.

I used the example of a negative culture because it is as prevalent as it is vexing. But you can apply the I VALUE IT principles to any other problems involving teams, even if you don't lead the effort. As an active participant, you can nudge the leader or the group to create an inclusive environment, to develop a vision, to build on strengths, and to listen. You can play a part in making sense of the situation, coming up with unique solutions, and implementing strategies. The more you practice these roles the faster you will master the art of teamwork.

Of all the skills and roles we reviewed in this chapter, think of one or two that can help you, or that can help others. Perhaps you want to become a better listener, or a better leader. You might want to become a more inclusive host. Lack of procedural fairness may be prevalent at work. Think of ways to increase voice and choice among staff. If you follow the GREASE method, pick one goal, move toward it gradually, make it easy to experience small wins, reinforce yourself for sticking with it, and get support from others.

5

Physical Well-Being

THE LAUGHING SIDE

The following humor stories teach you two things about physical well-being: avoid hospitals, and never leave home without laxatives. Reading them might motivate you to take care of yourself, which is the subject of the next section. Since humor can put you in a good mood, and since a good mood improves learning, don't skip this section.

Waiting Room Woes

It took me a while to find the right waiting room in the hospital.

Me: Can you please tell me where the waiting room for nuclear multisyllable chromosomal endocrinal catheterization is?

Random person wearing a white coat in the hospital: Follow the green line.

Me: Which one?

Random person: The one on the floor.

After following the green line for forty-five minutes I ended up at a garbage dump full of green bins with a big sign on them: "Danger: Radiologic Biologic Morphologic Recycling." I somehow figured that my friend, who just had a multisyllabic procedure, wasn't there.

Me: Can you please tell me how to get to the information desk?

Different random person wearing a stethoscope around his neck and carrying a two-gallon Coke bottle in his pocket: Follow the red line.

Me: The one on the floor?

Same different random person, now drinking from two-gallon Coke bottle, drooling all over his stethoscope: Of course, moron!

After following the red line for ninety minutes I arrived at the information desk of Macy's. At that point I discovered that I was color-blind, but a nice lady guided me back to the hospital. I eventually found the department of nuclear multisyllable chromosomal endocrinal catheterization.

Me: Can you please tell me where I can find Isaiah Franklin, my friend, who just had a gastro morphologic orchiectomy?

Nurse carrying a three-gallon Coke bottle: He is doing well, but we also had to perform a myringotomy and a diverticulectomy abdominoplasty because he was constipated. He is in room 323. Just follow the yellow line.

Me: I'm sorry, I'm color-blind.

Nurse: Second door on the right.

Me: Can you also point me to the restroom?

Nurse: Just follow the smell.

Relieved that I had found my way back to the waiting area, I sat in the small room, turned off the annoying TV, which usually advertises discounted gonadectomies, and turned on my Kindle for some quiet time. No sooner did I start reading than three incredibly loud women sat next to me, talking in Spanish, in detail, about their father's scrotoplasty. To add insult to injury they turned on the TV and started watching *La Rosa de Guadalupe* in Univision. I pretended I did not speak Spanish to avoid unsolicited conversation about scrotoplasties or Fidel Castro, but I could not help being distracted by the telenovela. A very big woman was trying to rescue a very young woman from what looked like a very bad pimp. She succeeded, but only temporarily. As soon as the very big lady drove away with the very young lady, the very bad pimp telephoned another pimp who brought ninety-eight other pimps to the rescue house, where it seemed like very young girls were rehabilitating themselves from a life of very bad things. The ninety-nine pimps came with very big guns to the house and then there was a very long commercial break. The commercials advertised Dos Equis beer with seminude women hugging Camaros and the Mexican soccer team selling tortillas.

To distract myself I fantasized: What if I pressed the emergency button by the stretcher next to me? What if I responded to a code blue and showed up at the emergency room before the real doctors? (I have only a PhD, which in Jewish families is as good as a high school diploma.) What if I walked into one of the rooms and conducted a diverticulectomy abdominoplasty on some random patient? Any of these options would have been better than suffering all the scrotoplasty talk, but my superego took over and I resigned myself to watching *La Rosa de Guadalupe*.

As I was getting into *La Rosa de Guadalupe*, the phone of the lady next to me started ringing uncontrollably. The phone owner, who was describing in gruesome detail the scrotoplasty to her mother and sister, could not be bothered to answer. The conversation got even louder when the Spanish-speaking nurse offered us in the waiting room some Jell-O, which I would never touch because it must have colorant, sugar, and 2,987 different kinds of germs. As they swallowed the green Jell-O, my companions asked the nurse how their relative was doing. Displaying great surgical erudition, the nurse went on and on for forty-five minutes describing more body parts than you would ever learn in a whole season of *Grey's Anatomy*. At that point I wanted to have a morphologic orchiectomy myself. Alternatively, I would have swum to Guantanamo for some quiet time.

Missing LAX

Few people like to admit that their happiness revolves around their bowel movements. I used to be one of them, keeping bowel movements to myself. I grew up in a house where defecation existed only in other people's houses. Although I grew up in the sixties, my mom was still living in the Victorian era. After forty-five years of intensive therapy I can now claim a major Freudian achievement: use the word *defecation*.

There was a time when I was oblivious to my bowel movements. Ignorance was bliss. I really don't know how that was possible, but one day my bliss came to a sudden and complete stop. I was visiting my brother's family in Mexico City. I had to miss my nephew's bar mitzvah due to work, so I decided to come and visit them during the winter break for a week. We were living in Canada at the time, so escaping to Mexico for a week sounded like a great idea. That was, until my brother fed me so much meat and white bread that I got Montezuma's constipation. All of a sudden, I became painfully aware of my stomach and entire digestive tract: large intestine, small intestine, and the whole nine yards. I was in pain. That started a love-hate relationship with my colon.

My colonic hypervigilance turned into trauma when my good friend Geoff Nelson introduced me to his naturopath, Jim Farquharson. Jim told me in casual conversation that four to five bowel movements a day is normal.

WHAT?

Friends don't do this to each other. Friends don't introduce you to friends like Jim. Since that moment on, I could not help but obsess about my once-a-day bowel movement. Friends don't tell friends they poop five times a day. That's cruel. How can that be possible?

But I'm nothing if not methodic, so I started to experiment with foods. I was determined to poop five times a day. While I did not reach that goal, a lot of good things happened along the way. My consciousness about healthy eating, for instance, grew tenfold.

Some pertinent background: I grew up in Argentina. We used to eat meat three times a day, and not just a little, but a lot, and not just steak, or chicken, but everything, and I mean everything: large intestine, small intestine, tongue, cow brains, testicles, veins, coagulated blood, the works. Although I lived in Argentina only until I was sixteen years old, I'm sure that I ate enough meat to last several lifetimes. Determined to conquer constipation, I started eliminating meat, which was great for my elimination system. Then went white bread; dairy followed. I slowly discovered that my digestive tract did not much like these foods. I gradually overcame my obsession, learned to count my blessings, and ended up a vegan. In my family's eyes I went from colon-centric to eccentric. How could an Argentinean give up meat!?

While my colonic health is good, remnants of worry remain: whenever I travel I put a laxative in my suitcase, just in case. I never use it, but it's good to have. I never know what people will feed me when I travel. And since most of the world is pretty oblivious to the needs of vegans, I have to be ready to face constipation.

Some more background: I do quite a bit of travel, and I've made it a bit of a science to pack everything into a carry-on suitcase, no matter how far, or for how long I go. To prove to myself, and Ora, my wife, that I can be flexible, I decided to take to Taiwan a carry-on and a small bag. After all, I was going to a conference; I had to take a suit and could not fit everything into a carry-on suitcase. So in a moment of bravery, and against my best judgment, I decided to send one of my two pieces of luggage, only to worry during the long flights from Miami to Taipei that the small bag I sent, containing my laxative, would end up in Mongolia.

Sure enough, I land in Taipei, take my carry-on, and proceed to the carousel to collect my small brown bag (all my bags are brown, as are most of my clothes, watches, shoes, and underwear), only to discover that it was not there. Worrying that my anxiety would quickly turn into a panic attack, I started thinking about contingency plans: have to get to a pharmacy, must find restaurant with beans, should send Ora a text to overnight me Senokot. But my anxiety was such that ruminations took over: how do I tell my hosts, waiting for me in the lobby, that my laxative did not arrive? It is seven in the morning. Can they take me to a pharmacy? What else did I put in the brown bag?

Meanwhile, the ground crew assured me that my bag would get to my hotel within two to three days. Three days! The specter of constipation was too much to bear.

My gracious hosts, two graduate students waiting for me in the airport, were worried that something had happened to me. It took me a while to fill out the paperwork to have my bag delivered, whenever it would get to Taiwan from Kazakhstan. I finally came out of customs, the last passenger, to meet them. After a few pleasantries, we took the speed train to T'ai-nan. Settled in the hotel, I discovered that my brown bag contained not only my laxative, but also my exercise clothes, and shoes. If there is one thing that I'm more rigid about than regularity, it's my exercise routine. The prospect of not exercising for three days was worse than the fear of constipation. Counting the time until my hosts would pick me up for the opening ceremony of the conference, I hurried to buy running shoes, a pair of shorts, and, of course, some laxatives.

My lucky day! Next to the hotel there was a pharmacy. Just as I entered I found B12. Vegans must take B12 to prevent a host of neurological complications that make constipation look like a walk in the park. My B12s were in my brown bag on its way to Estonia, but I had found a solution. Feeling elated, I proceeded to look for laxatives, only to find out that the only thing in the entire pharmacy with English labels was a bottle of B12. I paced up and down the aisles in hopes of finding a clue, a picture, or a sign that would lead me to a laxative. Unfortunately, I could not tell apart a laxative from a pregnancy kit. It was all in Chinese.

Overcoming years of repressive Victorian education, I timidly approached the pharmacist and mumbled the word *laxative*, only to encounter a puzzled look. Of course the pharmacist spoke no word of English, and I spoke no word of Chinese. All of a sudden the meaning of "lost in translation" hit me like a ton of bricks. I had no idea what she thought I was asking for. At that point I had two choices: either mimic constipation or walk away. However, it dawned on me that I had no idea how to simulate constipation. I feared that if I held my stomach and grimaced she would think I had food poisoning or pancreatic cancer. I quickly scanned my brain for old episodes of *Whose Line Is It Anyway?* to find the appropriate simulation, but I drew a blank. I left the pharmacy determined to master Mandarin in two days. It was that or constipation until LAX—the Los Angeles airport—a name that sounded like a cruel joke at the time.

My only hope for a bowel movement now was either a plate of raw beans or vigorous exercise. With no beans in sight I rushed to the nearest department store to buy running shoes and a pair of shorts. I knew I should not have sent my brown bag in the cargo. That should teach me a lesson. While I was worried sick about my digestive health, my bag was probably in Angola being used to smuggle arms.

I finally got to the department store and discovered that no one spoke English there either. I speak other languages, but I figured if they don't speak English they wouldn't speak Hebrew, Spanish, Italian, or Portuguese either. At least it was easy to point to shoes. After a few misdirected attempts, I went to the sporting goods section to meet a very pleasant Taiwanese who, you guessed it, did not speak a word of English. I showed her with my fingers the number 8 (US shoe size), and I pointed to some white shoes. She proceeded to bring me nine boxes of shoes, none of them white, none of them eight. After forty-five minutes, which is forty-four more than I can bear in any store, we found a pair of gray Nikes that would go well with my long-running Nike pants, in my brown bag, if I ever got it back from Nicaragua.

Then I proceeded to select a pair of shorts. I will spare you the ensuing miscommunications, but after a similar eternity, she found a suitable pair. I was never so happy to get to a cashier, but the clerk interrupted the exchange to say something that sounded like "tax refund." Under the circumstances I could only imagine that she remembered she had to offer me a tax refund because I was, obviously, a foreigner. Although at that point I was ready to pay whichever price for the sporting goods, I thought that I should be responsible with my money and get my tax refunds. I know you are thinking that I'm making this up, but I swear it's true.

The nice lady took me up several flights by the hand until we reached what looked like THE TAX REFUND OFFICE. The clerk requested my passport. I handed it to her, and while they copied the information they put in front of me a piece of paper in Mandarin, and, finally, English. They pointed to the English section, which they asked me to read and sign. At that point I was so desperate to go for a jog that I was ready to admit that I was the Unabomber, only to discover what the English said: "If you are getting the tax refund, you are not supposed to use any of your purchases in Taiwan. They must remain closed in a zipped bag until you leave the country." I had just spent three hours in a stupid department store, the likes of which I hate, to buy some running gear, only to be told that I cannot use the darn shoes until I get to LAX. Overcome by frustration, I grabbed the bags, my passport, and took off.

THE LEARNING SIDE

Being mindful of your own body is essential for health and wellness. After my yoga classes, during the relaxation period, our instructor asks us to visualize different parts of the body. She wants us to notice how they feel. She thinks we need to increase our awareness. Of course, the LAX story brings bodily awareness to neurotic heights, but I'm just amazed how unaware I was of my body until I had a severe case of constipation. There is often a disconnect between body and mind. The more attention we pay to our bodies, the more likely we are to do something about it. The more aware we are, and the more we do to prevent common ailments, the less we'll have to visit hospitals. It is true that my story about waiting rooms exaggerates the suffering involved in going to hospitals, but not by much.

Hospitals are the embodiment of reactive medicine. We often go there when we have failed to prevent a preventable condition such as hypertension, lung cancer due to smoking, obesity, or stress. The vast majority of physical illnesses are preventable, including cardiac arrest and the many complications deriving from obesity.[1] But just to be clear, hospitals do not prevent disease. At best, they help us cope with them.

People's notion of health is often a visit to the doctor or the pharmacy to buy the latest miracle cure. This is all reactive medicine. It is costly, and it involves a lot of side effects, aggravations, and stress, not to mention a small fortune in copayments and uninsured procedures. Prevention is cheaper and easier. Remember the old adage that "an ounce of prevention is worth a pound of cure"? It is absolutely true. There are certain conditions that even the best hospitals in the world cannot cure.

This idea was brought home to citizens of Soho in London in September 1854. On the 31st of August a cholera epidemic broke out, and in ten days it killed five hundred people. Physicians didn't know how to cure cholera, and even if they did, there wouldn't be enough doctors, nurses, and hospital beds to treat those afflicted with the disease. The demand for medical services exceeded the ability of the health system to care for them. But even if it did, there would always be new cases to contend with. Curing people with cholera did nothing to prevent new cases from emerging.

The only solution to the problem was prevention. This is what Dr. John Snow thought. Through detective work, he was able to find the root cause of the epidemic. Gross alert! People had been drinking water contaminated with fecal matter and other toxins from the Broad Street pump. When Dr. Snow concluded that most people who had been dying had been drinking contaminated water from the Broad Street pump, he discovered the cause of the problem. On September 7, he met with city officials to share his findings. On September 8 public health workers stopped the cholera epidemic by removing the handle from the pump. Preventing people from drinking polluted water stopped the disease.[2]

John Snow didn't know how to cure cholera, but even if he did, there would never be enough doctors to treat all the patients affected by the disease. Instead of trying to cure all the new cases, which he couldn't, he decided to prevent new cases altogether. And prevent he did. By finding the root cause of the problem, he was able to avert many more deaths. His solution was more humane, efficacious, and cheaper than trying to cure dying patients.

My mentor George Albee, former president of the American Psychological Association, taught me that *no mass disorder afflicting humankind has ever been eliminated, or brought under control, by treating the affected individual.* The only way to effectively cope with HIV/AIDS is through prevention. The same goes for cholera and for many other epidemics like obesity. Even effective treatment of those with HIV/AIDS does not prevent the occurrence of new cases. Saving one patient does not do anything to stop the disease from killing others. The only way to eradicate permanently the disease is through prevention. Just like John Snow stopped the cholera epidemic through prevention, so we can eliminate the many diseases associated with obesity, hypertension, dangerous levels of cholesterol, and stress.

The good news is that there are effective ways to prevent these conditions, and they are cheaper and safer than going to hospitals. The only side effects of prevention are positive! If you successfully prevent diseases associated with being overweight, you will gain confidence to conquer other challenges in life, like smoking, excessive drinking, sedentary lifestyle, and stress.[3]

Physical Well-Being Defined

Physical well-being refers to our level of satisfaction with our body. Physical wellness is about energy and vitality on the positive side, and lack of pain and disease on the negative side. Adequate body function depends on proper nutrition, physical activity, and adequate sleep, among other things. Despite all we know about nutrition and physical activity, millions of people suffer from preventable diseases. Food can be a great healer or a devastating killer, but people seem oblivious to what they eat and drink.[4]

As a health nut, I try to maintain a healthy lifestyle regardless of where I am, which can be a challenge while I travel because the fit is often horrendous. At home, though, the fit is optimal. Instead of trying to strengthen my willpower, I modified the environment around me to make it easy to stay healthy. I live across the street from the university where I work. This way I avoid traffic and can increase physical activity by walking more. The fitness center is a four-minute walk from our house. Our fridge and pantry are stocked with healthy foods. We eat a plant-based diet. We go to restaurants that offer healthy options. At work, I instilled a culture of healthy eating at functions and parties. Slowly but surely I improved the fit between my physical aspirations and my environment. I have come to believe that it is all about the fit.

Physical Fit

One of the greatest fallacies of the modern era is that we have great willpower. We have willpower, but not great willpower, and unless we train it, and we use it, we lose it.[5] Just like we build muscle through resistance training, our willpower develops through gradual exposure. If the environment is overwhelmingly tempting, and we have had no training, chances are we will fail. We will fail when tempted with junk food and the comfort of the couch. Just like the love of broccoli and exercise must be nurtured, resistance to junk food and the couch must be fostered.

Healthy environments don't require great willpower, but toxic ones do. In North America, the nutritional environment is quite atrocious. If we were more humble as a species, we would have a better chance of enhancing our physical well-being because we would train our willpower and improve the context at the same time.

For people to experience health and wellness there must be a fit between what people bring to the equation, and what the environment has to offer. If the context is nutritionally awful, it would behoove us to change ourselves to resist the bombardment of salt, sugar, and fat that is present in most processed foods.[6] That is one option. It is an option predicated on the fact that we can walk around fast-food outlets and restaurants full of junk and say NO THANKS, I WOULD RATHER EAT MY CELERY STICK. Try doing that when you are hungry for lunch and all your buddies are going to Fat Central. It is hard. The environment overwhelms you with nutritionally empty calories and addictive choices full of grease, salt, and sugar. For that kind of heroism, you need a ton of willpower, which most people lack.

A second option is to change the environment to make it healthier. Now we have two options instead of one: we can change the environment or we can try to change our habits. We must do both. We must improve our capacity for personal wellness and we must change the environment at the same time. If we rely exclusively on willpower, we are cheating ourselves of enormous opportunities to create health. It is time to try a new approach I call environmental healthification. (My dictionaries tell me that *healthification* is not a word. Well, it is now. By healthification I mean the process of creating healthy places.)

The nutritional landscape consists of our homes, workplaces, restaurants, shopping centers, airplanes, trains, schools, parks, and communities. This is what food psychologist Brian Wansink calls our food radius.[7] When you think that most humans in wealthy countries eat three meals a day and snack midmorning and midafternoon, you end up with five opportunities to provide your body nutrition or junk; you healthify or putrefy your body every time. (My dictionaries tell me that *healthify* is not a word either; too bad, because this word is long overdue. Healthify means making something healthier.)

Healthification is the process of changing our surroundings so that our willpower doesn't have to be tested so often. Like our muscles, overexertion depletes our energy. Confronted with succulent foods and scrumptious desserts, depleted willpower has no chance. Instead of straining our willpower, we have to work on alimentary design. Some environments are naturally healthy. When Dan Buettner visited centenarians, he found them in cities and villages that are naturally good for them. He found them in places that require lots of walking. He met them in communities with plenty of fruits and vegetables. He was amazed by the social support network they all had. Stress was low; joy and friendships were high.[8]

Since most of us cannot easily move to Okinawa, Sardinia, or the Nicoya Peninsula in Costa Rica, where most centenarians live, we have to think of what we can do in our own backyard to make it healthier. Politicians, academics, and nutrition experts work on policy. You can work on your own food radius: your home, work, and community.

Studies demonstrate that the availability and attractiveness of food make a huge difference in our consumption patterns. Brian Wansink has studied this topic in depth and has come to the conclusion that the most effective way to get slim is by design. That is, by constructing an environment around you that is full of healthy options, minimal in bad options, and all around good for you.

Instead of exposing us to tempting situations all day long he advocates altering the surroundings. You can bring a healthy lunch to work. You can buy healthy foods in the supermarket. You can preselect restaurants with plenty of tasty and healthy items on the menu. You can use smaller plates. You can limit your trips to the buffet to just one. You can place healthy snacks at eye level in school cafeterias. You may call this the architecture of nutrition.[9] If you don't have it naturally around you, like in the Nicoya Peninsula, you can create it.

The architecture of my sleep was poor. My sleep had a bad fit with coffee. Until twenty years ago coffee was part of my daily routine. I liked coffee. It was part of my life—regular in the morning, decaf at night. For as long as I had decaf in the evening, I was fine. But on the few occasions that I was served regular coffee by mistake, I had a hell of a time falling asleep. I don't blame waiters for getting sick of my repeated calls to ensure that the coffee was decaf. I was a real pain, until one night a waiter probably got fed up with my decaf neurosis and served me, by mistake or by design, real coffee in the evening.

It was a night to remember. We were living in Waterloo, Ontario. It was winter and it was snowing outside. The temperature was way below freezing. I was so overstimulated that I put on my jogging suit and went outside for a run in the middle of the night. I had way too much caffeine in my system to fall asleep. Instead of sleeping I had racing thoughts. Jogging was the only cure for my excess caffeine. That was the last day I had coffee. My neurosis and my coffee didn't get along. Good buy, bad fit. I traded something I minimally liked, which lasted for a few minutes, for something I loved, which lasted for seven hours every night for the rest of my life: sleep. I healthified my environment. Coffee was out, sleeping was in.

But healthification applies not only to food or sleep. It also pertains to physical activity. You can design your day so that you walk more. You can get off the bus or train a couple of stops before your destination and walk. You can take the stairs instead of the elevator. You can leave your exercise clothes by your bed so when you get up in the morning you are reminded to go to the gym. You can have walking buddies. Some of these opportunities require collaboration from friends and relatives, but some are totally within your control.

Physical Fitness

To achieve an optimal fit you need to work on both sides of the equation: person and environment. Wherever you start, you need to pick up some skills. To improve your physical fitness you need to acquire some life fitness. Many people get discouraged when they start an exercise routine and desist shortly thereafter. Others become disheartened because they compare themselves to people in much better shape. They think that they will never achieve the sexy physique or svelte silhouette of their neighbors. That is the wrong comparison to make. Our point of reference should be ourselves: where we are today and where we want to go. In short, who do we want to become? These are the right questions. If you want to feel better physically, there are things you can do starting today, like eating better, moving more, and eliminating behaviors or products that will affect your sleep.

But before you start, it is helpful to go back to one of our basic values: self-care. Think about what this means for you. Do you want to increase your energy levels? Do you want to avoid pain? Do you want to be around to enjoy your grandchildren? What gives you meaning in life? What can you do to pursue your goals and ambitions? Can you eat better? Can you exercise more? Can you drink less alcohol and more water? Getting healthier is about mattering, to yourself and to those you love. It all goes back to self-care.

Values are vehicles to meaning. In addition to self-care, perhaps you make meaning through self-determination. If that is the case, you probably want to discern what it means to exercise autonomy over your diet and your exercise routine. Are these based on your own decisions or are they based on cultural norms? Have you thought about the influence of advertising and commercial interests on how you eat? If you value self-determination, you probably want to question the source of your healthy or unhealthy habits. In this section we will review some skills to help you realize the values of self-care and self-determination.

In previous chapters you mastered the basics of GREASE. Any change process to increase fit, fitness, and fairness requires Gradual goals, Reinforcements, Easy targets, Alternatives, Support, and Education. Now we can dive deeper into the science of personal change. To help you achieve your physical well-being goals, you can leverage any one of seven drivers of change: Behaviors, Emotions, Thoughts, Interactions, Context, Awareness, and Next Steps (BET I CAN). The BET I CAN drivers offer multiple points of entry into the process of health improvement, such as changing a single behavior, modifying the context, challenging some negative thoughts, or increasing your awareness about health.

The application of the GREASE method to the BET I CAN drivers can guide your efforts to improve physical fitness. You can set a gradual and achievable goal like increasing your walking three minutes per day. This is the application of a gradual approach to changing a specific behavior. To maintain the walking routine you can do a simple thing: use one of the many available apps to record how many minutes of walking you do every day. This is an easy way to reinforce your new behavior. Another easy action is to reward yourself, not by eating an ice cream bucket, but by telling yourself that you are getting healthier every day. In doing so you are reinforcing a thought and a positive emotion.

To activate positive emotions you can share with an empathic friend your excitement about your health journey. People who lose weight or incorporate exercise into their daily routine feel a reinforcing surge of vitality. Relish it. Be mindful of your renewed vigor.

You can challenge negative thoughts such as "It's all genetics," "I've tried it before," and "I will never get healthier." You can confront this negative self-talk by doing something really easy: three more minutes of walking every day, or half a teaspoon of sugar less in your coffee. These are easy and gradual ways to challenge negative thoughts and introduce healthier behaviors. You can also begin writing a new story about your life. Past is not destiny. The bridge between past and future is the present. The story you tell about yourself can change with half a teaspoon of sugar less a day.

Supportive friends and family can give you an enormous lift. Create your team of cheerleaders. My daughter-in-law Elizabeth started a "hydration club" with family and friends to remind one another to drink plenty of water.

Observing the context around you is a skill you can acquire. You can become a health detective. Spot the stairs to your office. Count how many steps between the ground floor and yours (fifty-five steps to my office). Spot the healthy outlets in the food court. Pay attention to cues in the environment. These are easy ways to increase your awareness and study your context. When is it that you eat the least healthy meal of the week? Is it when you go out for lunch on Friday with your colleagues? When is it that you have the worst night of the week? Is it when you drink regular coffee or have a late meal? You can educate yourself and raise your level of awareness about eating habits.

Reflecting is the way to leverage awareness. Assuming a curious attitude about yourself and the issues you are dealing with is not hard to do. Start by asking yourself questions. What are my values, why do I want to get healthy and for whom, what experiences shaped my behavior and my health? What do I need to know about issues affecting my physical well-being? Being curious is all about asking questions, and since most of us are quite self-centered, exploring our own dynamics should be intriguing.

The worst thing we can do is to accept traditions without questioning them. I often hear from my Argentinean relatives that "We've always eaten meat." From young people I hear "Everybody drinks." From Miami drivers I hear "Texting while driving is not a big deal." Conformity to unhealthy cultural norms is just harmful. In the Passover Haggadah, the least-developed child is the one who doesn't know how to ask questions. Challenging convention, asking why, and seeking better and better answers is part of the pursuit of wellness.

Every cycle of learning revolves around asking ourselves what to do next. "Next steps" is the last element of BET I CAN for a reason. Once you have learned how to utilize behaviors, emotions, thoughts, interactions, context, and awareness to your advantage, you should always ask yourself, what now? It does not have to be big or drastic. In fact, it is recommended to make the next step in the journey to health small but sustainable. Willpower is like a muscle. It requires training. When you train your muscles, you grow them gradually. First you expose them to certain weights and exercise routines. Once they reach a certain body mass, you can move to the next level. The same applies to willpower. You train yourself how to walk three more minutes or how to put a little less sugar in your tea every day. Before you know it, you are walking gingerly every day, sugar free.

The particulars of your new diet or physical activity plan can be discussed with experts or found in many websites and books. As each of us is unique, it takes some time to arrive at the right combination of foods that will work for you, but some facts are well known and documented. Cigarettes are toxic, too much fat is bad for your health, uncontrolled sugar intake is harmful, too much drinking affects your liver, fruits and vegetables are healthy for you, and sedentary lifestyles are dangerous.[10]

Having grown up in Argentina, I took it for granted that meat was a necessary part of my diet. I never questioned it. The same goes for milk. When I lived in Israel, I enjoyed dairy products without ever thinking they may be bad for me. As it turns out, my digestive system hated meat and dairy in equal parts. I also never thought that drinking water was so vital to all my organs. I was nutritionally clueless. I had to educate myself about the context of my life and how traditions and unquestioned habits were affecting me.

When we moved to Canada, food was so cheap and abundant that I gained about twenty-five pounds in a matter of months. We visited Kentucky Fried Chicken often and ordered pizza with a two-liter Coke for movie night. I had to learn that this plentiful environment was not really great for me. Ora, who was much more nutrition-conscious than me at the time, got us on a path to health. Frequent constipation also helped.

With time, I discovered the diet that worked best for me. I had to learn how to become a vegetarian, and eventually a vegan. I had to learn how to find alternative sources of protein and what grains to eat. I also had to make sure my iron and B12 levels were adequate. It took some time, but with persistence I learned what worked for me. I became an avid reader of T. Colin Campbell, Caldwell Esselstyn, Dean Ornish, and Neil Barnard, all supporters of plant-based diets.[11]

I never used to be aware of the importance of water—coffee in the morning and Coke for lunch. I drink plenty of water now and eliminated soft drinks from my diet ages ago. I didn't learn all of this at once. The benefits of a plant-based diet may be obvious to many of you, but they weren't to me. The biggest change I had to make was to become a learner.

Life is never boring. New challenges appear. I may get sick tomorrow. With every new struggle, there is new learning involved. Fitness is about embracing a learning attitude. It is, I must say, quite liberating to be a lifelong learner because you never have to feel like you know it all. Adopting a curious attitude toward your physical well-being is enormously helpful. The biggest fitness achievement you can hope for is an inquisitive mind.

My experiences also say a lot about the importance of context. Living in Argentina, I was frankly unaware of alternative diets. Meat and potatoes ruled the day. Living in Israel, I greatly enjoyed dairy products, without ever questioning if milk and cheese were really good for me, which obviously they weren't. Living in Canada, I was excited about how cheap and abundant food was. The environmental context pretty much dictated what I ate. Of all the GREASE strategies, I started with education, but I soon followed with gradual goals, alternatives, and easy targets. I got a lot of support from my wife, and I often reinforced myself for becoming healthier. Today I am in excellent physical shape but still use all these techniques to maintain a healthy weight.

We now have GREASE techniques that can be applied to behaviors, emotions, thoughts, interactions, and the context of our lives. Of all the aspects of BET I CAN, the C for Context is probably the best place to start. To make the context work for us, we have to healthify it. Brian Wansink is an expert at this. His studies showed, time and again, that the way we structure our environments, from our kitchen to our office, can make a huge difference in our waistline. His research demonstrates that it is easier to change the environment than to change our motivation, especially when it comes to food. It makes sense, then, to tackle context first.[12]

To create a healthy kitchen, according to Wansink, we have to pay attention to the furniture, the counter, the cupboards, the pantry, the fridge, and even the dishware. To begin with, he recommends removing lounge-type chairs because they invite prolonged stays in the kitchen. The longer we stay there, the more likely we are to keep eating. He recommends removing the TV from the kitchen for the same reason. The counters should display a fruit bowl with two or more types of fruits. The counter should not have any of the following: bread, chips, candy, cookies, snacks, or breakfast cereals. There is a method for the refrigerator as well: precut fruits and vegetables on the center shelf, less-healthy snacks hidden from view, any veggie leftovers stored in clear containers, and non-vegetable leftovers covered with aluminum foil to make them less visible.

The cupboards should also feature healthy snacks front and center. It is ideal if the pantry is not in the kitchen. As for the dining table, he recommends eating salad and vegetables first, and using small serving bowls and serving spoons instead of tongs. Every person should have a glass of water in front of them. Plates should be no bigger than ten inches in diameter and non-water glasses should be tall and thin. Wansink thinks of everything! As I compare our own kitchen to his ideal one, I see we're doing pretty well.

We always have clear plastic containers with freshly cut veggies: carrots, celeries, peppers, cherry tomatoes, broccoli, cauliflower. We take them to work or eat them at home for snacks. Ready-to-eat veggies are always front and center in the fridge. Our main shelves are full of berries: blueberries, raspberries, blackberries, strawberries. We consume lots of them for breakfast. There is no meat in our house, so there is plenty of room for vegetables in our fridge and whole grains and legumes in our pantry. Ora likes chocolate, so there is always a dark one at home, but she consumes it infrequently and in small quantities. Our freezer is full of homemade soups, in all the colors of the rainbow. We rarely if ever eat processed foods at home. We keep water and herbal teas always at hand. We have soft drinks only for guests. A bottle of Coke can stay in our fridge for months.

To create a healthy kitchen, you must create healthy shopping habits. Wansink recommends going for fruits and vegetables first at the supermarket. He also suggests using the front half of the shopping cart for fruits and veggies. In Williamsburg, Virginia, as well as in Toronto, Canada, he found that when people are encouraged to use the front half of the cart for fruits and veggies, they end up buying more of them. You buy healthier food, you consume healthier food. You get the point by now: we eat with our eyes!

Wansink's methods are meant to create a healthy context where water, fruits, and vegetables are always within reach, and where sugary, processed, and salty foods are hidden. He is invoking the first E in GREASE: easy. Make it easy to drink more water and to munch on veggies and fruit.

At home, we also use the A for alternatives. Since we eat mostly a vegan diet, we have to find alternatives to animal protein, so we consume lots of nuts such as almonds, pecans, and walnuts and a variety of legumes such as beans, lentils, and chickpeas. Once in a while we have some soy. Since we don't care much for starches, white pasta, or white bread, we eat lots of quinoa, brown rice, and whole wheat pasta. When we pine for a crunchy treat, lightly salted brown rice cakes do the trick.

Today we might get an "A" from Drs. Brian Wansink, T. Colin Campbell, Dean Ornish, Neal Barnard, and Caldwell Esselstyn, but it took us some time to get there. We did this very gradually. Ora and I supported one another; we reinforced each other for good behavior and educated ourselves about healthy eating. We went on two vegan cruises where we attended lectures on the benefits of a plant-based diet. I can say that we pretty much used all the GREASE tips to create a healthy lifestyle.

As we go out often to events and dinners, we sometimes have a healthy snack before we leave home. We pre-bean! Instead of arriving famished to a party where there may be no healthy options, we eat a small portion of beans or have a bowl of soup before we leave home. I know this probably sounds crazy, and perhaps it is, but it works for us. It prevents us from eating junk we later regret.

We socialize quite a bit and love going out with friends for dinner, so we discovered about half a dozen restaurants in our neighborhood that cater to vegans: Thai, Middle Eastern, Italian, fusion. Our friends are pretty accommodating, and we usually find some place that everyone is happy about. In Miami there is a growing number of restaurants that serve healthy and delicious food. We're lucky. In Nashville we struggled mightily.

When you think about what Wansink recommends, and what we do at my home, it is really a series of small, gradual, and easy changes that do not require Herculean effort. It is all about healthification of the environment, and it starts with simple behaviors, like removing cookies from the counter and placing veggies in the middle shelf of the fridge.

Eating well will also make you feel well. Exercise and healthy eating make you feel energetic. The emotions you derive from feeling great are very reinforcing. Thoughts such as "I will never change" are challenged with simple tweaks to the environment. If you must have a sweet snack in the afternoon, don't deprive yourself—just have a different kind of sweet: fruit instead of candy.

What's good for eating is good for exercising. If you rarely engage in physical activity, pick an easy target. Walk for five minutes every day. Increase it to ten next week, fifteen the one after that. Before you know it, you are walking half an hour a day. If it's hard to do it all at once, break it up; some at lunch, some after dinner. You don't need to join a gym and buy expensive athletic wear to get going. You can start at home. I happen to go to the gym a few times a week, like many people who like the routine, but it's not a must. Find out what works for you.

By combining GREASE with BET I CAN you have six techniques to apply to seven drivers of change, for a grand total of forty-two options to choose from. To get started, pick one combo. If you like Wansink's approach, reconfigure your kitchen, or leave your exercise clothes next to your bed to remind you to exercise in the morning. One gradual change at a time will reaffirm your self-determination and reinforce your self-care.

Physical Fairness

Self-care and self-determination are foundational values, but so is a sense of fairness. Many people want to eat nutritious foods but don't have access to them. Others want to exercise outside, but their environment is dangerous. We are in fairness territory now.

Fairness is the quest to provide people what they deserve, and to expect from them what they owe others. It is about getting a fair share. When it comes to physical well-being, there are four fairness issues that deserve attention:[13]

- Access to proper information
- Access to proper nutrition
- Access to physical activity opportunities
- Access to adequate health care

I put access to proper information first because without knowledge and education, all the fruits and veggies in the world won't make a difference. Food companies are so dependent on ignorance for their profits that they resist efforts to label food. The tobacco industry knew for years that their product was harmful but withheld information to maximize revenues.

Schools do a poor job of educating for physical health and wellness. Many of them receive sponsorships from large food corporations that install vending machines on their premises. Other schools limit physical activity because it is thought to take time away from preparation for high-stake testing.

Public service announcements present no competition to the billions of dollars spent on marketing junk. Physicians are not much help either. Few of them engage in serious conversations about the impact of nutrition on health. They spend more time prescribing drugs than a healthier lifestyle. The scarcity of credible information leaves consumers to fend for themselves. Some get educated, but many don't. Ironically, those who need it most tend to be less informed.

People in poor communities also suffer from lack of access to fresh food. They live in food deserts—places where you cannot get nutritious ingredients even if you want to. This is a food justice issue. You may blame adults for making bad choices, but children cannot be held responsible for not knowing what they need to know. This tends to happen in the same communities where it's difficult to go outside for a walk because it's dangerous. Triple whammy: no information, no access to affordable healthy foods, and no safe place to walk.

Lack of access to preventive and clinical care is also a health justice issue. Having lived in Canada for fifteen years, I had the opportunity to sample universal health care. The system is not perfect, but nobody is denied care because insurance companies are trying to save money. If access to health care is a fundamental human right, depriving children and parents of such is a human right violation. There are cases where no amount of health fitness can prevent catastrophic illnesses. In these circumstances we need universal and equitable access to health care. Many countries have done it, with lesser costs than the United States. An environment that deprives citizens of nutritious foods, information, access to health care, and places to exercise is a bad fit for humans.

Know Yourself, Help Yourself

You have strengths and you have stress. While the former can bolster your physical well-being, the latter can destroy it. Let's start with strengths. If you're reading this, you learned how to read, and you are curious about well-being, unless some professor is forcing you to do it, in which case you have strengths because you're attending school, and you know how to follow instructions. Celebrate!

Life is a series of undertakings. Holding this book in your hands represents an act of strength. You are resourceful. If you think about all you've accomplished in life—meaningful relationships, a steady job, a degree, a second language, staying alive—you will discover that perseverance, focus, self-regulation, and organization played a role. These are tools at your disposal. If you finished high school, you must have applied yourself to a task. If you finished college, you must have learned how to delay gratification. If you completed a graduate degree, you probably had to put up with obnoxious professors. How did you write your thesis? How did you get your first job? You probably did all these things with a mixture of self-determination, self-care, and a good amount of grit. You may have more strengths than you realize.

You can develop an inventory of your personal strengths. You may be conscientious, caring, intelligent, passionate, and driven. To improve your physical well-being you need to harness these skills and apply them to a plan of action. Research says that you should not have more than two goals at a time.[14] Choose one or two physical well-being goals and strive to achieve them gradually, just like you did to complete your thesis, master a second language, or learn how to play a musical instrument. You probably did all these things one step at a time. If you are able to keep a steady job, you must be somewhat conscientious. Apply your focus, energy, and passion to conquering an aspect of physical wellness: better nutrition, better sleep, more physical activity, fewer cigarettes.

Your plan should encompass as many of the GREASE techniques as possible. If you want to eliminate sugary drinks from your diet due to risk of diabetes, start gradually, reinforce yourself, and make it easy to reach for alternatives, like water. Enlist support from your family and friends, and get educated on the benefits of water and the costs of sugar to your health.

You may have strengths in other I COPPE domains of life. You may enjoy great interpersonal relationships and economic well-being. If that is the case, what can you do to leverage strengths in these areas to help you with physical well-being? Can you commit to improve your nutrition with a caring friend? Can you afford to buy healthier food, even if it's a little more expensive? The best way to help yourself is to enlist the strengths you already have: friends, family, focus.

If you're alive, you're bound to experience stress from time to time. In moderation, and with adequate coping skills, most of us can handle it quite well. But in excess, it can cause real damage to our immune system. Stressors can be mixture of occupational, economic, interpersonal, communal, or psychological challenges. When demands on our system exceed our capacity to cope, we experience stress. If our close relationships are conflictive, and our boss is a real pain, stress is bound to affect our mood and eventually our health. This is why we must monitor well-being in all spheres of life. Many psychosomatic conditions are a reflection of stress. From time to time, we should reflect on our overall well-being to prevent problems in one department spilling over to others. The best prevention to hypertension may be to terminate an abusive relationship, or just to change jobs.

Know Others, Help Others

If you're an educator, you're responsible for your students. If you're a manager, you're in charge of employees and customers. If you're a parent, you're looking after your kids. Whatever role you occupy in society, chances are there are people who rely on you for guidance. To foster their physical wellness, observe their environments and study their behaviors. Use the BET I CAN drivers of change to understand their behaviors, emotions, thoughts, interactions, contexts, and levels of awareness. They all impact their physical wellness.

If you're a school principal, can you change the design of the cafeteria to make healthy choices more visible to kids? After all, they do tend to eat what they see first. If you're a restaurant owner, can you replace big plates with smaller ones? If you're an HR professional, can you make it easier for employees to go to the wellness center? These are all contextual changes that have small but incrementally powerful effects. Healthier employees are more effective, and healthier students learn better.

Are there some hidden Broad Street pumps in your environment? If John Snow came to visit your workplace, what would he discover? Would he scold you for having too many candy bowls around your office? Would he tell you to put a fruit bowl in the middle of the staff room instead of potato chips?

Most people react negatively to attempts to control their behavior. When Mayor Bloomberg wanted to ban monster-size soda drinks in New York, he encountered vigorous opposition and a serious backlash.[15] People perceived this as an assault on their self-determination. There is a lesson here. Giving people more choices is more effective than curtailing people's freedom. I happen to agree that we need to change the environment, but we have to do it in a way that works with people's psychology, and not against it. Therefore, I suggest you involve people in the healthification of their environments. Healthification without consultation leads to resistance.

Our need for self-determination is bound to reject efforts to control our behavior, regardless of how stupid and self-defeating our behavior might be. A gradual approach that presents plenty of easy and healthy alternatives, coupled with reinforcements, is the way to go. GREASE can help you promote the physical fitness of those you care for. Raise awareness, redesign the context, reinforce healthy behavior, review alternatives, and most importantly, provide a good role model.

6

Psychological Well-Being

THE LAUGHING SIDE

The following stories exaggerate only a little our quest for meaning. Well, at least *my* quest. What could grant more meaning and recognition in life than the Nobel Prize, and what could be more satisfying than helping your own son?

Nobel Prize: I'm Not Bitter

As everybody knows, self-esteem is central to psychological well-being, but the phone call never came. I freed up most of my days for the last weeks of October in anticipation of the phone call from the Nobel Committee, but it never came. Although I'm not bitter, I have to admit I'm surprised. Considering that I was nominated in several categories, it was hard to believe that, once again, I was skipped over for the Nobel Prize. Admirers the world over recommended me in several fields. Here's a short list of categories and my corresponding achievements:

1. *Anthropology*: Immigration from lawless countries, when combined with a high concentration of plastic surgery billboards, in regions with annual average temperatures above 86 Fahrenheit, results in reckless driving and higher-than-average Medicare and tax fraud.
2. *Linguistics*: Based upon observational studies in Hialeah, a suburb of Miami, I discovered that no matter how long or how well Hispanics speak English, they cannot bring themselves to use the word *but* instead of the Spanish *pero*. They can speak flawless English, but the *but* will never replace the genetically and culturally imprinted *pero*.
3. *Complaining*: This one was recommended by a *Miami Herald* reader who commented that I was the biggest tool in the world for complaining so much about everything. I am very gratified by his newfound sense of irony and humbled by his nomination.
4. *Literature*: This one is obvious.

5. *Chemistry*: I discovered that no matter how tasteless the food is in our house, if you add liquid aminos, which is an all-purpose condiment made from soy, it prevents vomiting.
6. *Regularity*: 1.4 per day
7. *Peace*: I moved to Israel from Argentina in 1976. In 1977 Anwar el-Sadat came to the Holy Land and in 1979 signed the peace agreement between Egypt and Israel with Menachem Begin. Say no more.
8. *Medicine*: The failed launch of Obamacare caused heartburn to the Democrats. The successful launch caused heartburn to the Republicans.
9. *Economics*: When the GDP (Gazillion Debt per Person) of the United States is equal to or higher than the gap between the actual and reported rate of inflation in Argentina, the Chinese burst into laughter and go on a shopping spree, growing consumer demand and raising commodity prices in Australia, leading to record sales of beer and wine Down Under.
10. *Psychology*: I discovered that when members of a particular political party lose the elections, they develop electile dysfunction, which is characterized by regression to the temper tantrum age of two, the impulse to destroy the country, and political suicide.
11. *Physics*: In Miami the wavelengths of the colors yellow, green, and red are the same.

Not since Leonardo da Vinci has anyone come up with so many discoveries to improve the human condition, but I'm not bitter. I'm just curious. At first I thought that the Nobel Committee did not pick me because I was Jewish, but then I read about all the Jews who were given the Nobel Prize and I figured it must be something else.

I wonder if my nomination went to spam. No, wait, I wonder if the paper copies were not delivered because of the government shutdown. That must be it! USPS must have not delivered the package! While I was worried sick that my scientific and artistic attainments did not reach Nobel level, there is a more sensible explanation: my materials did not reach the committee. Next year I will UPS the submission, with a copy via FedEx. I tell you, you cannot trust government services.

I know what you are thinking, that I'm full of s--t, pero I want you to know that I did have an uncle who received the Nobel Prize in Medicine. César Milstein, who received the Nobel Prize in 1984, was married to my dad's cousin, Celia Prilleltensky, which goes to show that in my family we are smart enough to marry Nobel material, which is not a far cry from getting the Nobel Prize ourselves.

I know I'm getting close because Daniel Kahneman, a psychologist, like me, who lived in Israel and then the United States, like me, received the Nobel Prize in 2002. Last year, the writer Alice Munro, who is Canadian, like me, received the Nobel Prize in Literature for writing short stories, like me. My uncle César Milstein left Argentina because of political instability, like me. I just have to make sure that my materials get to the Nobel Committee in time next year. I'm already working on the press release. I'm blocking off the entire month of October. The phone call is coming. I know it.

Irrational, but Not Incompetent

My wife and I made plenty of irrational decisions in our lives. For example, moving to Nashville, or buying an apartment in Manhattan without ever seeing it. But once we make irrational decisions, we deal with them very competently. In contrast, there are plenty of people who handle any decision, rational or irrational, most incompetently. Due to our Seasonal Irrational Decision Disorder (SIDD), Ora and I encountered many of these people this summer.

It all started when we decided to invest in a little place in New York City. That would allow our son and his wife to finally leave the ridiculously expensive and ludicrously small rental they were sharing with some insects in the Lower East Side. My competent wife turned her office at home in Miami into logistics central and handled most aspects of the search and purchase. She ably dealt with real estate agents, lawyers, contractors, movers, and utility companies. I pitched in by calling the cable company in New York. This is a company that starts with V and rhymes with horizon, but I am afraid to identify it due to fear of reprisals.

Given that our son and his wife were teachers, and had no time during office hours to contact all these services, Ora and I decided to do it, for which Matan and Elizabeth are immensely grateful. Ora and I look at it as padding for our eulogies. So lucky me, I called the company that starts with V and rhymes with horizon. I needed to transfer the Internet account from the Lower East Side rental to the new place in East Harlem. I told them the account was in our son's name and gave them the number to locate it. They didn't think twice about stopping the service in his old place without even asking him. I would have expected the V Company to request an email or a letter from my son authorizing the transaction, but no, they trusted me, which seemed both irrational and incompetent, but hey, it made life easier for us. Unfortunately, that was the only thing that was easy about the company that rhymes with horizon.

Ora lined up the walkthrough for the new place, the closing at the lawyer's office, and the movers. I booked the contractor and the V Company. Our son, who had already seen the new place a few times, went to IKEA in Brooklyn and coordinated the delivery of new furniture. He also arranged for a friend to help us put together the furniture, which came in no less than fourteen gigantic boxes. Getting a friend with building expertise was a very rational decision. Matan knew that he couldn't trust me with building a two-piece stool more than he could trust himself, so his friend Willy saved the day. What a charming guy. He put together all the IKEA furniture with a big smile. But before all of this took place, Ora and I had to get to New York from Miami, which of course entailed a stop at MIA. This is where irrational and incompetent blended seamlessly and deliciously.

After we obtained our boarding passes and sent our luggage we headed for security. But before you meet a TSA agent, you must show your boarding passes to an official directing traffic at the security lines. One line was for TSA pre-check passengers, one for wheelchair users, and one for the masses. Ora was both TSA pre-check and wheelchair user, which completely puzzled the lady directing traffic. I couldn't tell whether her decision was irrational, incompetent, or both, but she sent Ora to the TSA pre-check, which had a very long lineup, almost as long as the regular line.

Given that Ora goes through a special search anyway because she uses a scooter, I could not understand the logic behind sending us to a long lineup when the wheelchair line was completely empty. When I approached her and asked if we could use the wheelchair line, she said that we are TSA pre-check, to which I replied that my wife also uses a scooter and it would be much faster to go through a line that was empty. She seemed confused but eventually let us use the wheelchair line.

It is possible that there is some logic behind her decision that completely escapes me, so before I turn into a complete judgmental tool, let's explore her thinking. Some options for her reasoning:

1. "I'm facing two people. Both with TSA pre-check, but only one with wheelchair. Two is bigger than one, so I need to send them to the pre-check line." Somewhat rational, but incompetent.

2. "One is in a wheelchair, but both have TSA pre-check. The line for pre-check is long, the line for wheelchairs is empty. I will send them to pre-check." Irrational, incompetent, and, of course, anti-Semitic.

3. "The lady uses a scooter. The line for wheelchairs is empty. She cannot use her pre-check anyway because she goes through a special search. She will be better off going through the wheelchair line. But since she lives in Miami, she is probably faking her disability, like most people in Miami, just to get a disabled parking permit, like my aunt Sofia, my cousin Lourdes, and my uncle Francisco (Panchito). I bet a hundred dollars that she is faking the disability. In fact, she reminds me of my aunt Sofia. Oh mi tia Sofia, que pobrecita, pero que mentirosa. I will show this Prilleltensky couple! Pre-check." In the context of Miami, this is not irrational, just disablist.

The flight was uneventful and the taxi ride to the apartment we rented was fine. La Guardia has plenty of taxis with ramps, which is awesome. In Miami, to get a taxi with a ramp in June you have to book it in January, the year before.

The two-bedroom apartment we rented in East Harlem, close to the new place, was spacious in New York terms, and it had a laundry room and a nice supermarket with a juice bar across the street. We were happy. Matan and his wife, Elizabeth, would spend the week with us there. Their landlord didn't allow them to stay an extra week in the rental until they took possession of the new place; so the four of us camped out in East Harlem.

The superintendent at the rental place was both rational and competent, which presented a nice contrast to the MIA gestapo. He got us a laundry card and explained how to use the machines. As I was shoving clothes into the washer, I noticed that the instructions in Spanish and English were contradictory. As the picture shows (see figure 6.1), where it says "Detergent

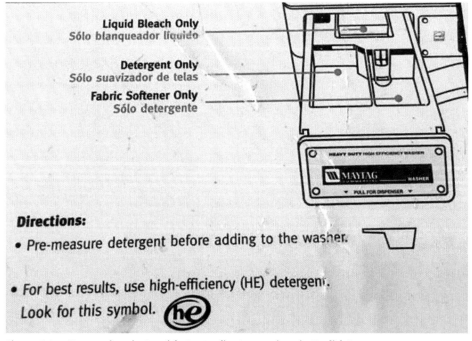

Figure 6.1. "Instructions in Spanish Contradict Instructions in English"

Only" in English it also says "Sólo suavizador de telas," which means "only fabric softener," and where it says "Fabric Softener Only" in English, it says "Sólo detergente," which means "only detergent." You would expect that in a country with over fifty million Spanish speakers, in East Harlem, which is not called *El Barrio* for nothing, somebody would know how to get instructions right in both languages, but no. Oh the incompetence!

But lest we get too judgmental about New York, we have our share of incompetence here in Miami, which will surprise no one. Last week I walked into the restroom of a new restaurant in Coral Gables and read a sign on hand-washing procedures with incomprehensible Spanish translation (see figure 6.2).

The translation of "Whenever else you feel you should" (wash your hands) sounds like my grandmother trying to speak Spanish with Yiddish grammar. Worse yet, the translation of "Dirty Hands Spread Disease" makes absolutely no sense in Spanish: "Las Manos Sucias se Deje Crecer la Contaminación." What the f$%*&?

We flew on a Sunday. Monday we fed the kids breakfast before they went to school. They were both teachers in the Lower East Side. Quite a schlep from East Harlem, so we all got up early, made fruit, eggs, cereal, and for a moment Ora and I felt like young parents sending kids to school. The charm of the moment dissipated quickly when I had to wash all the dishes in a kitchen without any supplies. It may be rational in New York terms to leave a rental apartment without any dish soap, broom, dustpan, paper towels, soap, or toilet paper, but in my books this is totally incompetent. We paid over $2,300 for a week in this place, and I expected at least a broom. When I discovered the state of the place, I became a little paranoid and started worrying about the landlord having our credit card number.

To make sure she wouldn't charge the damage deposit, I started documenting the existing scratches on the wood floors. I took pictures of all the existing scratches to make sure I could win in court. Considering that she had our credit card number, my decision to take 257 pictures of the floor was, in my mind, both rational and competent, if a little time consuming. Once I stopped worrying about the damage deposit, I started worrying about food.

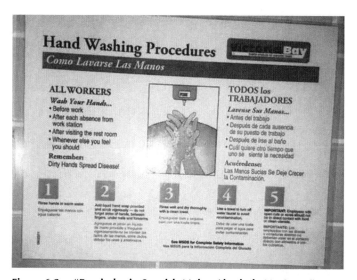

Figure 6.2. "Reminder in Spanish Makes Absolutly No Sense"

Ora and I are healthy vegans, which pretty much eliminates 125 percent of the restaurants in East Harlem. While I'm the carb grab police, Ora is the oil patrol. No white rice, pasta, or bread for me, no oil for her. In sum, we ruin every outing with our kids by talking about the health quotient of the meal.

The first night we ordered from *seamless*, an addictive app that lets you order from a wide variety of restaurants in New York City. Our first choice was Seasoned Vegan in Harlem. It was pretty good, but nothing special. Still, it was appealing enough that Ora and I wanted to go back for lunch the next day. It was far, about fifteen blocks. But Ora's scooter was fully charged, and I love walking, so we decided to go.

The idea of walking about fifteen blocks was not irrational, but not checking if the restaurant was open for lunch was incompetent. We met the owner, who chatted with us at the front of the restaurant and told us that they open at 5 p.m. It was noon, and we were starving. Our choices were either to walk to the Upper East Side or take the bus. We went for the bus. Faster, we thought. But buses in New York require exact change, and who walks around with exact change these days? The other method of payment was a metro pass, which you can only get in metro stations, but since most of them are not wheelchair accessible, we pretty much gave up on that.

So we engaged in a relentless pursuit of change. Several laundromat change machines later, we boarded the bus for the Upper East Side. We got off near Eighty-Fifth Street. I found some app pointing me to vegan restaurants "near me." I discovered Candle 79 at the corner of Seventy-Ninth and Lexington. We had already walked a good twenty-five blocks, and we needed to walk another fifteen or so. I thought it was a little irrational to spend nearly two hours, walk about forty blocks, and get a bus to get lunch, but we finally made it.

It was worth the wait! We spent less than one second looking at the menu when, in unison, we ordered the black bean soup, which was delicious, filling, and satisfying. We also had an amazing veggie dish with polenta, which was to die for. As if the food wasn't rewarding enough, Sam Waterston (Jack McCoy from *Law and Order*) sat at the table next to us. This made the whole New York experience complete. We took the bus on Third Avenue to return to the apartment in East Harlem. Our lunch expedition took four hours, which is average for workers in the Miami airport, so we didn't feel so bad.

Tuesday was the big day. The walkthrough for the new apartment was scheduled for 11:15 a.m., and the closing at the lawyer's in midtown for 1 p.m. This was the first time Ora and I actually saw the apartment, other than in pictures. We were pretty happily surprised, except for the layers of dirt glued to the oven, and the food stains adorning the fridge, outside and inside. At the closing we met the previous owner, who looked cleaner than the apartment where he lived.

Ora and I sat quietly for most of the closing while the lawyers and a representative from the title company engaged in real estate talk:

Our lawyer to title guy: Do we know if there ever was involuntary alienation or a judgment lien and/or an appeal to the Landmarks Commission prior to ascertaining the existence of a J-51?

Title guy: There was only a negative pledge and a recurring Notice of Lis Pendens before the courts issued a nonconforming use injunction, but there is nothing to worry about.

Other lawyer: The radon tests were negative, though.

Our lawyer to Ora and me: It's all okay, nothing to worry about. It just means that the writ of attachment may take a while.

Ora and I kept munching on the peanuts our realtor provided. She was hoping to secure from us referrals for similarly clueless buyers.

I'm sure there was a level of rationality to all this talk, but it completely eluded me. I was just happy there were fewer papers to sign than when you buy a doghouse in Miami. I just hope we end up owning the condo in East Harlem, and not just paying for it.

To reassure us, the previous owner did give us a key and a fob, which is an electromagnetic entry device that Google couldn't find what it really means. What the previous owner couldn't give us, though, was the correct key to the mailbox. The guy had two mailboxes with similar keys, one for our condo and one for the mailbox at his office, and he couldn't distinguish between them. Incompetence?

Mr. Disoriented gave us what he thought was the right key to the mailbox, only to call me thirty minutes later to tell me that he had given us the wrong one. The poor guy had to come from his office in Brooklyn to East Harlem to give us the right mailbox key later that evening.

By the end of the closing it was 3 p.m., and Ora and I had not had lunch. We found a Thai restaurant next to the office building and were happy to munch on some veggies. As it started pouring, we decided to take the subway back to East Harlem instead of the bus. We had been warned that not all stations in NYC are wheelchair accessible, but I asked a person at the information desk at Penn Station and she reassured us that this station was 100 percent accessible. She even gave me a map with all the accessible subway stations in NYC. I asked if there was an accessible station in East Harlem, and she pointed to one on 125th Street, which was close to our place. After a labyrinth of elevators we finally ended up at the uptown platform of the 5 line.

When the train approached the station, we saw a gigantic gap between the train car and the platform. We were sure the scooter would get stuck there, causing me premature widowhood. We were not quite ready for it and let the train go. As we were about to retrace our steps to take the bus, we saw a metro officer who knew about wheelchair access to the trains. She directed us to a spot on the platform marked with a wheelchair sign. She told us that the gap there was narrower.

We felt relieved, until the next train arrived, at which point we realized that the gap remained the same. What changed this time was our ability to make sound judgments, and in the rush of it all we decided to go for it. In a split-second decision, we thought we could make it, and we did. Once in the train, Ora and I looked at each other and we thought that we were as stupid for doing this as the official who thought the gap there was safe. Once again, we behaved irrationally but competently. We did it. We managed to push the scooter fast enough to make it into the train, but in retrospect it was one of the most dangerous and nonsensical things we ever did.

Aboard the train we began worrying about the exit. What if there was a huge gap at the 125th station? The scooter was facing west and Ora could barely maneuver it, as people were on top of each other like sardines. We entered the train from the east side, so we figured we would also exit from that side. We talked to two very nice guys behind us, who promised to help. Fortunately, the exit at 125th Street was from the west side of the train, so we didn't have to make a U turn; just to push ahead. That sounded simple enough, but there was a moron standing in front of us who refused to move an inch to let the scooter go by. What kind of asshole stands in the way of a lady in a scooter!? One way or another, we managed to get off, safely.

After so much irrationality and incompetence it was so nice to deal with the contractor and the movers who, by stereotypical standards, are supposed to give you a hard time. The contractor was a soft-spoken man from Chile, Esteban. Together with his son, Andrew, they helped us with painting, sanding the floors, electrical work, and other minor repairs. They were kind, empathic, and helpful, and mostly punctual.

A bigger positive surprise was dealing with the three Serbian guys who did the move. The man in charge, Goren, was a friendly giant. He was a teddy bear. He told us to take our time, and that if we wanted something moved again at the end, they can do it. Goren was an island of tranquility in the tempest of a move. Even the IKEA guys came on time. Three in a row: contractor, movers, and IKEA. The cable company, however, kept sending me emails with various times, just to keep us guessing. I learned, by the way, that most cable companies are email happy. AT&T in Miami sends me emails explaining how to read my bill, as if I have nothing better to do. The V Company, in turn, keeps sending me welcome emails, again and again and again.

After several phone calls to the cable company rhyming with horizon, a technician finally showed up. He was a friendly guy who spent most of the time complaining about his employer. Upon completion of the installation we tried to connect to the Wi-Fi and it worked, for exactly forty-five minutes. That was annoying. Long story short—true story—they had to come THREE MORE TIMES to get the router to work properly. So in total they came FOUR TIMES to get the Internet to work. But as it turned out, that was the beginning, not the end of the nightmare with Verizon (oops).

To make life easier, I put on automatic payment everything: car lease, credit card, Comcast, AT&T, life insurance, pool service, condo fees, bribes to city officials, everything. So it was only natural that I would want to do the same with Verizon (oops again). I clicked on one of the seventeen emails I had received from them in the last hour to set up automatic pay. After I completed the registration process for a new user, it told me that I already had an online account, which I never set up. As a good detective, I thought that the system perhaps still linked the new account number to the old account number, which was in our son's name, so I asked our son for his username and password, which he provided, which Verizon (what the heck) rejected.

What followed was a Kafkaesque interminable loop of the system asking me security questions:

- Name of my elementary school
- Name of my first pet
- My mother's maiden name
- Year in which the Ottoman Empire was founded by Oghuz Turks

Once I entered what I thought were correct answers, I eagerly waited for the system to send me the username or password, but no, instead, I kept getting messages, in large red font, to the effect that "the combination of your email, answers, or attitude is incorrect." The cortisol I secreted during this episode was enough to create a nuclear stress bomb, which I plan to detonate next time a Verizon rep says, "Is there anything else we can do for you today?"

THE LEARNING SIDE

Winning the Nobel Prize can certainly make you happy, satisfied, and fulfilled. But most human beings never get the phone call from the Nobel Committee, which is why we need to come up with more achievable goals. In my case, working with my wife to help our son is a source of meaning and satisfaction. It is also an opportunity to feel useful and capable. After all, we may be irrational, but not incompetent!

Most of us derive a sense of meaning from two sources: relationships and experiences of mastery. Feeling recognized for our efforts is also a source of mattering. Being recognized by the Nobel Committee is certainly a big honor, and reason to be proud, but don't worry, in this section we will concern ourselves with achievable goals, not impossible ones.

Psychological Well-Being Defined

Psychological well-being is largely about conversations we have with ourselves.[1] We are constantly evaluating our life: Am I satisfied with life? What do others think of me? Do I measure up? Call this the *evaluative* dimension. But psychological well-being is also about experiences and how we feel: happy, sad, stressed, excited, content, depressed. Call this the *experiential* side. The third and final component of psychological well-being has to do with flourishing, mattering, and meaning. This is usually called the *eudaimonic* side of well-being.[2] *Eudaimonia* is a Greek term that translates more or less into "human flourishing." Much has been written about eudaimonic well-being, but most authors agree that it contains some essential elements: achievements, personal growth, supportive relationships, self-acceptance, and the pursuit of meaning. In my view, all these elements can be integrated under the concept of mattering.

In the first chapter of the book I introduced the I COPPE Scale of Well-Being, which is a tool to assess evaluative well-being. The scale measures satisfaction with various domains of life. If I ask you to evaluate your life as a whole, you can easily say how satisfied you are. If I ask you how you're feeling right now, you can report your emotional state without problems. These two aspects of psychological well-being are pretty easy to grasp. But if I ask you about meaning and mattering in your life, you may pause for a moment, because we don't talk often about these things. Nonetheless, this is a crucial element of psychological well-being.

Figure 6.3 shows the two core components of mattering: meaningful recognition and meaningful impact. Recognition is about being acknowledged and feeling valued. We all have a need to feel recognized for who we are. We thrive when others afford us an opportunity to be who we are, authentically, without having to cover any aspect of our identity, such as the fact that we may be gay or lesbian.[3] Recognition is intrinsic to a sense of dignity. It is about honoring your unique strengths, identity, and biography. Acceptance is fundamental to our humanity. Indeed, our humanity is affirmed when we experience unconditional positive regard.[4] Acceptance and recognition make us feel like we belong to a community. These emotions lead to a sense of mattering; to a feeling that we count.

While recognition is about belonging to a community, impact is about making a difference. Much has been written about the importance of self-efficacy and feelings of mastery, and for good reason. They are essential to survival. Life requires that we negotiate complicated situations, relationships, and environments. When we do so successfully, we derive great meaning. When we feel that we can make a difference, we affirm our sense of agency. As can be seen in figure 6.3, recognition emanates from three sources: self, relationships, and community, which also happen to be sites of impact.

It is evident why we need to be recognized and affirmed by others, but let's not forget that we need to accept and love ourselves too. There are three main pathways to experience self-recognition: self-care, self-acceptance, and self-esteem. The more we take care of ourselves and the more we accept our individuality, the more self-recognition we'll experience.

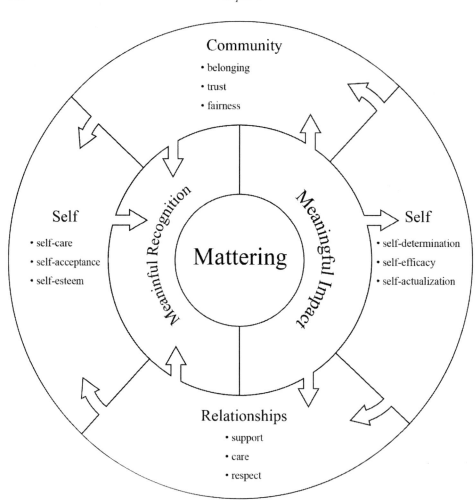

Figure 6.3. "Elements of Mattering"

Self-acceptance is about living peacefully with who we are and not hoping, trying, or pretending to be someone else. That would not be meaningful self-recognition; that would be meaningless emulation.

You'll remember that self-care was one of the key values introduced in chapter 1. When it comes to relationships, we also go back to the main values: care, respect, and support. Together, these principles bolster our sense of mattering. It starts in infancy with a secure attachment to caregivers and extends later in life to friends, peers, and romantic partners. We rely on these relationships to make us feel like we matter.

Communities can also afford us recognition through trust, belonging, fairness, and equality. International studies show that places that are high on fairness tend to be high on psychological wellness. Denmark is such a place. The Danes are fierce about equality and fairness. They also trust their neighbors and have a sense of belonging. As a result, it's not surprising that they often report the highest level of psychological well-being in the world.[5]

In summary, recognition by self, others, and community is a source of meaning. We feel that we matter to ourselves and to others.

For all its importance, however, caution must be exercised when granting or getting recognition, for too much of it can easily lead to entitlement. The other extreme is equally harmful, for too little of it can result in invisibility. When people feel invisible, their dignity is diminished. Too much recognition, on the other hand, is often associated with too little concern for others. Some people are obsessed with self-aggrandizement and entitlement, so much so that they show little regard for others.[6]

If you were ever invited to a party where nobody paid attention to you, you can get what I mean by invisibility. If you were ever an immigrant, or a person with a disability, and the context was not welcoming, you can understand what it means to feel excluded. Marginalized groups like gays and lesbians, or racial minorities, experience rejection repeatedly. Throughout history, minorities had to contend with efforts to assimilate to "mainstream society." The same occurred with colonization. Indigenous populations in the United States, Canada, Australia, and New Zealand were forced, despite protestations, to embrace the colonizers' culture.[7]

While discrimination may not be so blatant anymore in some countries, the stress associated with stigma and stereotype is real and prevalent. These are some of the negative consequences of lack of recognition.

The second pillar of mattering is meaningful impact, which is the experience of making a positive difference in the world. We have an opportunity to make an impact in three spheres of life: self, relationships, and community. Psychologists from various persuasions contend that we achieve a sense of meaning through self-determination, self-efficacy, and self-actualization. Self-determination refers to our ability to make decisions and live according to our values. The two essential ingredients of self-determination are voice and choice. We want to have a say in matters affecting our lives, and we want to exercise choice. Few values throughout history have been as consistent and universal as liberty and freedom. We fiercely protect our self-determination. It is a building block of meaning and mattering, and has been recognized by eminent researchers of well-being such as Carol Ryff and others.[8]

Self-efficacy, a brilliant insight articulated by Albert Bandura, refers to feelings of mastery and competency.[9] We can make a difference in our lives by acquiring skills and dexterity in music, sports, art, parenting, teaching, languages, social change, and others. When we have goals to achieve at work, we practice self-efficacy by meeting deadlines and delivering high-quality products. We can practice self-efficacy on our own health by aiming to improve our nutrition. The perception that we are capable of making a difference in our relationships, health, and work feeds our sense of mattering.

Self-actualization, a concept proposed by Abraham Maslow, refers to our drive to fulfill our potential.[10] Some of us may have great potential as athletes, nurses, or writers. The pursuit of meaning and self-actualization contributes to our sense of mattering because we feel engaged. We are progressing toward a goal. We are proactively seeking higher ground. But just to be sure, these accomplishments don't have to rival the Nobel Prize. We all have goals that are unique to our own circumstances, and we all have individual histories that are going to influence our path to self-actualization. There is no formula for self-actualization. The path will look different for each one of us, but what's important is to move forward in pursuit of meaning.

Viktor Frankl, a Holocaust survivor and author of the famous *Man's Search for Meaning*, claimed that people derive meaning from love, action, and even suffering.[11] His book details the pursuit of meaning under the horrid conditions of concentration camps. Quoting

Nietzsche, he lived by the motto that *he who has a why to live can bear almost any how*. Amidst unbearable suffering, Frankl found solace in invoking the presence of his wife, dreaming of finishing a book, and caring for fellow prisoners. According to him, these small acts of meaning saved his life. For most of us, it is hard to understand how one can survive, let alone make meaning, under such dehumanizing conditions, but for Frankl, these were all opportunities to become more human.

While the reality of the Holocaust may be too gruesome for most of us to comprehend, we can certainly relate to people who have converted tragedies into social goods. We often see people who experience cancer, or the death of a child, turn their energies to a related cause. Fighting cancer and preventing violence are different ways to find meaning in suffering. We often see parents who dedicate themselves to a cause to celebrate the memory of their child. Of course, nothing can replace the loss of a human being, but we see time and again individuals afflicted by tragedy who do their best to improve the human condition. For them, it's a way to make meaning. The same process takes place for individuals who have been wrongly convicted or who have been victims of abuse. Survivors of sexual abuse turn their attention to prevention, while survivors of oppressive systems, like orphanages, become advocates for change.

But Frankl was clear that suffering was not necessary for meaning. He believed that relationships and accomplishments are the main sources of meaning. Indeed, mattering can be experienced in interactions with other human beings. Relating with care and respect are foundational values.[12] Getting and giving support promote both recognition and impact. When we improve somebody's life, even in a small way, we matter. We certainly matter to that individual, but we also matter to ourselves.

Contributing to community, through trust, belonging, and fairness, is a source of mattering. While great leaders like Mandela did so in a major way, most of us can find small ways to help. Healthy communities, as we saw in chapter 3, excel in all these domains. And they don't get to be healthy by chance. Their health and well-being is the result of human action. Conditions of trust, belonging, and fairness elicit the best in people. People are more caring, compassionate, and fair when they see their neighbors behave that way. On the other hand, when they witness violence and incivility, it is harder to behave in virtuous ways.

The benefits of making an impact, and the various means to do so, are clear, but impact is not without risks. Just like too much recognition can lead to entitlement, too much need for impact can degenerate into domination. And just like too little recognition can lead to invisibility, too little impact can lead to helplessness. What conditions lead to recognition or rejection? What circumstances enable or inhibit impact?

Psychological Fit

For mattering to emerge, we require the right set of conditions. Under conditions of oppression and neglect our physical and mental health are bound to suffer. This was recently brought home in the findings of a major commission studying women's health. The report, published in the prestigious *Lancet* in 2015, made several recommendations that are completely in line with the mattering model. As far as recognition is concerned, the commission urged professionals and policy makers to value, count, and compensate women. As far as impact is concerned, it recommended to empower and to enable women.[13]

The authors conducted extensive analyses of contextual factors, across dozens of countries, affecting the health of millions of women. They concluded that women's health depends on the goodness of fit between their needs and circumstances. Depression and anxiety are among the leading causes of suffering for women. Conditions of insecurity, exploitation, and margin-alization result in mental anguish that can be drastically alleviated in a culture of recognition, respect, trust, and equality. This influential study brought to sharp relief the dictum that without fairness there is no wellness.[14]

As the authors note, women need to be valued and enabled. This is the equivalent of saying that they need to be recognized and empowered to experience self-determination. Presently, many women around the world are undervalued and disempowered. To improve their physical and mental health we must improve the fit between their needs and their surroundings.

Cultures of trust, belonging, and fairness afford opportunities to feel accepted and cared for. Relationships based on caring, respect, and support nourish self-worth. Messages that we are loved and lovable get internalized into self-acceptance and self-care. Conversely, stereotypical messages that we are deficient, foreign, weird, or abnormal impair our cognitive and psychological functioning. This phenomenon is called stereotype threat and was formulated by social psychologist Claude Steele.[15]

Stereotype threat refers to the perception that the group I belong to is deficient or inadequate in some way. This perception need not be conscious. It can be subtle or even unconscious, but if we feel threatened by a stereotype, our performance is going to suffer. Whites do not believe they have the same natural athletic abilities as blacks. Some women get the message that they are not as strong in math as men. Blacks get the message that they may not be as intellectually capable as whites.

These stereotypes, trafficked in our culture, have real consequences. Steele explored stereotype threat in a variety of groups and found that once this perception is in the air, athletic or intellectual performance is impaired. When women are under the threat of the cultural stereotype that they cannot do math as well as men, they do not perform as well. But when this threat is eliminated, by telling them, for example, that both men and women perform equally well on the test, their performance is indeed equal to men's. Steele's research goes to show that subtle cultural messages of incompetence affect how we function. Furthermore, it demonstrates that thoughts that are in the air have a way of getting into our mind, and under our skin.

We make judgments of people quickly, automatically, and often unconsciously. When these judgments are negative, there are real psychological consequences for the subject of our verdicts.[16] If we happen to like a person, she will benefit from it. If we happen to stigmatize her, she will suffer. And given that humans are comparing machines, and highly status conscious, we often tend to put people down to elevate ourselves. This is what Susan Fiske calls "scorn down."

A good fit builds on people's strengths. Just as parents celebrate their children's accomplishments, we need to cherish the uniqueness of our friends, colleagues, and romantic partners. The more we accept them, the more they will accept themselves. The more we support them, the more resilient they will be in the face of adversity. Most of all, the more empowered they will feel to make an impact. Self-efficacy is built over years of small successes: learning to read, to ride a bike, or to throw a ball. They all contribute to feelings of self-esteem and self-efficacy. Indeed, mattering starts at home, but not all home environments are good for kids.[17]

Introverted kids prefer solitary play. If we push them to interact with others, just because we think it's good for them, we're not in tune with their constitution. We know a case where pushy parents demanded machismo from their son—a gentle soul. It was painful to watch as the child tried to live up to his parents' expectations. The mismatch could not have been more obvious. Meaningful recognition is about accepting diversity. We come in different forms, sizes, and predilections. Trying to force us into predetermined molds goes against self-determination.

Opportunities for genuine voice and choice contribute to mattering. This is why we must establish participatory mechanisms, at home, school, work, and community. As noted in chapter 3, voting in local elections makes people feel in control of their destinies. Their participation also increases their psychological and physical well-being.

The need for voice has found a catalyst in social media. Trillions of selfies, Facebook messages, and tweets represent, in large degree, our thirst for self-expression. For millions of people social media has provided an outlet to broadcast their—sometimes frivolous, sometimes thoughtful—ideas.

To summarize the factors that can make for a good fit, we can look again at figure 6.3. To achieve a sense of mattering, we need environments that foster meaningful recognition and enable meaningful impact. These conditions are achieved when communities promote trust, belonging, fairness, and equality. Closer to home, we need relationships characterized by care, respect, and support. When all these conditions are met, it is easier to experience self-acceptance and self-determination, but for these positive scenarios to emerge, we need skills.

Psychological Fitness

Parenting is the art of creating the most conducive environment for optimal child development. For the first few years of life, the responsibility for person-environment fit resides with parents, caregivers, and teachers. As we mature, the responsibility gets transferred onto us. We may wish to blame our parents and teachers for all our ills, but at some point we need to take responsibility for our lives. If we find ourselves in toxic situations, we need to get out, or change them. Needless to say, this is easier said than done, which is why we need to master certain skills. Many of us experience enormous stress. This is the archenemy of well-being. Thankfully, in the last couple of decades mindfulness training has proven effective in reducing stress. Through meditation, people experience gains in self-acceptance and psychological well-being. To achieve these goals, we have to train for mindfulness and other skills.[18]

In an ideal scenario, children and adults would benefit from people, events, and cultures that foster inner peace, self-acceptance, control, mattering, and plain happiness. Under these circumstances, the chances of feeling empowered are pretty high. Deprived of nurturance, psychological well-being plummets, not for all, but for many. Some of us are quite resilient and learn to cope with negative environments, but not without suffering. Feelings of neglect can be overcome, but not without pain.[19]

Resilient people learn how to cope with adversity. They leverage one or more of the BET I CAN drivers of change to overcome hardships. Their psychological fitness depends on how well and how many drivers of change they can engage. Pick interactions for instance. To overcome neglectful relationships they learn how to show and receive affection from others. Take thoughts. Some of them reframe disappointments into stories of learning and growth.[20] Our son the chess player has had to compete against very strong opponents throughout his career. He's had his share of losses, but he has always managed to learn from mistakes and to integrate adversity into his pursuit of excellence. Awareness is closely related to mindfulness. By learning to become mindful, present, and calm, we are better able to deal with stress in our lives. Training makes perfect.

Using BET I CAN you are able to DO, FEEL, THINK, RELATE, OBSERVE, REFLECT, and ACT in ways that can improve the fit between your personality and the context of your life. For some, the easiest point of entry into the process of change is action. For others it is thinking. Some change through observation and reflection, and others through interaction with role models. The routes to resilience and psychological well-being are as diverse as the personalities involved.

When I lost my parents at the age of eight, I was confused, sad, and fearful. With nurturance from my aunt, who adopted my siblings and me, a process of healing was put into motion. My positive interactions with her and with friends began to fill a huge emotional void. I was active. I did things. I was involved in soccer and in a youth movement. I felt love from family and friends, and with time, I learned to fend for myself, something that looked impossible when Mom and Dad passed away in a car accident.

The quest for psychological well-being can be helped with skill development. My healing would have been facilitated by adults acquainted with emotional literacy. Today it seems incredible that nobody would talk to a kid about his experience of parental loss, but in 1967, in Argentina, the most common way to deal with loss was repression.

We are all agents of psychological well-being, not just recipients of it. It behooves us to know how to help one another, how to be good listeners, and how to foster a climate of growth and affirmation. With such support, we are more likely to feel capable and in control of our destiny.

Some of the skills associated with interpersonal and community well-being come in handy, as they constitute two of the three spheres of recognition and impact. Relationships that make us feel that we matter are characterized by caring, respect, and support. A key skill to support others and show them we care is good listening. As noted in chapter 2, there are five steps to listening:

1. Park intrusive thoughts.
2. Identify hidden needs, feelings, and beliefs in the other person.
3. Share, with humility, what you think the other person needs, feels, or believes.
4. Ask open-ended questions.
5. Refrain from judgment.

Practicing good listening will help you build relationships that matter, to you and to the other person. In addition to responding to others with care, you need to know how to assert your needs. To refresh your memory, in chapter 2 we listed the following five strategies to express your needs in relationships:

1. Identify your personal needs, feelings, and beliefs.
2. Express them in non-blaming terms.
3. Make "I" statements.
4. Assert your rights for safety and self-expression.
5. Distinguish between relationships that need dialogue and those that need termination.

The key to building healthy relationships is to nurture the "we" instead of the "me." Using the language of "we" to identify beliefs and to meet certain needs will foster bonds of reciprocity. As can be seen in figure 6.3, supportive relationships contribute to meaningful recognition and to self-care as well.

In chapter 3 we covered a set of skills to build community. Since community is such an integral part of mattering, and mattering is central to psychological well-being, let's review I VALUE IT:

- Inclusive host
- Visionary
- Asset seeker
- Listener
- Unique solution finder
- Evaluator
- Implementer
- Trendsetter

Some of these strategies bolster meaningful recognition. An inclusive host makes you feel like you belong to the community. A visionary considers ways to promote fairness and equality in processes and outcomes. A good listener builds trust. An asset seeker acknowledges your strengths, uniqueness, and potential. Lucky is the person who lives in such community, for she will experience more self-acceptance and higher self-esteem. When those around us are skilled community builders, we benefit greatly. When we develop these competencies ourselves, we can make a positive difference in their lives as well.

The question now is how to cultivate self-care, self-acceptance, and self-esteem. A useful approach developed by Steven Hayes is called acceptance and commitment therapy (ACT).[21] His model encourages, as meditation does, to accept unwelcome thoughts and emotions as part of our life. This is step one. Step two is to commit to live according to our values, and in the process to challenge negative assumptions about ourselves.

According to Hayes, we've internalized expectations that we must be happy and that we must feel a certain way to be a complete person. He challenges us to create our unique path to life and self-determination and to stop avoiding negative feelings. He believes that by accepting negative thoughts and emotions as part of life, we are more in touch with ourselves. The goal is not to perpetuate suffering, of course, but again, as in mindfulness meditation, to contemplate these negative thoughts without feeling trapped by them. In our BET I CAN model, this is analogous to the A for awareness.

We have to cultivate awareness of all our states, positive and negative. The theory behind ACT is that acceptance can help us get in touch with ourselves, in a caring way, and move in a positive direction. Instead of living according to a litany of "shoulds," we could embrace who we are and how we feel, and love ourselves the way we are.

Once we embrace who we are, and how we feel, we can determine for ourselves how we want to lead our lives. We can choose certain values to guide our journey. This is what meaningful recognition and meaningful impact are all about. In this book I've proposed the values of self-care, self-determination, respect, caring, sense of community, and sense of fairness because there is great support for them among psychologists and philosophers. Your job is to define for yourself what values should guide your path to meaning and mattering.

There is great alignment between ACT and mindfulness-based stress reduction (MBSR). The latter has been popularized by Jon Kabat-Zinn and proven effective in dealing with unwelcome thoughts and feelings. What MBSR shows is that it is possible to live with intruding thoughts without letting them control your life.[22]

Martin Seligman, founder of the positive psychology movement, claims that in order to cope with depression, it is not enough to fight bad things such as negative thoughts and emotions. We must also build positive experiences and thoughts that will foster meaning, happiness, satisfaction, and flourishing. Seligman recommends a series of exercises to build positive experiences, such as counting blessings, writing down three things that went well today, expressing gratitude to people who've helped you in some way, and building on your strengths.[23] The last one is particularly important because individuals with depression tend to ignore their assets. One of the assignments Seligman gives his clients is to write a one-page positive introduction in which they recount how they used their strengths in a concrete way.

As noted earlier, we all have strengths of the head, heart, or hand. We can contribute to others our time, our support, or our ideas. Doing so will make us feel useful. In our BET I CAN model, these actions are manifestations of the B for behaviors. Seligman assigns concrete tasks to his clients. Engaging positively with others, through gratitude, or with oneself, through character strengths, is a reminder that we are not defined by our depression. Negative emotions may be part of us, but they don't define us.

What is common to Viktor Frankl, Martin Seligman, Carol Ryff, and Steven Hayes is the active pursuit of meaning. Through recognition of strengths and values, they assert the agency within us. Of course, it helps if we can enjoy supportive and nurturing environments, but their research shows that even if we don't, there are ways to cultivate meaning and fight for fairness.

Psychological Fairness

Happiness, satisfaction, and meaning are central to psychological well-being. They represent, respectively, expressions of experiential, evaluative, and eudaimonic well-being. All of them rely on a combination of opportunity and responsibility. The more opportunities we have to feel loved, the easier it will be to act fairly toward ourselves.

It may sound counterintuitive to act unfairly toward oneself, but it is entirely possible. Some people dislike themselves. They engage in self-mutilation and other forms of self-harm, from anorexia to suicide. One way to think about these problems is to classify them as pathologies. Another way is to think about lack of personal fairness. All the authors reviewed in the previous section implored us to think not just in terms of pathologies, but also in terms of values. They refuse to define the human experience strictly in terms of destiny and deficiency. They all invoke our ability to act in accordance to certain values. These values make us humans. Fairness is widely recognized as a universal value. If we can act fairly toward others, why should we not act fairly toward ourselves?

We are fully capable of taking responsibility for our actions. This is a definitional moment of the human experience. This is how we're different from other species. We can follow a set of principles that elevate our humanity. If we do this toward others, there is no reason we should not do it toward ourselves. The call to personal fairness questions why we torture ourselves with punishing ruminations about our lack of worth.

While many psychologists and psychiatrists treat self-harming behaviors as pathological, I think there is also merit in thinking about them as a failure of personal fairness. Just as Seligman encourages us to practice gratitude and forgiveness toward others, we should also practice it toward ourselves. This is not to undermine the severity and complexity of self-harming behaviors, but rather to offer another way to think about them. I believe that we can talk about self-deprecation not just in medical and psychiatric terms, but also in moral terms.

Is it possible that you are unfair to yourself? If you are, you are not upholding the value of fairness. And if you cherish this value, you're going to have to do something about it, just as you would if you discovered that you were treating another human being unfairly. This is the commitment part in ACT; taking responsibility for your behavior, and acting with self-compassion.

Know Yourself, Help Yourself

The Office of National Statistics (ONS) of the United Kingdom conducts an annual population survey with the following four questions:[24]

1. Overall, how satisfied are you with your life nowadays? (evaluative well-being)
2. Overall, to what extent do you feel things you do in your life are worthwhile? (eudaimonic well-being)
3. Overall, how happy did you feel yesterday? (experienced well-being)
4. Overall, how anxious did you feel yesterday? (experienced well-being)

Answering these questions will help you know yourself a little better. The I COPPE survey introduced in chapter 1 (see also the appendix) will also give you an idea about your evaluative psychological well-being.

What's more, the I COPPE scale will tell you how you're doing overall and in the six domains of life. If you're doing well in most domains of life, chances are you will be doing well in the psychological domain too. The I COPPE framework offers six avenues for promoting happiness, satisfaction, and meaning: interpersonal, communal, occupational, physical, psychological, and economic. If any of your three types of psychological well-being—evaluative, experienced, or eudaimonic—are low, it would be good to think of ways to also improve the other I COPPE domains.

When it comes to mattering, as we saw earlier, we matter through relationships and community. What's going on for you in these spheres of life? It is helpful to think about well-being holistically. Think about well-being panoramically. Consider the full spectrum of your life through the lens of I COPPE. Finding joy or despair in relationships, work, or community may be a key to your psychological well-being.

In summary, know how well you're doing in the evaluative, experienced, and eudaimonic dimensions. In addition, determine how your satisfaction in other domains of well-being are impacting your psychological well-being. Chances are that increases or decreases in the other domains are raising or lowering your psychological well-being.

Your level of psychological well-being may be a reflection of the quality of meaningful recognition and impact you are experiencing in relationships, work, or community. Knowing, however, is not enough to change a situation.

You may know that your relationships are not helping your psychological well-being, or that your work is stressing you out, but the question is what to do. The first step is to identify an achievable goal that will enhance your well-being and improve your self-efficacy. Making an impact in your life is both an intrinsic and extrinsic good. It is intrinsic because it is good to feel better, matter more, and experience more satisfaction in life. But it is also extrinsic in that it helps build your confidence for tackling other issues.[25]

Let's go with something doable that has proven beneficial in reducing stress and improving psychological well-being: mindfulness meditation. Engaging in a sustainable practice of meditation requires the start of a new behavior—the B in BET I CAN. Assume you want to meditate daily because it is good for you. You are aware that this will help you—the A in BET I CAN.

We can use the GREASE techniques to make it happen. First, start gradually. Do it for three minutes a day and increase the length gradually. Reinforce yourself for getting started. Find a time when it is easy and convenient to do it. Perhaps before you go to work, or after your exercise routine. If you take the train to work, you can do it with your earphones and your eyes closed. Do whatever works for you. Tell your partner that you are doing this and encourage him to do so as well. Support one another. If the meditation technique you are using is not working for you, try an alternative. There are many apps with guided meditation. Educate yourself about the different options and their results. The method developed by Jon Kabat-Zinn has been studied extensively with positive outcomes for a variety of issues, including stress.[26]

Remember that your first step toward psychological well-being does not have to be huge. It has to be doable. This will enhance your self-efficacy and self-determination. If meditation is not for you right now, pick another technique that will be of interest. Psychological well-being is closely related to physical well-being. If you lead a sedentary lifestyle, how about starting a walking routine? Remember, you don't have to become an athlete, or the best-looking person in the gym. Your goal is to get going and try different avenues until one feels right for you.

We develop meaning in diverse ways. Start by identifying an area of I COPPE that appeals to you, and give it a try. If you embrace a growth mindset, you will approach life with an open mind. If you fail, you will learn from it. If you endorse a fixed mindset, you will approach life with a fatalistic attitude. If you fail, you will think that happiness, or satisfaction, or meaning, is not in the cards for you. Conversely, if you adopt a growth mindset, you will strive to find meaning, happiness, and satisfaction in different ways. The actual search will give you meaning. This is what the research on mindset has shown. It is not just about the outcome, but also about the process of growing and learning. Your plan should not be about winning, but about growing.[27]

Know Others, Help Others

If your goal is to help others improve their psychological well-being, you have to define your radius of impact. Are these people close to you? Are they family members? Are they coworkers? Do you want to improve the psychological well-being of newcomers to your community? After you decide who you want to help, you have to get to know them. The listening skills identified in chapter 2 come in handy. As you listen, think about mattering in their lives. Do they get meaningful recognition from friends and family? Do they feel valued at work? Are they welcome in this community? Do the same for impact. Do they feel empowered to make a difference? Can they influence the community where they live?

To help others start by recognizing their strengths. Sometimes people don't even see how good they are at certain things. We all possess gifts of the hand, heart, or head. We can offer others a lending hand, a word of support, or a great idea. These are assets that we possess. However, due to histories of abuse, neglect, or self-doubt, people ignore their own strengths. You can be immensely helpful to others if you work with them to recognize and build on their strengths. This is one of the main contributions of Seligman and his positive psychology movement: identify and nurture signature strengths, in yourself and others.

Next, instead of focusing only on fighting negative symptoms, such as depressive thoughts, promote their well-being by engaging with them in meaningful and fun experiences. The popularity of the medical model has led us to think that if we want to help others, the only way to do so is to eliminate bad things. This is one way. The other way is to build positive things. Seligman has shown that engaging in experiences that matter, such as expressing gratitude and building positive relationships, can help with depression. It is not all about eliminating rumination and other depressive symptoms. We promote well-being also by fostering supportive relationships, contributing to the community, and practicing self-determination along the way.

To put strengths into motion, we need to do whatever we can to enable action. This is what empowerment is all about. Teaching kids how to ride a bike without training wheels is an act of empowerment. We're there until they find their stride, and then we let go. Mastery and independence are vital to psychological well-being.

When we try to help others, we must resist the temptation to focus on their deficits and to blame them for their misfortune. None of the following help:

- "If you only applied yourself at school, all these problems would go away."
- "If you weren't so lazy, you could succeed."
- "Your problem is that you cannot motivate yourself."
- "You had it coming."

Statements like these are bound to elicit resistance and feed self-doubt. They are the exact opposite of meaningful recognition. They are meaningless exhortations at best, and meaningful put-downs at worst. None of them show caring, respect, or support.

But to help others we also need to pay attention to the community in which they live. Fairness, equality, belonging, and trust are hallmarks of community well-being. We can help individuals through friendship and mentoring, but we can also help groups by becoming involved in civic organizations and social justice movements. If we care about equality, we can join the fight for access for people with disabilities. If we care about belonging, we can become inclusive hosts of newcomers. In other words, there are institutional ways to help others, which can be very powerful because they impact the lives of thousands.

In summary, to help others we can start by recognizing their unique strengths and encouraging them to apply their gifts. Since we are part of their environment, enacting caring, respect, support, belonging, trust, and fairness will go a long way. Focusing on strengths instead of deficits and empowerment instead of blame will build meaningful recognition and meaningful impact.

7

Economic Well-Being

THE LAUGHING SIDE

Who are we kidding? Rationality has very little to do with financial decisions. Our financial well-being has something to do with the cost of living, but also with the cost of seeing. We buy with our eyes, and not with our heads. But if buyers are irrational, so are sellers. The following humor stories set the stage for understanding economic transactions and their impact on economic well-being.

Financial Colonoscopy

A big part of the American dream is to own a big mortgage, and a little piece of a home. If owning one home in America is a good thing, owning two must be awesome. So my wife and I bought our first, and then our second home in Miami. We have a lovely house in Coral Gables, next to the University of Miami where I work, and a condo in Hollywood Beach, Florida, where we spend holidays. The two poor immigrants were now part of the American dream.

Then we started thinking that our perfectly fine twelve-hundred-square-foot condo in Hollywood was not good enough for us. So we, the embodiment of rationality, thriftiness, prudence, and frugality, acquired on an impulse a third home, and a third mortgage. Ora and I saw a unit for sale in the same building of our condo in Hollywood, and we fell in love with it. All of a sudden the view from our condo, which had mesmerized us for the last two years, was not spectacular enough. All of a sudden the place was not big enough to accommodate our son and his wife, who come to visit only a few times a year, and never complain about sleeping in the den. All of a sudden we needed more. Frugal us turned into consumers are us.

Our congenial mortgage broker, who had helped us with previous loans, told us that we would have no problem getting a third mortgage. "For you, no problem" she said. Reassured, we proceeded to put an offer at full price, and then some, to make sure that we got this particular unit. At a moment's notice, rationality went out the window. But what a window that was! With unobstructed views of the Atlantic Ocean and the Intracoastal Waterway, we fell in love with the place the way suckers fall prey to whatever the Property Brothers sell them on TV.

Never mind years of training in impulse control and careful planning of finances. On a whim, we committed to a third property, and a third mortgage. This was when our American Dream turned into our American Nightmare.

The process began simply enough, requesting salary statements, W2 forms, printouts of bank accounts; the usual stuff of mortgage applications. We were promised a loan at 80 percent of the value of the condo, and we did have the remaining 20 percent in the bank, the result of careful planning and obsessive savings. Then the appraisal came, and we were told that we were paying $15,000 above appraised value. We had to sign a letter acknowledging that we were paying above market value. Sign we did, but we were told that we would get only 75 percent of the original estimated value of the condo. I got a little worried, but we could do it.

Then the mortgage company had to look into the financials of the condo association and our credit score going back to the destruction of the Second Temple. After an interminable series of emails, phone calls, faxes, texts, scans, pdf files and more emails, phone calls, texts, and scans, we were told that the building did not pass certain Fannie Mae and Freddie Mac mortgage certificate of estoppel reserves escrow HUD deed warranty of good behavior, and that the mortgage company would be able to give us only 70 percent of the value of the house. That was the first time we heard about such possibility. I started getting a little more worried.

We did have money to cover the differential, but in a bank account in Australia. To make up the difference, we would have to transfer from overseas a few thousand dollars. I hasten to point out that this is all legal, and that I always religiously declare all my bank accounts here and abroad. I know in Miami it is hard to believe, but it is all clean money, and it is all our money, the result of saving and careful planning that went out the window the minute we walked into the unit with the water views.

Despite my assertions to the mortgage company that the money overseas was money that we had transferred there for saving purposes, they needed to see evidence that I had transferred the money from my US account to my overseas account and that we were not operating some money laundering scheme. That meant that I had to go back months and years in bank statements and find out exactly when I transferred the money, and provide printouts of my bank accounts, here and overseas, before, during, and after the transfer of money, so that the underwriter could see that the money was ours and did not belong to some Colombian cartel.

Meanwhile, I kept getting emails, texts, pdf files, and faxes about more estoppel letters, escrow statements, HUD warranty deeds, underwriting, reserves, appraisals, inspections, and forms to sign. Every time I looked at the computer there was another email from the mortgage company requesting twenty more documents going back years about every financial transaction that I had ever done or considered doing. At that point, I thought that the Inquisition would have been a breeze.

Because Ora and I were so rational, controlled, measured, and prudent, we made our offer *unconditional* to make sure that we got THIS unit and that NOBODY ELSE did. So we could not get out of the deal on account of not getting a mortgage. Well, perhaps the inspection could save us, but it happened so early in the process that the mortgage company had not yet initiated its Inquisition. So, in summary, we were stuck, and we were being screwed by a mortgage company that kept blaming Freddie Mac and Fannie Mae and JP Morgan and Countrywide and the Democratic Party for putting in place so many requirements for a second home mortgage. And every day the mortgage broker would contact us to let us know that there is a NEW law that they did not know about that pretty much required that they conduct a financial colonoscopy of our entire family.

All I could think about at this stage was Kafka. We were in the midst of a Kafkaesque play, and there was no way out. Every time I wanted to transfer money from Australia to cover all the unanticipated costs, I knew that I had to produce more paper than the Amazon forest could produce in a year. I dreaded going to the computer to read the new requirements and the emails going back and forth between the various mortgage company employees, our lawyer, and us about estoppels, escrows, underwriting, insurance, inspections, appraisals, taxes, condo fees, reconciliation fees, flood insurance, HUD warranty deeds, reserves, transfers of money, new printouts of bank accounts, and new salary stubs. Whatever I had submitted last month was no longer valid, so it was a Sisyphean financial boulder all over again.

Ora kept reinforcing me and praising my patience and organizational skills for being able to produce the Amazonian quantity of paperwork required. As I tried to cope with the tsunami of requests, I asked myself, "And why do we need this headache?" At that moment I realized that we had just become full-fledged Americans.

Dos and Don'ts of Selling

"It's Dick Cheney's company, American made," said the shop owner, as he tried to sell me a backpack made by Halliburton. "And I'm supposed to like it because it's Cheney's company?!" I said, to which the owner, noting my displeasure, swiftly replied: "But it was a long time ago, don't worry about it, he is no longer involved in the company." I can see somebody trying to sell me a product associated with Scarlett Johansson, but Dick Cheney! This exchange brought home for me what is wrong with the American economy: instead of plastering stores with pictures of Scarlett Johansson, they tell you that goods were made by Dick Cheney. No wonder we had a recession.

A few days later I found myself in an optical store trying progressive glasses for the first time. The delightful store manager was telling me that my brain would get used to the blurry peripheral vision. "What if I have a car accident while getting used to them?" She said not to worry, "Just bring the broken glasses and we will replace them." That was the second revelation about American retail in a week: optical stores fail to sell life insurance with progressive lenses. Great missed opportunity.

As I was experimenting with the glasses in the store, trying to read emails from my phone and signs in the store, Betsy (not her real name) suggested that I walk around the mall for a few minutes to see how I felt. She told me that my brain would get used to it, but what if *I* did not get used to it? My brain is one thing; I'm quite another. I don't really care what my brain does; I care about how *I* feel.

My progressive lenses experience lasted exactly forty-five minutes, enough to come home, try them in front of the computer, and drive back to Aventura Mall to return them. To read a sentence I had to point with my head toward it, calibrating my vision as if I was a sniper trying to shoot words with my eyes. I phoned the store, and Betsy told me that I need to give it some time and that my brain would adjust to it. I don't care about my brain; I care about *me* adjusting to the darn thing. I'm going to recommend that if they want to increase sales, they show more empathy toward clients and less sympathy toward their brains.

People in real estate can also use a bit of empathy training. My wife and I have had our share of buying and selling houses (and thanks to my business acumen, losing tons of money doing so). More than once we've had agents trying to convince us of the unparalleled features of a dump. As you are trying to prevent an argument with your spouse, doing your best to handle all the stress, and attempt to memorize the seventy-eight houses your spouse forced you to see, the agent would annoyingly ask, "What is it that you don't like about this house?" As you repress the urge to say, "That you are an idiot and should have never wasted my time with this dump," you slowly but surely go on to develop another ulcer.

And talking about arguing with your wife while house hunting, let me share a true story. When we were looking for a house in Melbourne, Australia, we were given an address to inspect a house. As we drove by, I told Ora that something looked strange about the house. There were video cameras all over the place. The house looked more like Guantanamo than a suburban residence. My brave wife sent me by myself to find out what was the story. I saw a neighbor and asked him why there were so many security cameras. The neighbor told me that the previous owner was a mafia guy and was gunned down by a rival team in the front lawn. His widow was now selling the house. When I told Ora the story, she said that the house would probably sell for cheap and that we should look into this! It took me a while to convince Ora that the mafia sometimes doesn't keep good records, and somebody may come after me by mistake.

Selling insurance is admittedly hard, especially door to door, as in the old days. My father-in-law tells the story of a life insurance broker who tried to persuade him to purchase a policy by depicting morbid scenarios. "Imagine, Mr. Rapoport, that you die suddenly," to which my father-in-law promptly replied, "No, let's say that you die suddenly." Although my father-in-law is not superstitious, he did not want to tempt fate.

In the last couple of years we also witnessed the president trying to sell health insurance, and we all know how well that went. The president of the United States of America should have known better. Trying to launch a new venture is hard. You need to have good infrastructure and hire a bunch of web consultants from Montreal, as the government did. Instead of trying to institute a whole new health insurance system, Obama should have annexed Canada, and we all would have gotten government-provided care at affordable prices. Imagine the cost savings. Instead of invading Iraq, which is so far, and has a terrible medical system, we could have marched right next door and gotten public health insurance from Ontario, Manitoba, or British Columbia, depending on your time zone. Even Sarah Palin could have gotten free health care from Nunavut, which leads me to the mayor of Toronto and his failed attempt to sell an image of composure in light of revelations of drug abuse and undignified behavior.

Rob Ford, mayor of Toronto, should borrow a page from Barack Obama when it comes to apologies. While the president took responsibility for not invading Canada, Rob Ford should have taken responsibility for not running Miami-Dade, which is used to corruptions, instead of ruining Toronto's pristine reputation.

Whether you sell backpacks, glasses, real estate, or insurance, remember to know your audience. And most importantly, plaster your website with pictures of Scarlett Johansson.

THE LEARNING SIDE

No amount of rationality can get in the way of impulsive behavior. This was the hard lesson of buying a new condo. The vision of owning a new condo with magnificent views promised memorable experiences, but the purchase itself was incredibly stressful. In retrospect, we did the right thing, and we do experience great times there, not just us, but our kids as well. However, we were not prepared for the tedious and odious process. Before you buy, make sure you can afford it, and make sure the loan company discloses everything up-front.

We were in good financial shape, and other than the avalanche of paperwork, we could afford the purchase. Many, however, cannot, and make commitments that are way over their heads. Did you ever buy something that you really did not need, or could not afford? Is the stress associated with payments worth it? Have you thought of the paperwork related to more credit cards, more bills to pay, and more annoying phone calls to answering machines?

Shopping is an experience in itself, and I believe that some people like it. For me, it is usually traumatic. The aggravation is magnified when sellers show incompetence, obstinacy, or plain rude behavior. Both stories show the irrationality of buyers and sellers. If we want to improve our financial well-being, we would do well to come to terms with our irrational behavior.

Economic Well-Being Defined

Economic well-being relates to satisfaction with financial security. There is quite a bit of research on income and well-being. In handling money, it's important to save for the future and to spend it on memorable experiences rather than on material goods. Studies also show that the best way to use money to increase your well-being is by spending it on others and not on yourself.[1] In addition, we know that money is important for overall well-being, but after a certain threshold, the returns are not that high. Research has shown that well-being consists of much more than money. For people without basic economic resources, it is imperative to achieve a minimum level of financial security to experience physical and psychological well-being. But for those with an income of more than $75,000 per year, accumulating more money will usually not make a big difference in most aspects of well-being.[2]

Economic Fit

To experience financial well-being, we require a fit between cost of living and cost of seeing, on one hand, and spending capacity, on the other. Cost of living is a composite number based on food, housing, transportation, and the like. Cost of seeing is more complex. It refers to how much it costs to buy objects or experiences that we covet but we don't really need. These are objects invented by companies and marketed by experts to make money. This is what consumerism is all about; spending on stuff we see but don't really need. I call this the cost of seeing because we're bombarded with visually appealing images of products we don't need. The pictures in the ads are awesome, so we come to believe that if we purchase a certain garment or gadget our sex appeal will go through the roof. Many men and women regard themselves as museum pieces. The way they dress and adorn themselves makes them look like exhibition artifacts.

To afford the cost of living and the cost of seeing, we need to have either earning capacity or inherited wealth. The latter benefits only a small portion of the population. Most of us struggle with the former. In an ideal scenario, we acquire skills through education that can be exchanged for a good salary in the marketplace. We make enough to cover the cost of living, and if we can afford it, some of the cost of seeing too. The problem starts when the cost of seeing and the allure of consumerism exceed our spending capacity. Of course, for some people the cost of living is a problem too. Earning depends on many factors, one of which is education. Minimum wage is another. Societies with large inequalities in education, health, and wealth make it hard for vast segments of the population to afford the basic cost of living, to say nothing of the cost of seeing.[3]

If you dissect the fit between cost of living and cost of seeing on one hand, and earning capacity and inherited wealth on the other, you can pretty much identify the sources of your economic well-being. These four factors can help you identify leverage points for financial stability. Cost of living is usually related to location. Ora and I did part of our graduate studies in Winnipeg, Manitoba, where the cost of living was quite low. In contrast, Matan, our son, did his graduate studies in New York City, where the rent is ridiculously expensive. Ora and I worked in Winnipeg for a few years, and then moved to Waterloo, Ontario, where the cost of living was also reasonable. Matan decided to stay in New York City. To live well in the Big Apple you have to make much more money than Ora and I needed in either Waterloo or Winnipeg. People's financial well-being is closely tied to cost of living.

The second factor to consider is the cost of seeing. Are you enthralled by the latest gadgets and garments? Do you feel the urge to own the latest car model? What about wines? Eating out too often? Do you camp outside the Apple store for three days to be the first one to buy the latest iPhone?

Some friends of ours, with good incomes, were eating their salaries in restaurants. It wasn't until their accountant showed them how much they were spending eating out that they started to save. The ease of access to more and more credit cards doesn't help. Spend today, pay whenever.

The third factor in the equation is earning power. If you have a great job that can pay for the cost of living and the cost of seeing, and still save for retirement, you are in good shape. For many of us, that is not the case. With the cost of higher education for our children, catastrophic medical bills, and cyclical recessions, life is not so easy. Some people relocate when they retire to spend less. Some relocate just to get a job.

Unless you invented some contraption in your garage and became an instant millionaire, played basketball like Michael Jordan or LeBron James, or looked like Scarlett Johansson or Hugh Jackman, you have to work really hard to make a living. Most of us had to put ourselves through school, endure some sacrifices, and control our spending impulses. Assuming society affords us fair opportunities, it is up to us to roll up our sleeves.

The fourth factor is inherited wealth. Consider yourself lucky if you are in that category, and don't waste your resources.

Whether you are rich or struggle to make a living, you will need some skills to enhance your earning power or protect your fortune. This is where fitness comes in.

Economic Fitness

To improve your financial well-being you can play with revenues or expenditures. You either find ways to increase the former or reduce the latter. If you are in the lucky category of family money, you need to learn how to protect your assets. If you are in the work-hard-to-make-a-living category, you need to learn two kinds of skills: content and process. The former refers to some expertise, like engineering, plumbing, teaching, finance, or medicine.[4] The latter refers to emotional intelligence: how to regulate your emotions, delay gratification, dedicate yourself, cooperate with others, lead, commit to a task, and persevere.[5] Success at work depends on the ability to integrate expertise with interpersonal acumen and self-regulation. No small task. It takes many years to prepare in an area of expertise, like nursing, or computer programming, and it takes careful mentoring to nurture emotional intelligence.

Aptitude and attitude are refined over years of formal and informal education. The ability to self-regulate, carefully cultivated by parents and mentors, will help you resist frivolous spending and live frugally, if that is what you need. Exposure to the right environment is essential in developing economic fitness. Opportunities to attend good schools and to learn from role models play a huge role in economic well-being. Provided with the right opportunities, the responsibility falls onto us to make good use of them. When we are deprived of such chances, it is time to worry about fairness, not just fitness.

Research has actually shown that the stress associated with poverty interferes with economic planning and sound financial judgment. Poverty and immediate necessity preclude long-term calculations that people with more cushion can afford. Circumstantial stressors reduce the ability of the poor to engage in long-range considerations such as retirement or saving for a house. These look beyond reach. The priority is to get through the day.[6]

Growing inequality and pervasive poverty require fitness, not just in economic well-being, but also in social justice. The skill to challenge injustice is just as important as the skill to make a living. They are a very different set of skills, but in some contexts, our ability to challenge inequality is the only thing that will make a difference in the long run. This is what Muhammad Yunus did when he created the Grameen Bank in Bangladesh. Trained at Vanderbilt University in economics, Yunus returned to Bangladesh to improve the economic well-being of his fellow citizens. What he discovered was that poor people worked very hard, but were unable to get out of poverty due to indebtedness to loan sharks. To start their own small businesses poor people needed loans, but the only loans they could get charged astronomical interest rates. As a result, no matter how hard they worked, they were always paying debt that prevented them from getting out of poverty.

What Yunus did was to create a new financial institution, the Grameen Bank (Grameen means village), that provided loans to poor people at reasonable interest rates. Instead of teaching poor people to beat the odds, which was impossible under those conditions, he changed the odds. All that poor people needed to get out of poverty was a fair chance. Yunus went on to win the Nobel Peace Prize with the Grameen Bank, and millions of people were lifted out of poverty. His approach to poverty alleviation was based on financial fitness and fairness prowess.[7]

Economic Fairness

When we talk about poor children, we often feel compassion. When we talk about poor adults, we often feel contempt. Blaming them for their misfortune is not uncommon. The problem with blaming adults, however, is that we ignore the fact that many of them grew up poor. At one point they were the kid we felt compassion for, and at another they became the object of our disdain. We assume, erroneously, that by the time they reach a certain age, these adults are supposed to have the capacity, motivation, and wherewithal to overcome poverty. The adult is the product of the child. If the child was neglected, raised in decrepit conditions, and exposed to violence instead of violins, the outcome will be less than optimal.[8]

We artificially dichotomize between adults and children. Of course adults should assume responsibility for their destiny, but it is entirely unpsychological and unscientific to pretend that the adult can overcome poverty of language, social skills, study habits, frugality, and prudence without a radical change in learning opportunities.

It is beautifully simplistic and utterly seductive to blame the poor for their fate. Simple solutions are appealing to our cognition. They are neat and don't tax our morals or thinking too much: "If they weren't lazy, they would be okay. After all, this is the land of opportunity." But this thinking assumes that we can expunge histories of deprivation. We cannot. We can help people beat the odds if we change the odds, but changing the odds requires leveling the playing field.

We think that if we create one more community college access program, everyone will be ready for a career. Millions drop out of school because they are not ready for college or career. Fairness is about meeting people's needs where they are at. If they require remediation, so be it. If they require earlier interventions to prevent dropping out of high school, so be it. Fairness is about providing all children equal opportunities to learn content and process skills. Unless we teach all children rich content and emotional regulation from a young age, and unless we ensure a calm, reassuring, stable, and supportive environment, the independent and mature economic self we all wish for will remain an illusion.

It is all about readiness to learn, and readiness to work. We ignore the preconditions for learning and working at our own peril. Among other adversities, research shows that kids who grow up in poverty have smaller brains and compromised cognitive abilities.[9] This is one of the terrible costs of poverty. There is no question that many poor kids overcome adversity, but they start life with many strikes against them.

We want young adults who are not ready for the workforce, or college, to perform miracles. Human development does not work like that. Success stories—like mine, by the way—serve to reinforce simplistic thinking. If Isaac, who was an orphan, and an immigrant, and had to escape Fascism and anti-Semitism, could overcome adversity, get a PhD, and become a well-functioning adult, so can anybody. This seductive narrative omits important facts. I had, as a child, great love from an aunt who raised me. I grew up in an intellectual environment. My private school gave me a scholarship. The state of Israel paid for most of my first two university degrees. When you look at resilient cases, there is always more than meets the eye.

Many poor kids do not have a single adult who is crazy about them. Many go to schools with poor resources and with overworked, underpaid, and often unprepared teachers. With no role models available, it is hard to imagine a bright future. When poor children, like me, do have a single adult who is crazy about them, the chances are much better. Psychological compensation does wonders. You can experience great trauma, as I did as a kid, but with the right supports, you can overcome it and thrive. Unlike me, many poor kids have parents who are poor, traumatized, and who were abused as kids.

Economic well-being will not be achieved for vast sectors of the population unless there is a massive investment in early childhood education, parenting, and public health. Fairness dictates that all children receive, within a certain range, similar opportunities.[10]

When we talk about fairness in economic well-being, we must be precise about who we are talking about. I might complain that I did not get a big enough raise last year, but I do pretty well already. I have buffers against economic adversity. I have savings and a good job. Many, however, worry constantly about food and rent.

Know Yourself, Help Yourself

If you have some money to spend, there is research on how to spend it. In *Happy Money: The Science of Smarter Spending*, Elizabeth Dunn and Michael Norton studied the happiness return of various ways of spending money.[11] There are five ways to increase your happiness by spending your hard-earned money.

Buy experiences instead of material goods

Research suggests that buying experiences such as trips, meals with friends, walks in nature, and concerts deliver more happiness than another pair of shoes, a bigger house, or a luxury car. Experiences are ways to nurture mattering, either through relationships or self-actualization. Taking a course is an experience. Refining our musical talent through practice is an experience of mastery. Experiences are more engaging than objects.

Make it a treat

We get habituated to good things, and they slowly lose their appeal. After a while, eating too much chocolate loses its appeal. Indulging in treats once in a while enhances its pleasure value. Since we get used to all kind of things, including good ones, it is preferable to limit our consumption of them to maximize the joy they deliver. This principle applies to lattes as much as to chocolate.

Buy time

If you can afford someone to clean your house, do it. Buying time is a great investment because it allows us to pursue things we find meaningful and enjoyable. For me, buying the condo I referred to in the story was an incredible time investment. I think that eventually it resulted in many positive experiences, but when I was in the midst of the financial colonoscopy, all I could think of was how I could be using the time to do something else. The same goes for shopping of any kind. When I have to buy something, I usually get in and out of a store in record time. I usually know what I need and spend the least amount of time needed to perform the transaction.

A universally hated activity is commuting. People regard it as a stressful waste of time. To buy time, and prevent the stress, when we moved to Miami we bought a house next door to the university where Ora and I work. This has been an amazing investment. I get to the office in three minutes and avoid the stress associated with reckless drivers. I have time to come home for lunch, and I save lots of time that I dedicate to exercising, learning, reading, and writing, not to mention spending time with my adorable wife.

Pay now, consume later

Booking and paying for a vacation ahead of time enables you several months of anticipation. This way, you not only enjoy the actual trip, but also the excitement of getting ready. You can see pictures of the beach and imagine yourself having a great time. You can picture your family by the pool sipping piña coladas. In actual fact, many vacations are not as great as predicted, but the anticipation makes you happy. Perhaps we should satisfy ourselves with the planning and cancel the actual trip. This way we get to enjoy the anticipation and save the money for something else!

Invest in others

Spending money on other people delivers more happiness than spending it on oneself. We get a surge in mattering when we contribute to the well-being of others. This is because we are relational beings through and through. By making a positive difference in someone's life we derive a sense of pride and satisfaction. This is the definition of meaningful impact. Supporting others is also part of meaningful recognition. We help, and get recognized for it. Two for one. This is a good investment.

Knowing your spending habits can certainly help you improve your economic well-being. Do you tend to spend more on objects than experiences? Do you indulge in lattes every day? Are there opportunities for you to outsource some chores so you have more time to engage in meaningful activities? Can you move closer to work? When was the last time you spent on others? Do you savor the anticipation of a great adventure?

Dunn and Norton make good recommendations, but by their own account they are useful only to people who have money to spend on adventures or lattes. The reality of many people is vastly different. They struggle with basic necessities and cannot live on minimum wage. To suggest that they buy experiences instead of material goods is a cruel joke because they have money for neither.

While it is true that growing up in poor conditions sets you up for a life of challenges, it is also true that you are not a demographic statistic. Although in population terms upward mobility is very difficult for people with low levels of education, in individual terms many people do get out of poverty. What can we learn from them? They usually get an education, develop good relationships with mentors, save for a rainy day, go to extraordinary lengths to advance themselves, and make some sacrifices along the way.

Without parents to support me, and zero dollars in the bank, as an undergraduate student I had a difficult choice to make. I wanted to study history and philosophy, but I doubted I could get a job with these degrees, so I studied psychology instead. I've thoroughly enjoyed being a psychologist, but at the time it was a pragmatic decision. Perhaps I would have enjoyed being a poor philosopher, but the prospect of waiting tables or driving taxis to maintain my philosophical interests was not too appealing to me. That was why I chose to study a subject with professional opportunities.

I was an immigrant without full command of either language of study in Israel: Hebrew and English. I grew up speaking Spanish, and after eighteen months in Israel to finish high school, I was not quite ready for studying psychology in Hebrew, and English, at the university. At one point I wanted to drop out because it seemed just too difficult, but I somehow stuck with it. After I finished my BA I miraculously got accepted into a prestigious master's program in clinical child psychology at Tel Aviv University, which I finished with flying colors. By then I had mastered both languages, and grew in confidence.

To pursue better professional and economic opportunities, Ora and I moved quite a bit. We migrated from Israel to Canada, from Canada to Australia, and from Australia to the United States. We also moved within Canada and the United States. We were after the right fit. Along the way we both got doctorates and eventually landed great jobs. Upon reflection, we used many of the GREASE techniques.

First, we had clear professional and economic goals. To achieve these goals we thought that moving to Canada would be a good move. Ora got a job as a teacher and I as a school psychologist. We both continued our studies at the University of Manitoba. To become qualified for a doctoral program, I took English courses. Ora took some evening courses toward her master's degree. It was all very gradual, really, the first principle of GREASE. We also reinforced ourselves for making progress. We both had full-time jobs and we both took a pretty full load of courses. It was like juggling two full-time jobs. It was not very easy, but we got a lot of support from Ora's parents, who helped us with babysitting and housing.

I did not study history or philosophy, but I found a pretty good alternative. Psychology has been good to me. Finding alternatives is an important part of economic prosperity. Many people who grow up in poverty are very savvy about negotiating life's challenges, as are immigrants. If one door closes, they keep looking for the one with a small opening.

A combination of aptitude and attitude can help you get ahead financially. That was certainly the case with me. I kept studying and working hard, and knew how to get along with folks. It worked for me. But, to return to the demographic approach, not everyone has a chance to cultivate aptitude and attitude. This is why we need to do our best to help others.

Know Others, Help Others

As a teacher, parent, mentor, or manager, you have an opportunity to develop aptitude and attitude in people. Due to their diverse backgrounds, some may need to learn how to optimize their spending, in which case Dunn and Norton can help; but others may need more basic skills. Yet others may need our help in challenging conditions of inequality that perpetuate poverty. To view ourselves as useful helpers, we need to know what other people need. To exhort willpower when basic skills are not present is not going to help. The prescription must be based on correct diagnosis.

For middle-class folks struggling to save, some financial literacy might help. Perhaps they need to learn about the high costs of seeing, and not just the high costs of living. For people struggling to make ends meet, mentoring and support can help. Activating networks can help in getting your friends a job. Sharing tips for job interviews and strategies for success would be great. But if we want to lift millions out of poverty, we might have to do what Yunus did, or get involved in social movements for equality.

The opportunities for involvement are enormous. You can support high-quality public education to make sure all kids develop aptitudes and attitudes that will serve them well in the job market. You can get involved in the movement for affordable housing. You can express support for a decent minimum wage and join the fight for women's rights. You can push governments to implement proven approaches to poverty alleviation. If you care about evidence, you cannot dismiss these recommendations as merely ideological or political, for they are based on persuasive research.[12] Economic well-being is about fit, fitness, and fairness. Some may need to refine their economic fitness, but for many, the real cure is fairness.

Quiz

It is now time to review what we've learned so far.

> *Myth*: If you go to some hospitals in California, you will pay $24 for a Tylenol with codeine pill that has a market price of $0.50.
> *Fact*: You will not pay $24. You will pay instead $37 for a single Tylenol pill!
> *Myth*: A stitch in time saves nine.
> *Fact*: I don't know what stitches you are talking about, but in most hospitals around the country, nine stitches will cost you about $4,500.

These facts are true. I know they are true because they were reported by the *New York Times* on December 3, 2013. Granted, that newspaper does have a liberal bias, but even if they exaggerated a bit, you still end up with a pretty big number. Let's say the *New York Times* reports that a Tylenol pill costs $37, and Fox News says it costs $23; you still end up with an average of $30, which is enough to build a small hospital in Kiribati.

Let's face it. If you don't want to become a victim of overpriced pills or medical procedures, you must invest in wellness. But before we jump into dangerous territory, such as getting up from the couch to eat a piece of broccoli, let's assess your overall well-being. Answer the following quiz:

Interpersonal well-being: When you need emotional support . . .

a. You hug strangers at random in the mall.
b. You post tragic messages on Facebook and stare intently at the screen for hours in the hope that somebody will feel pity for you and throw you a word of sympathy.
c. You flip channels until you find a reality TV show with characters more pathetic than you.

If you answered *a*, you should wash your hands often. If you answered *b*, you should go to meetup.com and start a Desperate Anonymous group. If you answered *c*, you are like 99.9 percent of Americans.

Community well-being: When there is crime in your neighborhood . . .

a. You blame the police.
b. You blame the National Rifle Association.
c. You blame Obamacare.

If you answered *a*, you are in trouble because the police will come after you next. If you answered *b*, you are a delusional, self-hating, anti-American communist sympathizer, or Piers Morgan. If you answered *c*, you are watching too much Fox News.

Occupational well-being: When you are not satisfied with your work . . .

a. You spend 95 percent of your time at work on the Internet looking for another job.
b. You spend 85 percent of your time at work on the Internet posting nasty messages about your boss.
c. You spend 75 percent of your time at work pretending that you are working.

If you answered *a*, you are like 95 percent of Americans. If you answered *b*, you are like most reality TV characters. If you answered *c*, you are like the remaining 5 percnet of the country.

Psychological well-being: When you feel stressed . . .

a. You smoke three packs of cigarettes per day.
b. You send your wife to the gym.
c. You buy a stress-reduction book on Amazon.

If you answered *a*, don't get near me with that awful smell. If you answered *b*, you will be able to smoke in peace. If *c* is your answer, be careful the book is not delivered by a drone that will confuse you with a terrorist.

Physical well-being: When you feel the urge to exercise . . .

a. You sit tight and wait until it passes.
b. You go to the mall and buy new exercise clothes.
c. You buy an exercise video from Amazon.

If you answered *a*, you are like 99 percent of Americans. If you chose *b*, you are like 98 percent of Americans. If you chose *c*, the drone will eventually get you.

Economic well-being: When you max out on your credit card . . .

a. You have been buying too many exercise clothes you will never use.
b. You blame Obamacare.
c. You get a new credit card.

If you answered *a*, you can become the competition for Lululemon. If you answered *b*, no need to worry because you will eventually get a job at Fox News. If you answered *c*, you are like 99 percent of college graduates.

Now sum up how many of your answers are *a*, *b*, and *c*. If you answered *a* more than three times, you can become a wellness coach and start getting suckers to buy your videos. If you answered *b* more than four times, you have a tendency to blame others for your problems and you very likely have eczema. If you answered *c* twice or more, you should try to get your cholesterol level below 400 and eat more kohlrabi. The alternative is to pay $30 for a Tylenol pill, or become a vegan like me.

Appendix

I COPPE Scale of Well-Being

This scale evaluates your overall well-being as well as your level of well-being in six domains of life: Interpersonal, Community, Occupational, Physical, Psychological, and Economic.
Instructions: Read each question and circle the appropriate number on the vertical scale.

1. On the vertical scale, the top number ten represents the best your life can be. The bottom number zero represents the worst your life can be. When it comes *to the best possible life for you,* on which number . . .

Table A.1.

do you stand now?	did you stand a year ago?	will you stand a year from now?
10	10	10
9	9	9
8	8	8
7	7	7
6	6	6
5	5	5
4	4	4
3	3	3
2	2	2
1	1	1
0	0	0

2. This set of questions pertains to relationships. The top number ten represents the best your life can be. The bottom number zero represents the worst your life can be. When it comes to *relationships with important people in your life,* on which number . . .

Table A.2.

do you stand now?	did you stand a year ago?	will you stand a year from now?
10	10	10
9	9	9
8	8	8
7	7	7
6	6	6
5	5	5
4	4	4
3	3	3
2	2	2
1	1	1
0	0	0

3. This set of questions pertains to your community. The top number ten represents the best your life can be. The bottom number zero represents the worst your life can be. When it comes *to the community where you live*, on which number . . .

Table A.3.

do you stand now?	did you stand a year ago?	will you stand a year from now?
10	10	10
9	9	9
8	8	8
7	7	7
6	6	6
5	5	5
4	4	4
3	3	3
2	2	2
1	1	1
0	0	0

4. This set of questions pertains to your main occupation. The top number ten represents the best your life can be. The bottom number zero represents the worst your life can be. When it comes to *your main occupation (employed, self-employed, volunteer, stay at home),* on which number

Table A.4.

do you stand now?	did you stand a year ago?	will you stand a year from now?
10	10	10
9	9	9
8	8	8
7	7	7
6	6	6
5	5	5
4	4	4
3	3	3
2	2	2
1	1	1
0	0	0

5. This set of questions pertains to your physical health and wellness. The top number ten represents the best your life can be. The bottom number zero represents the worst your life can be. When it comes to *your physical health and wellness,* on which number

Table A.5.

do you stand now?	did you stand a year ago?	will you stand a year from now?
10	10	10
9	9	9
8	8	8
7	7	7
6	6	6
5	5	5
4	4	4
3	3	3
2	2	2
1	1	1
0	0	0

6. This set of questions pertains to your emotional and psychological well-being. The top number ten represents the best your life can be. The bottom number zero represents the worst your life can be. When it comes to *your emotional and psychological well-being,* on which number

Table A.6.

do you stand now?	did you stand a year ago?	will you stand a year from now?
10	10	10
9	9	9
8	8	8
7	7	7
6	6	6
5	5	5
4	4	4
3	3	3
2	2	2
1	1	1
0	0	0

7. This set of questions pertains to your economic situation. The top number ten represents the best your life can be. The bottom number zero represents the worst your life can be. When it comes to *your economic situation,* on which number

Table A.7.

do you stand now?	did you stand a year ago?	will you stand a year from now?
10	10	10
9	9	9
8	8	8
7	7	7
6	6	6
5	5	5
4	4	4
3	3	3
2	2	2
1	1	1
0	0	0

SCORING INSTRUCTIONS

1. Add up the three scores for each question. For example, if you had a 6, 7, and 8, respectively, for each one of the three columns in question 1, your total score is 21.
2. Divide that number by 3. For example, if you got a 21 in question 1, your final score is a 7.
3. Insert that number in the table below:

Table A.8.

Domains of Well-Being	My Final Score
Overall	
Interpersonal	
Community	
Occupational	
Physical	
Psychological	
Economic	

4. Scores of 7 and above place you in the *thriving* category. Scores of 5 and 6 place you in the *struggling* category. Scores of 4 and below place you in the *suffering* category.

Details of the psychometric properties of this scale may be found in the following references:

Myers, N. D., Prilleltensky, I., Jin, Y., Dietz, S., Rubenstein, C., Prilleltensky, O., & McMahon, A. (2014). Empirical contributions of the past in assessing multidimensional well-being. *Journal of Community Psychology, 42*, 789–98.

Prilleltensky, I., Dietz, S., Prilleltensky, O., Myers, N., Rubenstein, C., Jin, Y., & McMahon, A. (2015). Assessing multidimensional well-being: Development and validation of the I COPPE scale. *Journal of Community Psychology, 43*, 199–226.

Acknowledgments

I would like to thank Myriam Marquez, former editorial page editor of the *Miami Herald*, for giving me an opportunity to publish my first humor columns there. Nancy Ancrum, the current editor, continues to publish my work in the paper, for which I'm very grateful. Dave Lawrence thought that the *Herald* might be interested in my work and introduced me to Myriam. I appreciate Dave's help very much. I also want to thank Michael Lewis, publisher of *Miami Today*, for publishing my columns and submitting the one on Beckham to the National Newspaper Association competition. That piece, reproduced in the book, won second place for Best Humorous Column (I can hear my late Jewish mother: *why not first place?*). Both the *Herald* and *Miami Today* have allowed me to republish some of my stories in this book.

I am also indebted to Tom Koerner, vice president and publisher of the education division of Rowman & Littlefield, for showing a keen interest in this book. Carlie Wall, Bethany Janka, and Rachel Wing at Rowman & Littlefield, was also very professional and helpful throughout the publication process. Mitch Kaplan, owner of the iconic Books & Books in Miami, was very supportive and offered to help in different ways.

At work, my friend and executive assistant extraordinaire, Yvette Carpintero, has helped during the last ten years in more ways than I can possibly remember. Thank you, Yvette. In general, the University of Miami has been a wonderful place to pursue my scholarly work and writing. My research team at the School of Education and Human Development has been magnificent. I thank Samantha Dietz, Adam McMahon, Nick Myers, and Ora Prilleltensky for productive and enjoyable conversations that have enriched this book. In addition, I had informative discussions about wellness, fairness, and humor with my doctoral students Johnathan Duff, Carolyn Rubenstein, and Susie Patterson. I am also indebted to the following friends and colleagues for reading the book and offering their support: Ros Ben-Moshe, David Blustein, Iain Butterworth, Mitch Earlywine, Michelle Grossman, Harold Levine, Michael Lewis, Talma Lobel, Geoff Nelson, Eduardo Padrón, Ken and Lisa Rosen, Martin Seligman, Laura Smith, and Len Syme.

My sister Myriam (Cachi) Prilleltensky has been a wonderful cheerleader for many years. She has always shown a sincere interest in my writing. My wife Ora is the love of my life and the first one to read anything I write. She laughs at my jokes and reminds me that if I want to keep my day job, there are certain things I should not publish. She also thinks I'm cute, which is why I married her. She is a wonderful writer herself and has provided sound advice for the book. It is a joy to live with a loving and laughing partner like Ora. We have been having fun together in four countries, in several languages, even in places like Nashville, for the last thirty-three years. Our son Matan, the best writer and smartest member of the family, offered constructive feedback. Matan is not only brilliant but hilarious. He sees the comic side of every situation. But above all, he is a true mensch. I'm the luckiest husband and father. I'm also a lucky son, even if I did not get to enjoy my parents for long. I inherited a good sense of humor from my dad, who unfortunately died in a car accident with my mom nearly fifty years ago, when I was eight years old. I think they would have enjoyed the book.

Notes

PREFACE

1. Nabi, R. (2015). Emotional flow in persuasive health messages. *Health Communication, 30*(2), 114–24. doi:10.1080/10410236.2014.974129.

2. Cann, A., Holt, K., & Calhoun, L. G. (1999). The roles of humor and sense of humor in responses to stressors. *Humor: International Journal of Humor Research, 12*(2), 177–93. doi:10.1515/humr.1999.12.2.177; Cann, A., & Kuiper, N. A. (2014). Research on the role of humor in well-being and health. *Europe's Journal of Psychology, 10,* 412–28. doi:10.5964/ejop.v10i3.818; Cann, A., & Collette, C. (2014). Sense of humor, stable affect, and psychological well-being. *Europe's Journal of Psychology, 10,* 464–79. doi:10.5964/ejop.v10i3.746; Crawford, S. A., & Caltabiano, N. J. (2011). Promoting emotional well-being through the use of humor. *Journal of Positive Psychology, 6,* 237–52. doi:10.1080/17439760.2011.577087; Earleywine, M. (2011). *Humor 101.* New York, NY: Springer; Klein, A. (1998). *The courage to laugh.* New York, NY: Jeremy P. Tarcher/Putnam; Klein, A. (1989). *The healing power of humor.* Los Angeles, CA: Jeremy P. Tarcher; Maiolino, N. B., & Kuiper, N. A. (2014). Integrating humor and positive psychology approaches to psychological well-being. *Europe's Journal of Psychology, 10,* 557–70. doi:10.5964/ejop.v10i3.753; Marcuse, F. L. (1988). *Humor is no laughing matter.* New York, NY: Vantage Press; Martin, R. A. (2007). *The psychology of humor: An integrative approach.* New York, NY: Elsevier; Morrison, M. K. (2012). *Using humor to maximize living* (2nd ed.). New York, NY: Rowman & Littlefield; Morrison, M. K. (2008). *Using humor to maximize learning.* New York, NY: Rowman & Littlefield.

CHAPTER 1

1. Dunn, E., & Norton, M. (2013). *Happy money: The science of smarter spending.* New York, NY: Simon & Schuster.

2. Fiske, S. (2012). *Envy up, scorn down: How status divides us.* New York, NY: Russell Sage.

3. Myers, N. D., Prilleltensky, I., Jin, Y., Dietz, S., Rubenstein, C., Prilleltensky, O., & McMahon, A. (2014). Empirical contributions of the past in assessing multidimensional well-being. *Journal of Community Psychology, 42,* 789–98; Prilleltensky, I., Dietz, S., Prilleltensky, O., Myers, N., Rubenstein, C., Jin, Y., & McMahon, A. (2015). Assessing multidimensional well-being: Development and validation

of the I COPPE scale. *Journal of Community Psychology, 43,* 199–226; Rath, T., & Harter, J. (2010). *Well-being: The five essential elements.* New York, NY: Gallup Press.

4. Lyubomirsky, S. (2007). *The how of happiness: A new approach to getting the life you want.* New York, NY: Penguin Books; Norcross, J. C. (2012). *Changeology: 5 steps to realizing your goals and resolutions.* New York, NY: Simon & Schuster; Weick, K. (1984). Small wins. *American Psychologist, 39*(1), 40–49.

5. Berkman, L. (1995). The role of social relationships in health promotion. *Psychosomatic Research, 57,* 245–54; Bookwala, J., Marshall, K. I., & Manning, S. W. (2014). Who needs a friend? Marital status transitions and physical health outcomes in later life. *Health Psychology, 33*(6), 505–15. doi:10.1037/hea0000049; Buettner, D. (2008). *The blue zones: Lessons for living longer from the people who've lived the longest.* Washington, DC: National Geographic; Buettner, D. (2010). *Thrive.* Washington, DC: National Geographic; Cacioppo, J., Reis, H., & Zautra, A. (2011). Social resilience: The value of social fitness with an application to the military. *American Psychologist, 66,* 43–51. doi:10.1037/a0021419; Cohen, S. (2004). Social relationships and health. *American Psychologist, 59,* 676–84. doi:10.1037/0003-066X.59.8.676; Coombs, R. H. (1991). Marital status and personal well-being: A literature review. *Family Relations: An Interdisciplinary Journal of Applied Family Studies, 40*(1), 97–102. doi:10.2307/585665; Gandy, W. M., Coberley, C., Pope, J. E., & Rula, E. Y. (2014). Well-being and employee health—How employees' well-being scores interact with demographic factors to influence risk of hospitalization or an emergency room visit. *Population Health Management, 17*(1), 13–20. doi:10.1089/pop.2012.0120; Horwitz, A. V., White, H., & Howell-White, S. (1996). Becoming married and mental health: A longitudinal study of a cohort of young adults. *Journal of Marriage and the Family, 58*(4), 895–907. doi:10.2307/353978; Kim, H. K., & McKenry, P. C. (2002). The relationship between marriage and psychological well-being: A longitudinal analysis. *Journal of Family Issues, 23*(8), 885–911. doi:10.1177/019251302237296; Koball, H. L., Moiduddin, E., Henderson, J., Goesling, B., & Besculides, M. (2010). What do we know about the link between marriage and health? *Journal of Family Issues, 31*(8), 1019–40. doi:10.1177/0192513X10365834; Ornish, D. (1997). *Love and survival: The scientific basis for the healing power of intimacy.* New York, NY: Harper and Collins; Symoens, S., Van de Velde, S., Colman, E., & Bracke, P. (2014). Divorce and the multidimensionality of men and women's mental health: The role of social-relational and socio-economic conditions. *Applied Research in Quality of Life, 9*(2), 197–214. doi:10.1007/s11482-013-9239-5.

6. Hystad, P., & Carpiano, R. M. (2012). Sense of community-belonging and health behavior change in Canada. *Journal of Epidemiology and Community Health, 66,* 277–83. doi:10.1136/jech.2009.103556; Kawachi, I., & Berkman, L. (2000). Social cohesion, social capital and health. In L. Berkman & I. Kawachi (Eds.), *Social epidemiology* (pp. 174–90). New York, NY: Oxford University; Peterson, N. A., Speer, P. W., & McMillan, D. W. (2008). Validation of a Brief Sense of Community scale: Confirmation of the principal theory of sense of community. *Journal of Community Psychology, 36,* 61–73. doi:10.1002/jcop.20217; Ross, N. (2002). Community-belonging and health. *Health Reports,* 13, 33–39; Shields, M. (2008). Community-belonging and self-perceived health. *Health Reports, 19,* 1–9.

7. Clark, A. (2010). Work, jobs, and well-being across the millennium. In E. Diener, J. Helliwell, & D. Kahneman (Eds.), *International differences in well-being* (pp. 436–64). New York, NY: Oxford University Press; Harter, J., & Arora, R. (2010). The impact of time spent working and job fit on well-being around the world. In E. Diener, J. Helliwell, & D. Kahneman (Eds.), *International differences in well-being* (pp. 398–435). New York, NY: Oxford University Press; Prilleltensky, I., Dietz, S., Prilleltensky, O., Myers, N., Rubenstein, C., Jin, Y., & McMahon, A. (2015). Assessing multidimensional well-being: Development and validation of the I COPPE scale. *Journal of Community Psychology, 43,* 199–226; Prilleltensky, I., & Prilleltensky, O. (2006). *Promoting well-being: Linking personal, organizational, and community change.* Hoboken, NJ: Wiley.

8. Chmiel, M., Brunner, M., Martin, R., & Schalke, D. (2012). Revisiting the structure of subjective well-being in middle-aged adults. *Social Indicators Research, 106,* 109–16. doi:10.1007/s11205-011-9796-7; Cohen, E. H. (1999). A facet theory approach to examining overall and life facet satisfaction relationships. *Social Indicators Research, 51,* 223–37. doi:10.1023/A:1007019526236; Gonzalez, M.,

Coenders, G., Saez, M., & Casas, F. (2010). Non-linearity, complexity and limited measurement in the relationship between satisfaction with specific life domains and satisfaction with life as a whole. *Journal of Happiness Studies, 11*, 335–52. doi:10.1007/s10902-009-9143-8; Keyes, C., & Simoes, E. (2012). To flourish or not: Positive mental health and all-cause mortality. *American Journal of Public Health, 102*, 2164–72. doi:10.2105/AJPH.2012.300918; Nieboer, A., Lindenberg, S., Boomsma, A., & Van Bruggen, A. C. (2005). Dimensions of well-being and their measurement: The SPF-IL scale. *Social Indicators Research, 73*, 313–53. doi:10.1007/s11205-004-0988-2; Pavot, W., & Diener, E. (2008). The Satisfaction with Life Scale and the emerging construct of life satisfaction. *Journal of Positive Psychology, 3*, 137–52. doi:10.1080/17439760701756946.

9. Dixon, R. A., & Backman, L. (Eds.). (1995). *Compensating for psychological deficits and declines: Managing losses and promoting gains.* Mahwah, NJ: Lawrence Erlbaum.

10. Diener, E., & Biswas-Diener, R. (2008). *Happiness: Unlocking the mysteries of psychological wealth.* Malden, MA: Blackwell.

11. Fredrickson, B. A. (2009). *Positivity.* New York, NY: Three Rivers Press; Fredrickson, B. A., & Kurtz, L. (2011). Cultivating positive emotions to enhance human flourishing. In S. I. Donaldson, M. Csikzentmihalyi, & J. Nakamura (Eds.), *Applied positive psychology: Improving everyday life, health, schools, work, and society* (pp. 35–47). New York, NY: Routledge.

12. Block, P. (2009). *Community: The structure of belonging.* San Francisco: Berrett-Koehler; McKnight, J., & Block, P. (2012). *The abundant community: Awakening the power of families and neighborhoods.* San Francisco: Berrett-Koehler; Nelson, G., Kloos, B., & Ornelas, J. (Eds.). (2014). *Community psychology and community mental health: Towards transformative change.* New York, NY: Oxford; Putnam, R. (2000). *Bowling alone: The collapse and revival of American community.* New York, NY: Simon & Schuster.

13. Dunn, E., & Norton, M. (2013). *Happy money: The science of smarter spending.* New York: Simon & Schuster.

14. Duncan, G., & Murnane, R. (2014). *Restoring opportunity: The crisis of inequality and the challenge for American Education.* Cambridge, MA: Harvard Education Press; Easterlin, R. A., & Sawangfa, O. (2007). *Happiness and domain satisfaction: Theory and evidence.* Paper presented at the Conference on New Directions in the Study of Happiness, University of Notre Dame. Retrieved from http://dornsife.usc.edu/IEPR/Publications /IEPR_07.5_EasterlinSawangfa.pdf; Florit, E. F., & Lladosa, L. E. V. (2007). Evaluation of the effects of education on job satisfaction: Independent single-equation vs. structural equation models. *International Advances in Economic Research, 13*(2), 157–70; Putnam, R. (2015). *Our kids: The American dream in crisis.* New York, NY: Simon & Schuster; Tsou, M. & Liu, J. (2001). Happiness and domain satisfaction. *Journal of Happiness Studies, 2*, 269–88.

15. Diener, E., Helliwell, J., & Kahneman, D. (Eds.). (2010). *International differences in well-being.* New York, NY: Oxford University Press; Diener, E., Scollon, C., & Lucas, R. (2009). The evolving concept of subjective well-being: The multifaceted nature of happiness. *Social Indicators Research Series, 39*, 67–100; Gallagher, M., Lopez, S., & Preacher, K. (2009). The hierarchical structure of well-being. *Journal of Personality, 77*, 1025–49. doi: 10.1111/j.1467-6494.2009.00573.x; Huppert, F. A., & Linley, P. A. (2011). *Happiness and well-being: Critical concepts in psychology; Vol. III: Causes and correlates of happiness and well-being: What makes us happy.* New York, NY: Routledge; Seligman, M. (2011). *Flourish: A visionary new understanding of happiness and well-being.* New York, NY: Simon & Schuster; Stone, A., & Mackie, C. (Eds.). (2013). *Subjective well-being: Measuring happiness, suffering, and other dimensions of experience.* Washington, DC: National Academies Press.

16. Baumgardner, S. R., & Crothers, M. K. (2009). *Positive psychology.* Upper Saddle River, NJ: Pearson Prentice Hall; Frisch, M. B. (2006). *Quality-of-life therapy: Applying a life satisfaction approach to positive psychology and cognitive therapy.* Hoboken, NJ: John Wiley & Sons; Heintzelman, S., & King, L. (2014). Life is pretty meaningful. *American Psychologist, 69*(6), 561–74. doi:10.1037/a0035049; Prilleltensky, I. (2014). Meaning-making, mattering, and thriving in community psychology: From co-optation to amelioration and transformation. *Psychosocial Intervention, 23*, 151–54.

17. Biglan, A. (2015). *The nurture effect: How the science of human behavior can improve our lives and our world.* Oakland, CA: New Harbinger Publications Inc.

18. Ryff, C. (2014). Psychological well-being revisited: Advances in the science and practice of eudaimonia. *Psychotherapy and Psychosomatics, 83*, 10–28. doi:10.1159/000353263.

19. Prilleltensky, I., & Nelson, G. (2002). *Doing psychology critically: Making a difference in diverse settings*. New York, NY: Palgrave/Macmillan; Fox, D., Prilleltensky, I., & Austin, S. (Eds.). (2009). *Critical psychology: An introduction* (2nd. ed.). London: Sage; Prilleltensky, I. (1994). *The morals and politics of psychology: Psychological discourse and the status quo*. Albany, NY: State University of New York Press.

20. Prilleltensky, I., Nelson, G., & Peirson, L. (Eds.). (2001). *Promoting family wellness and preventing child maltreatment: Fundamentals for thinking and action*. Toronto, Ontario: University of Toronto Press.

21. Bandura, A. (1997). *Self-efficacy: The exercise of control*. New York, NY: Freeman; Bandura, A. (2006). Toward a psychology of human agency. *Perspectives on Psychological Science, 1*(2), 164–80. doi: 10.1111/j.1745-6916.2006.00011.x; Bandura, A., Jeffer, R. W., & Gajdos, E. (2005). The primacy of self-regulation in health promotion. *Applied Psychology: An International Journal, 54*(2), 245–54. doi: 10.1111/j.1464-0597.2005.00208.x.

22. Nelson, G., & Prilleltensky, I. (Eds.). (2010). *Community psychology: In pursuit of liberation and well-being* (2nd ed.). New York, NY: Palgrave/Macmillan; Prilleltensky, I. (1997). Values, assumptions, and practices: Assessing the moral implications of psychological discourse and action. *American Psychologist, 52*(5), 517–35.

23. Kabat-Zinn, J. (2005). *Full catastrophe living: Using the wisdom of your body and mind to face stress, pain and illness* (15th anniversary ed.). New York, NY: Bantam Dell.

24. Marmot, M. (2015). *The health gap*. New York, NY: Bloomsbury; Marmot, M. (2004). *The status syndrome*. New York, NY: Henry Holt.

25. Twenge, J. M., & Campbell, W. K. (2009). *The narcissism epidemic: Living in the age of entitlement*. New York, NY: Free Press.

26. Biglan, A. (2015). *The nurture effect: How the science of human behavior can improve our lives and our world*. Oakland, CA: New Harbinger Publications Inc.

27. Block, P. (2009). *Community: The structure of belonging*. San Francisco: Berrett-Koehler; McKnight, J., & Block, P. (2012). *The abundant community: Awakening the power of families and neighborhoods*. San Francisco: Berrett-Koehler.

28. Corning, P. (2011). *The fair society: The science of human nature and the pursuit of social justice*. Chicago, IL: University of Chicago; Prilleltensky, I. (2012). Wellness as fairness. *American Journal of Community Psychology, 49*, 1–21. doi: 10.1007/s10464-011-9448-8; Sun, L. (2013). *The fairness instinct*. Amherst, NY: Prometheus.

29. Chess, S., & Thomas, A. (1999). *Goodness of fit: Clinical applications, from infancy through adult life*. New York, NY: Routledge; Lewin, K. (1936). *Principles of topological psychology*. Columbus, OH: McGraw-Hill; Shonkoff, J. (2014). A healthy start before and after birth. In K. McCartney, H. Yoshikawa, & L. Forcier (Eds.), *Improving the odds for America's children* (pp. 28–39). Cambridge, MA: Harvard Education Press.

30. Baumeister, R. F., & Tierney, J. (2011). *Willpower: Rediscovering the greatest human strength*. New York, NY: Penguin Books; McGonigal, K. (2012). *The willpower instinct: Why self-control works, why it matters, and how you can get more of it*. New York, NY: Penguin.

31. Duhigg, C. (2014). *The power of habit*. New York, NY: Random House; Watson, D. L. & Tharp, R. G. (2014). *Self-directed behavior: Self-modification for personal adjustment*. (10th ed.). Belmont, CA: Cengage Learning.

32. Brookfield, D., & Wilson, K. (2009). Effect of goal setting on motivation and adherence in a six-week exercise program. *International Journal of Sport and Exercise Psychology, 7*(1), 89–100. doi: 10.1080/1612197X.2009.9671894; Lyubomirsky, S. (2007). *The how of happiness: A new approach to getting the life you want*. New York, NY: Penguin Books; Norcross, J. C. (2012). *Changeology: 5 steps to realizing your goals and resolutions*. New York, NY: Simon & Schuster.

33. Thaler, R., & Sunstein, C. (2008). *Nudge: Improving decisions about health, wealth, and happiness*. New Haven, CT: Yale University Press; Wansink, B. (2014). *Slim by design: Mindless eating solutions*. New York, NY: Harper Collins Publishers.

34. Norcross, J. C. (2012). *Changeology: 5 steps to realizing your goals and resolutions.* New York, NY: Simon & Schuster.

CHAPTER 2

1. Sue, D. (2011). *Microaggressions in everyday life.* Hoboken, NJ: John Wiley & Sons.
2. Kohn, M. (2008). *Trust: Self-interest and the common good.* New York, NY: Oxford.
3. Blow, A., & Hartnett, K. (2005). Infidelity in committed relationships II. *Journal of Marital and Family Therapy, 31,* 217–33; Buss, D. M., & Shackelford, T. K. (1997). Susceptibility to infidelity in the first year of marriage. *Journal of Research in Personality, 31,* 193–221; Whisman, M., & Snyder, D. (2007). Sexual infidelity in a national survey of American women: Differences in prevalence and correlates as a function of method of assessment. *Journal of Family Psychology, 21,* 147–54.
4. Twenge, J. M., & Campbell, W. K. (2009). *The narcissism epidemic: Living in the age of entitlement.* New York, NY: Free Press.
5. Berkman, L. (1995). The role of social relationships in health promotion. *Psychosomatic Research, 57,* 245–54; Cacioppo, J., Reis, H., & Zautra, A. (2011). Social resilience: The value of social fitness with an application to the military. *American Psychologist, 66,* 43–51. doi:10.1037/a0021419; Cohen, S. (2004). Social relationships and health. *American Psychologist, 59,* 676–84. doi:10.1037/0003-066X.59.8.676; Cohen, S., & Willis, T. (1985). Stress, social support, and the buffering hypothesis. *Psychological Bulletin, 98*(2), 310–57; Ornish, D. (1997). *Love and survival: The scientific basis for the healing power of intimacy.* New York, NY: Harper and Collins.
6. Lieberman, M. (2013). *Social: Why our brains are wired to connect.* New York, NY: Random House.
7. Fiske, S. (2012). *Envy up, scorn down: How status divides us.* New York, NY: Russell Sage.
8. Lewin, K. (1936). *Principles of topological psychology.* Columbus, OH: McGraw-Hill.
9. Nelson, G., & Prilleltensky, I. (Eds.). (2010). *Community psychology: In pursuit of liberation and well-being* (2nd ed.). New York, NY: Palgrave/Macmillan.
10. Lane, J. A., & Fink, R. S. (2015). Attachment, social support, and well-being during life transition in emerging adulthood. *The Counseling Psychologist, 43*(7), 1034–58. doi: 10.1177/0011000015592184; Levine, A., & Heller, R. (2010). *Attached.* New York, NY: Jeremy P. Tarcher/Penguin; Mikulincer, M., & Shaver, P. R. (2007). *Attachment in adulthood.* New York, NY: Guilford Press.
11. Baumgardner, S. R., & Crothers, M. K. (2009). *Positive psychology.* Upper Saddle River, NJ: Pearson Prentice Hall.
12. Gable, S. L., Gonzaga, G. C., & Strachman, A. (2006). Will you be there for me when things go right? Supportive responses to positive events disclosures. *Journal of Personality and Social Psychology, 9,* 904–17.
13. Baumgardner, S. R., & Crothers, M. K. (2009). *Positive psychology.* Upper Saddle River, NJ: Pearson Prentice Hall.
14. Ivey, A. E., Ivey, M. B., & Zalaquett, C. P. (2014). *Intentional interviewing and counseling.* Belmont, CA: Brooks/Cole; Weger, H. J., Castle, G. R., & Emmett, M. C. (2010). Active listening in peer interviews: The influence of message paraphrasing on perceptions of listening skill. *International Journal of Listening, 24*(1), 34–49. doi:10.1080/10904010903466311; Weger, H. J., Bell, G. C., Minei, E. M., & Robinson, M. C. (2014). The relative effectiveness of active listening in initial interactions. *International Journal of Listening, 28*(1), 13–31. doi: 10.1080/10904018.2013.813234; Winzurk, J. (2000). *Listening and observing.* Cincinnati, OH: South-Western Educational Publishing.
15. Gottman, J. M., & DeClaire, J. (2001). *The relationship cure: A 5 step guide to strengthening your marriage, family, and friendships.* New York, NY: Crown Publishers; Gottman, J. M., & Silver, N. (2000). *The seven principles for making marriage work.* New York, NY: Three Rivers Press.
16. Tornblom, K., & Vermunt, R. (Eds.). (2007). *Distributive and procedural justice: Research and social applications.* Burlington, VT: Ashgate.

17. Brosnan, S., & de Waal, F. (2003). Monkeys reject unequal pay. *Nature, 425,* 297–99. doi:10.1038/nature01963

18. Hatfield, E., Rapson, R., & Aumer-Ryan, K. (2008). Social justice in love relationships: Recent developments. *Social Justice Research, 21,* 413–31; Jory, B., & Anderson, D. (1999). Intimate justice II: Fostering mutuality, reciprocity, and accommodation in therapy for psychological abuse. *Journal of Marital and Family Therapy, 25*(3), 349–64; Miller, D. T. (2001). Disrespect and the experience of injustice. *Annual Review of Psychology, 52,* 527–53.

CHAPTER 3

1. Fiske, S. (2012). *Envy up, scorn down: How status divides us.* New York, NY: Russell Sage; Fuligni, A. (Ed.). (2007). *Contesting stereotypes and creating identities.* New York, NY: Russell Sage Foundation; Steele, C. (2010). *Whistling Vivaldi: How stereotypes affect us and what we can do.* New York, NY: Norton; Yoshino, K. (2006). *Covering: The hidden assault on our civil rights.* New York, NY: Random.

2. Putnam, R. D. (2000). *Bowling alone: The collapse and revival of American community.* New York, NY: Simon & Schuster.

3. Langer, A., Meleis, A., Knaul, F. M., Atun, R., Aran, M., Arreola-Ornelas, H., . . . Frenk, J. (2015). Women and health: The key for sustainable development. *The Lancet, 386,* 1165–210; Looman, M. D., & Carl, J. D. (2015). *A country called prison.* New York, NY: Oxford; Prilleltensky, I., Nelson, G., & Peirson, L. (Eds.). (2001). *Promoting family wellness and preventing child maltreatment: Fundamentals for thinking and action.* Toronto, ON: University of Toronto Press.

4. Hystad, P., & Carpiano, R. M. (2012). Sense of community-belonging and health behavior change in Canada. *Journal of Epidemiology and Community Health, 66,* 277–83. doi:10.1136/jech.2009.103556; Kawachi, I., & Berkman, L. (2000). Social cohesion, social capital and health. In L. Berkman & I. Kawachi (Eds.), *Social epidemiology* (pp. 174–90). New York: Oxford University; Peterson, N. A., Speer, P. W., & McMillan, D. W. (2008). Validation of a Brief Sense of Community scale: Confirmation of the principal theory of sense of community. *Journal of Community Psychology, 36,* 61–73. doi:10.1002/jcop.20217; Ross, N. (2002). Community-belonging and health. *Health Reports, 13,* 33–39; Shields, M. (2008). Community-belonging and self-perceived health. *Health Reports, 19,* 1–9.

5. Rath, T., & Harter, J. (2010). *Well-being: The five essential elements.* New York, NY: Gallup Press.

6. Nelson, G., & Prilleltensky, I. (Eds.). (2010). *Community psychology: In pursuit of liberation and well-being* (2nd ed.). New York, NY: Palgrave/Macmillan.

7. Buettner, D. (2008). *The blue zones: Lessons for living longer from the people who've lived the longest.* Washington, DC: National Geographic; Buettner, D. (2010). *Thrive.* Washington, DC: National Geographic.

8. Tavits, M. (2008). Representation, corruption, and subjective well-being. *Comparative Political Studies, 41*(12), 1607–30.

9. Frey, B. S., & Stutzer, A. (2002). *Happiness and economics: How the economy and institutions affect well-being.* Princeton, NJ: Princeton University Press.

10. Buettner, D. (2010). *Thrive.* Washington, DC: National Geographic.

11. Lavoie, F., Borkman, T., & Gidron, B. (1994). *Self-help and mutual aid groups: International and multicultural perspectives.* Philadelphia, PA: Haworth; Norcross, J., Campbell, L., Grohol, J., Santrock, J., Selagea, F., & Sommer, R. (2013). *Self-help that works.* New York, NY: Oxford University Press.

12. Inglehart, R. (2010). Faith and freedom: Traditional and modern ways to happiness. In E. Diener, J. Helliwell, & D. Kahneman (Eds.), *International differences in well-being* (pp. 351–97). New York, NY: Oxford University Press; Inglehart, R., Foa, R., Peterson, C., & Welzel, C. (2008). Development, freedom, and rising happiness. *Perspectives on Psychological Science, 3*(4), 264–85.

13. Levy, B., & Sidel, V. (Eds.). (2006). *Social injustice and public health.* New York, NY: Oxford University Press; Marmot, M. (2015). *The health gap.* New York, NY: Bloomsbury; McKenzie, J., &

Pinger, R. (2014). *An introduction to community and public health* (8th ed.). Burlington, MA: Jones Bartlett Learning.

14. Putnam, R. D. (2000). *Bowling alone: The collapse and revival of American community.* New York, NY: Simon & Schuster.

15. Prilleltensky, I., & Prilleltensky, O. (2006). *Promoting well-being: Linking personal, organizational, and community change.* Hoboken, NJ: Wiley.

16. Riessman, F. (1965). The "helper" therapy principle. *Social Work, 10*(2), 27–32.

17. Duncan, G., & Murnane, R. (2014). *Restoring opportunity: The crisis of inequality and the challenge for American education.* Cambridge, MA: Harvard Education Press; Kozol, J. (2012). *Fire in the Ashes: Twenty five years among the poorest children in America.* New York, NY: Crown; Putnam, R. (2015). *Our kids: The American dream in crisis.* New York, NY: Simon & Schuster.

18. Facione, P. A., Scherer, D., & Attig, T. (1978). *Values and society: An introduction to ethics and social philosophy.* Englewood Cliffs, NJ: Prentice-Hall; Miller, D. (1999). *Principles of social justice.* Cambridge, MA: Harvard University Press; Prilleltensky, I. (2014). Justice and human development. *International Journal of Educational Psychology, 3*(3), 287–305; Sandel, M. (2009). *Justice: What's the right thing to do.* New York, NY: Farrar, Straus and Giroux.

19. Corning, P. (2011). *The fair society.* Chicago, IL: University of Chicago Press; Prilleltensky, I. (2012). Wellness as fairness. *American Journal of Community Psychology, 49*, 1–21. doi:10.1007/s10464-011-9448-8; Tornblom, K., & Vermunt, R. (Eds.). (2007). *Distributive and procedural justice: Research and social applications.* Burlington, VT: Ashgate.

20. McKnight, J., & Block, P. (2012). *The abundant community: Awakening the power of families and neighborhoods.* San Francisco, CA: Berrett-Koehler; Rosenberg, Y. (2012). *Join the club: How peer pressure can transform the world.* New York, NY: Norton.

CHAPTER 4

1. Achor, S. (2010). *The happiness advantage: The seven principles of positive psychology that fuel success and performance at work.* New York, NY: Random House; Clark, A. (2010). Work, jobs, and well-being across the millennium. In E. Diener, J. Helliwell, & D. Kahneman (Eds.), *International differences in well-being* (pp. 436–64). New York, NY: Oxford University Press; Harter, J., Schmidt, F., & Keyes, C. (2003). Well-being in the workplace and its relationship to business outcomes. In C. H. Keyes, J. (Ed.), *Flourishing: The positive person and the good life* (pp. 205–24). Washington, DC: American Psychological Association; Hall, D. T., & Mirvis, P. H. (2013). Redefining work, work identity, and career success. In D. Blustein (Ed.), *The Oxford Handbook of the Psychology of Working* (pp. 203–17). New York, NY: Oxford; Schwartz, B. (2015). *Why we work.* New York, NY: Simon & Schuster.

2. Blustein, D. L. (2006). *The psychology of working.* Mahwah, NJ: Lawrence Erlbaum; Pink, D. H. (2009). *Drive: The surprising truth about what motivates us.* New York, NY: Riverhead Books; Sisodia, R., Sheth, J., & Wolfe, D. (2014). *Firms of endearment* (2nd ed.). Upper Saddle River, NJ: Pearson FT Press.

3. Rath, T., & Harter, J. (2010). *Well-being: The five essential elements.* New York, NY: Gallup Press.

4. Aslund, C., Starrin, B., & Nilsson, K. W. (2014). Psychosomatic symptoms and low psychological well-being in relation to employment status: The influence of social capital in a large cross-sectional study in Sweden. *International Journal for Equity in Health, 13*(22), 1–10. doi:10.1186/1475-9276-13-22; Flatau, P., Galea, J., & Petridis, R. (2000). Mental health and well-being and unemployment. *Australian Economic Review, 33*(2), 161–81; Ganley, R. (2004). The psychological impact of joblessness. *Australian Social Policy 2002–03.* Australian Commonwealth Government, 179–200. Retrieved from http://www.dss.gov.au/sites/default/files/documents/05_2012/australiansocialpolicy2002-03.pdf#page=183; Jahoda, M. (1982). *Employment and unemployment.* Cambridge University Press; Murphy, G., & Athanasou, J. (1999). The effect of unemployment on mental health. *Journal of Occupational and Organizational Psychology, 72*, 83–99; Theodossiou, I. (1998). The effects of low-pay and unemployment on psychological well-being: A logistic regression approach. *Journal of Health Economics, 17*, 85–104.

5. Prilleltensky, I., & Prilleltensky, O. (2006). *Promoting well-being: Linking personal, organizational, and community change.* Hoboken, NJ: Wiley.

6. Autor, D. (2014). Skills, education, and the rise of earning inequality among the "other 99 percent." *Science, 344,* 843–51; Putnam, R. (2015). *Our kids: The American dream in crisis.* New York, NY: Simon & Schuster.

7. Goleman, D., Boyatzis, R., & McKee, A. (2002). *Primal leadership: Realizing the power of emotional intelligence.* Boston, MA: Harvard Business School Press; Weisinger, H. (2000). *Emotional intelligence at work.* San Francisco, CA: Jossey-Bass.

8. De Vogli, R., Ferrie, J., Chandola, T., Kivimäki, M., & Marmot, M. (2007). Unfairness and health: Evidence from the Whitehall II study. *Journal of Epidemiology and Community Health, 61,* 513–18; Elovainio, M., Kivimäki, M., & Vahtera, J. (2002). Organizational justice: Evidence of a new psychosocial predictor of health. *American Journal of Public Health, 92*(1), 105–8; Elovainio, M., Kivimäki, M., Steen, N., & Vahtera, J. (2004). Job decision latitude, organizational justice and health: Multilevel covariance structural analysis. *Social Science and Medicine, 58,* 1659–69; Kivimäki, M., Ferrie, J., Head, J., Shipley, M., Vahtera, J., & Marmot, M. (2004). Organizational justice and change in justice as predictors of employee health: The Whitehall II study. *Journal of Epidemiology and Community Health, 58,* 931–37; Mastroianni, M., & Storberg-Walker, J. (2014). Do work relationships matter? Characteristics of workplace interactions that enhance or detract from employee perceptions of well-being and health behaviors. *Health Psychology and Behavioural Medicine, 2*(1), 798–819. http://dx.doi.org/10.1080/21642850.2014.933343; Robbins, J. M., Ford, M. T., & Tetrick, L. E. (2012). Perceived unfairness and employee health: A meta-analytic integration. *Journal of Applied Psychology, 97*(2), 235–72. doi:10.1037/a0025408.

9. Colquitt, J. A. (2001). On the dimensionality of organizational justice: A construct validation of a measure. *Journal of Applied Psychology, 86*(3), 386–400; Colquitt, J. A., Conlon, D. E., Wesson, M. J., Porter, C. O. L. H., & Ng, K. Y. (2001). Justice at the millennium: A meta-analytic review of 25 years of organizational justice research. *Journal of Applied Psychology, 86* (3), 425–45.

10. Norcross, J. C. (2012). *Changeology: 5 steps to realizing your goals and resolutions.* New York, NY: Simon & Schuster.

11. Logan, D., King, J., & Fischer-Wright, H. (2008). *Tribal leadership: Leveraging natural groups to build a thriving organization.* New York, NY: Harper.

12. Adkins, A. (2015, January). Majority of U.S. employees not engaged despite gains in 2014. Retrieved from http://www.gallup.com/poll/181289/majority-employees-not-engaged-despite-gains-2014.aspx.

CHAPTER 5

1. Edlin, G., & Golanty, E. (2014). *Health and Wellness* (11th ed.). Burlington, MA: Jones & Bartlett Learning.

2. Hempel, S. (2007). *The strange case of the Broad Street Pump: John Snow and the mystery of cholera.* Los Angeles, CA: University of California Press.

3. Prilleltensky, I. (2005). Promoting well-being: Time for a paradigm shift in health and human services. *Scandinavian Journal of Public Health. 33,* 53–60; Prilleltensky, I., & Nelson, G. (2013). Prevention, critical psychology, and social justice. In E. Vera (Ed.), *The Oxford handbook of prevention in counseling psychology* (pp. 14–59). New York, NY: Oxford University Press.

4. Wansink, B. (2006). *Mindless eating: Why we eat more than we think.* New York, NY: Bantam-Dell.

5. Baumeister, R. F., & Tierney, J. (2011). *Willpower: Rediscovering the greatest human strength.* New York, NY: Penguin Books; McGonigal, K. (2012). *The willpower instinct: Why self-control works, why it matters, and how you can get more of it.* New York, NY: Penguin.

6. Moss, M. (2013). *Salt sugar fat: How the food giants hooked us.* New York, NY: Random House.

7. Wansink, B. (2014). *Slim by design: Mindless eating solutions.* New York, NY: Harper Collins Publishers.

8. Buettner, D. (2008*). The blue zones: Lessons for living longer from the people who've lived the longest.* Washington, DC: National Geographic.

9. Thaler, R., & Sunstein, C. (2008). *Nudge: Improving decisions about health, wealth, and happiness.* New Haven, CT: Yale University Press; Wansink, B. (2014). *Slim by design: Mindless eating solutions.* New York, NY: Harper Collins Publishers.

10. Edlin, G., & Golanty, E. (2014). *Health and Wellness* (11th ed.). Burlington, MA: Jones & Bartlett Learning.

11. Barnard, N. (2013). *Power foods for the brain: An effective 3-step plan to protect your mind and strengthen your memory.* New York, NY: Hachette; Barnard, N. (2011). *21-day weight loss kickstart: Boost metabolism, lower cholesterol, and dramatically improve your health.* New York, NY: Hachette; Campbell, T. C. (2014). *Whole: Rethinking the science of nutrition.* Dallas, TX: BenBella Books; Campbell, T. C., & Campbell, T. M. (2006). *The China Study.* Dallas, TX: BenBella Books; Esselstyn, C. B. (2007). *Prevent and reverse heart disease.* New York, NY: Penguin; Ornish, D. (2007). *The Spectrum: A scientifically proven program to feel better, live longer, lose weight, and gain health.* New York, NY: Ballantine.

12. Wansink, B. (2014). *Slim by design: Mindless eating solutions.* New York, NY: Harper Collins Publishers.

13. Segall, A., & Fries, C. J. (2011). *Pursuing health and wellness: Healthy societies, healthy people.* New York, NY: Oxford.

14. Brookfield, D., & Wilson, K. (2009). Effect of goal setting on motivation and adherence in a six-week exercise program. *International Journal of Sport and Exercise Psychology, 7*(1), 89–100. doi: 10.1080/1612197X.2009.9671894; Norcross, J. C. (2012). *Changeology: 5 steps to realizing your goals and resolutions.* New York, NY: Simon & Schuster.

15. Grunbaum, M. (June 26, 2014). New York's ban on big sodas is rejected by final court. *The New York Times.* Retrieved from http://www.nytimes.com/2014/06/27/nyregion/city-loses-final-appeal-on-limiting-sales-of-large-sodas.html?_r=0.

CHAPTER 6

1. Dweck, C. S. (2006). *Mindset: The new psychology of success.* New York, NY: Random House; Frisch, M. B. (2006). *Quality-of-life therapy: Applying a life satisfaction approach to positive psychology and cognitive therapy.* Hoboken, NJ: John Wiley & Sons; Greenberger, D., & Padesky, C. (1995). *Mind over mood: Changing how you feel by changing the way you think.* New York, NY: Guilford; Hays, P. A. (2014). *Creating well-being: Four steps to a happier, healthier life.* Washington, DC: American Psychological Association.

2. Baumgardner, S. R., & Crothers, M. K. (2009). *Positive psychology.* Upper Saddle River, NJ: Pearson Prentice Hall; Diener, E., & Biswas-Diener, R. (2008). *Happiness: Unlocking the mysteries of psychological wealth.* Malden, MA: Blackwell; Diener, E., Scollon, C., & Lucas, R. (2009). The evolving concept of subjective well-being: The multifaceted nature of happiness. *Social Indicators Research Series, 39,* 67–100; Fowers, B. (2015). *The evolution of ethics: Human sociality and the emergence of ethical mindedness.* New York, NY: Palgrave/Macmillan; Gallagher, M., Lopez, S., & Preacher, K. (2009). The hierarchical structure of well-being. *Journal of Personality, 77,* 1025–49. doi:10.1111/j.1467-6494.2009.00573.x; Huppert, F. A., & Linley, P. A. (2011). *Happiness and well-being: Critical concepts in psychology; Vol. III: Causes and correlates of happiness and well-being: What makes us happy.* New York, NY: Routledge; Lyubomirsky, S. (2007). *The how of happiness: A new approach to getting the life you want.* New York, NY: Penguin Books; Pawelski, J. O., & Moores, D. J. (2013). Introduction: What is the eudaimonic turn? and The Eudaimonic turn in literary studies. In J. O. Pawelski & D. J. Moores (Eds.), *The eudaimonic turn* (pp. 1–63). Lanham, MD: Rowman & Littlefield; Seligman, M. (2011).

Flourish: A visionary new understanding of happiness and well-being. New York, NY: Simon & Schuster; Shahar, T. (2007). *Happier: Learn the secrets to daily joy and lasting fulfillment.* New York, NY: McGraw Hill; Stone, A., & Mackie, C. (Eds.). (2013). *Subjective well-being: Measuring happiness, suffering, and other dimensions of experience.* Washington, DC: National Academies Press.

3. Yoshino, K. (2006). *Covering: The hidden assault on our civil rights.* New York, NY: Random.

4. Rogers, C. (1957). The necessary and sufficient conditions of therapeutic personality change. *Journal of Consulting Psychology, 21*(2), 95–103.

5. Buettner, D. (2010). *Thrive.* Washington, DC: National Geographic.

6. Twenge, J. M., & Campbell, W. K. (2009). *The narcissism epidemic: Living in the age of entitlement.* New York, NY: Free Press.

7. Nelson, G., & Prilleltensky, I. (Eds.). (2010). *Community psychology: In pursuit of liberation and well-being* (2nd ed.). New York, NY: Palgrave/Macmillan.

8. Prilleltensky, I., & Nelson, G. (2002). *Doing psychology critically: Making a difference in diverse settings.* New York, NY: Palgrave/Macmillan; Ryff, C. (2014). Psychological well-being revisited: Advances in the science and practice of eudaimonia. *Psychotherapy and Psychosomatics, 83,* 10–28. doi:10.1159/000353263.

9. Bandura, A. (1997). *Self-efficacy: The exercise of control.* New York, NY: Freeman; Bandura, A. (2006). Toward a psychology of human agency. *Perspectives on Psychological Science, 1*(2), 164–80. doi:10.1111/j.1745-6916.2006.00011.x; Bandura, A., Jeffer, R. W., & Gajdos, E. (2005). The primacy of self-regulation in health promotion. *Applied Psychology: An International Journal, 54*(2), 245–54. doi:10.1111/j.1464-0597.2005.00208.x.

10. Maslow, A. H. (1970). *Motivation and personality.* New York, NY: Harper & Row; Maslow, A. H. (1943). A theory of human motivation. *Psychological Review, 50,* 370–96.

11. Frankl, V. (2006). *Man's search for meaning.* Boston, MA: Beacon.

12. Gergen, K. (2009). *Relational being: Beyond self and community.* New York, NY: Oxford.

13. Langer, A., et al. (2015). Women and health: The key for sustainable development, *The Lancet, 386,* 1165–210.

14. Prilleltensky, I. (2012). Wellness as fairness. *American Journal of Community Psychology, 49,* 1–21. doi:10.1007/s10464-011-9448-8.

15. Steele, C. (2010). *Whistling Vivaldi: How stereotype affect us and what we can do.* New York, NY: Norton.

16. Fiske, S. (2012). *Envy up, scorn down: How status divides us.* New York, NY: Russell Sage; Kahneman, D. (2011). *Thinking, fast and slow.* New York, NY: Farrar, Straus and Giroux.

17. Chess, S., & Thomas, A. (1999). *Goodness of fit: Clinical applications, from infancy through adult life.* New York, NY: Routledge.

18. Arch, J. J., & Craske, M. G. (2006). Mechanisms of mindfulness: Emotion regulation following a focused breathing induction. *Behaviour Research Therapy, 44,* 1849–58. doi:10.1016/j.brat.2005.12.007; Chambers, R., Gullone, E., & Allen, N. B. (2009). Mindful emotion regulation: An integrative review. *Clinical Psychology Review, 29,* 560–72. doi:10.1016/j.cpr.2009.06.005; Davidson, R. J., & Dimidjan, S. (2015). The emergence of mindfulness in basic and clinical psychological science [Special issue]. *American Psychologist, 70*(7); Robins, C. J., Keng, S. L., Ekblad, A. G., & Brantley, J. G. (2012), Effects of mindfulness-based stress reduction on emotional experience and expression: A randomized controlled trial. *Journal of Clinical Psychology, 68,* 117–31. doi:10.1002/jclp.20857; Warren Brown, K., & Ryan, R. M. (2003). The benefits of being present: Mindfulness and its role in psychological well-being. *Journal of Personality and Social Psychology, 84*(4), 822–48. doi:10.1037/0022-3514.84.4.822; Williams, M., Teasdale, J., Segal, Z., & Kabbat-Zinn, J. (2007). *The mindful way through depression.* New York, NY: Guilford.

19. Biglan, A. (2015). *The nurture effect: How the science of human behavior can improve our lives and our world.* Oakland, CA: New Harbinger Publications Inc.

20. Dweck, C. S. (2006). *Mindset: The new psychology of success.* New York, NY: Random House; Frisch, M. B. (2006). *Quality-of-life therapy: Applying a life satisfaction approach to positive psychology*

and cognitive therapy. Hoboken, NJ: John Wiley & Sons; Hays, P. A. (2014). *Creating well-being: Four steps to a happier, healthier life.* Washington, DC: American Psychological Association; Meichenbaum, D. (2012). *Roadmap to resilience: A guide for military, trauma victims and their families.* Clearwater, FL: Institute Press.

21. Hayes, S. C., Strosahl, K. D., & Wilson, K. G. (2012). *Acceptance and commitment therapy: The process and practice of mindful change* (2nd ed.). New York, NY: Guilford; Luoma, J. B., Hayes, S. C., & Walser, R. D. (2007). *Learning ACT.* Oakland, CA: New Harbinger.

22. Kabat-Zinn, J. (2005). *Full catastrophe living: Using the wisdom of your body and mind to face stress, pain and illness* (15th anniversary ed.). New York, NY: Bantam Dell.

23. Seligman, M. (2011). *Flourish: A visionary new understanding of happiness and well-being.* New York, NY: Simon & Schuster.

24. Stone, A., & Mackie, C. (Eds.). (2013). *Subjective well-being: Measuring happiness, suffering, and other dimensions of experience.* Washington, DC: National Academies Press.

25. Lyubomirsky, S. (2007). *The how of happiness: A new approach to getting the life you want.* New York, NY: Penguin Books; Norcross, J. C. (2012). *Changeology: 5 steps to realizing your goals and resolutions.* New York, NY: Simon & Schuster; Watson, D. L., & Tharp, R. G. (2014). *Self-directed behavior: Self-modification for personal adjustment* (10th ed.). Belmont, CA: Cengage Learning.

26. Davidson, R. J., & Dimidjan, S. (2015). The emergence of mindfulness in basic and clinical psychological science [Special issue]. *American Psychologist, 70*(7); Kabat-Zinn, J. (2005). *Full catastrophe living: Using the wisdom of your body and mind to face stress, pain and illness* (15th anniversary ed.). New York, NY: Bantam Dell.

27. Dweck, C. S. (2006). *Mindset: The new psychology of success.* New York, NY: Random House.

CHAPTER 7

1. Dunn, E., & Norton, M. (2013). *Happy money: The science of smarter spending.* New York, NY: Simon & Schuster.

2. Graham, C. (2009). *Happiness around the world: The paradox of happy peasants and miserable millionaires.* New York, NY: Oxford University Press; Kahneman, D., & Deaton, A. (2010). High income improves evaluation of life but not emotional well-being. *PNAS, 107*(38), 16489–93.

3. Attewell, P., & Newman, K. (2010). *Growing gaps: Educational inequality around the world.* New York, NY: Oxford University Press; Duncan, G., & Murnane, R. (Eds.). (2011). *Whither opportunity? Rising inequality, schools, and children's life chances.* New York, NY: Russell Sage Foundation; Duncan, G., & Murnane, R. (2014). *Restoring opportunity: The crisis of inequality and the challenge for American Education.* Cambridge, MA: Harvard Education Press; Picket, K., & Wilkinson, R. (2010). *The spirit level: Why greater equality makes societies stronger.* London: Bloomsbury; Putnam, R. (2015). *Our kids: The American dream in crisis.* New York, NY: Simon & Schuster; Wilkinson, R. G. (2005). *The impact of inequality: How to make sick societies healthier.* New York, NY: The New Press; Wilkinson, R. G. (1996). *Unhealthy societies: The afflictions of inequality.* London: Routledge.

4. Autor, D. (2014). Skills, education, and the rise of earning inequality among the "other 99 percent." *Science, 344*, 843–51.

5. Vohs, K. D., & R. F. Baumeister (2011). (Eds.), *Handbook of self-regulation* (2nd ed.). New York, NY: Guilford Press.

6. Haushofer, J., & Fehr, E. (2014). On the psychology of poverty. *Science, 344*, 862–67.

7. Yunus, M. (2007). *Creating a world without poverty.* Philadelphia, PA: Perseus.

8. Aizer, A., & Currie, J. (2014). The intergenerational transmission of inequality: Maternal disadvantage and health at birth. *Science, 344*, 856–61; Duncan, G., & Murnane, R. (Eds.). (2011). *Whither opportunity? Rising inequality, schools, and children's life chances.* New York, NY: Russell Sage Foundation; Shonkoff, J. (2014). A healthy start before and after birth. In K. McCartney, H. Yoshikawa., & L. Forcier (Eds.), *Improving the odds for America's children* (pp. 28–39). Cambridge, MA: Harvard Education Press.

9. Noble, K. G., Houston, S. M., Brito, N. H., Bartsch, H., Kan, E., Kuperman, J., . . . Sowell, E. R. (2015). Family income, parental education and brain structure in children and adolescents. *Nature Neuroscience, 18,* 773–78.

10. Biglan, A. (2015). *How the science of human behavior can improve our lives and our world.* Oakland, CA: New Harbinger Publications Inc.; Duncan, G., & Murnane, R. (2014). *Restoring opportunity: The crisis of inequality and the challenge for American Education.* Cambridge, MA: Harvard Education Press; McCartney, K., Yoshikawa, H., & Forcier, L. (Eds.). (2014). *Improving the odds for America's children.* Cambridge, MA: Harvard Education Press; Putnam, R. (2015). *Our kids: The American dream in crisis.* New York, NY: Simon & Schuster.

11. Dunn, E., & Norton, M. (2013). *Happy money: The science of smarter spending.* New York, NY: Simon & Schuster.

12. Banerjee, A., Duflo, E., Goldberg, N., Karlan, D., Osei, R., Pariente, W., . . . Udry, C. (2015). A multifaceted program causes lasting progress for the very poor: Evidence from six countries. *Science, 348*(6236), 1260799:1–1260799:15; Gassman-Pines, A., & Yoshikawa, H. (2006). The effects of anti-poverty programs on children's cumulative level of poverty-related risk. *Developmental Psychology, 42*(6), 981–99; Langer, A., et al. (2015). Women and health: The key for sustainable development, *The Lancet, 386,* 1165–210; Marmot, M. (2015). *The health gap.* New York, NY: Bloomsbury; Smith, L. (2015). Reforming the minimum wage: Toward a psychological perspective. *American Psychologist, 70*(6), 557–65. http://dx/doi.org/10.1037/a0039579.

About the Author

Isaac Prilleltensky is vice provost for institutional culture and dean of the School of Education and Human Development at the University of Miami, where he is also the Erwin and Barbara Mautner Chair in Community Well-Being. He has published seven books and over one hundred twenty scholarly papers and book chapters. He is the recipient of the Distinguished Contribution to Theory and Research Award and the John Kalafat Applied Community Psychology Award, both from the Division of Community Psychology of the American Psychological Association (APA). He is also the recipient of the Lifetime Achievement Award of the Prevention Section of the Division of Counseling Psychology of APA. In 2015, he received an award from the National Newspaper Association for his humor writing. Isaac was born in Argentina and has lived and worked in Israel, Canada, Australia, and the United States. He lives in Miami with his amazing wife, Dr. Ora Prilleltensky. Their son Matan lives in New York City. Isaac can be reached at isaac@miami.edu.